Organizational
Power Politics

ORGANIZATIONAL POWER POLITICS

Tactics in Organizational Leadership

GILBERT W. FAIRHOLM

Westport, Connecticut
London

HF 5386.5
, F35
1993

Library of Congress Cataloging-in-Publication Data

Fairholm, Gilbert W.
  Organizational power politics : tactics in organizational
leadership / Gilbert W. Fairholm.
      p.   cm.
  Includes bibliographical references and index.
  ISBN 0–275–94420–4 (alk. paper)
  1. Office politics.   2. Leadership.   3. Power (Social sciences)
I. Title.
  HF5386.5.F35   1993
  658.4′095—dc20   92–20066

British Library Cataloguing in Publication Data is available.

Library of Congress Catalog Card Number: 92–20066
ISBN: 0–275–94420–4

First published in 1993

Praeger Publishers, 88 Post Road West, Westport, CT 06881
An imprint of Greenwood Publishing Group, Inc.

Printed in the United States of America

∞™

The paper used in this book complies with the Permanent
Paper Standard issued by the National Information Standards
Organization (Z39.48–1984).

10 9 8 7 6 5 4 3 2 1

Contents

List of Illustrations

Preface

Office politics, or organizational power politics, is a normal and routine part of organizational life. We all use power. It is an integral part of our lives. It permeates what we do and how we relate to others, and it dictates much of our success. Power is part of all of our relationships. It is a central element in leadership. Unfortunately many people have negative feelings about organizational politics. This attitude stifles full effectiveness on the job and limits our success.

Indeed, understanding power and how power is used, along with sensitivity to cultural values, provides the best means of understanding leadership and what leaders do. It helps us understand how leaders lead, what they do in exercising leadership, and why some people are leaders and other are not—even though they occupy the same or similar positions in our organizations and groups.

Power theory is also critical in helping us understand follower behavior. While a part of leader action, practical power use is also a critical and common feature of follower behavior. It is central to understanding relationships. Understanding power politics becomes a critical part of our quest for success in life regardless of the role played in the group hierarchy.

Unfortunately there has been little public discussion on this issue either in leadership terms or in general power use by either leaders or followers. This absence of discussion is especially true when we try to understand power in practical—applied—terms. Consequently, until recently, we have very little material available to help us understand how individuals use power and in what circumstances its use is most effective.

The decade of the eighties produced some important new insights about how individuals use power to lead others toward their (individual and group) goals. There is mounting evidence in the nineties of a shift toward accepting power politics as a legitimate topic for discussion and an integral element of leadership (Rost, 1991).

There is, now, a growing body of literature on the operational uses of power to supplement traditional sociological and political perspectives on power. The pages that follow attempt to integrate that knowledge base into a coherent system of organizational power tactics we can use to secure our desired outcomes in relationships with others. That is, this book attempts to tell readers how they can use power to lead others toward goals and vision values they believe will aid themselves and their group in attaining its potential.

My interest in power—and, consequently, the focus of this book—is in its applied, organizational dimension. This interest comes from a lifetime of personal involvement in organizations. I have seen power used and have used it many times to try to get accomplished what I felt to be important. As I look back on my experience with power as a professional manager, a professor of management, and as a leader or follower of many groups, the key fact is in its ambiguity. Perhaps the most severe impediment to clarity is in the lack of specific language to discuss and understand power politics. Another problem is the reluctance many people have in admitting that what they do in interpersonal relationships is use power to get their way.

This book pulls together some research findings on the subject of power and the specific tactics we use—or can use. My thesis is that organizational politics— that is applied power use—is an instrument of intended action. The focus is on power-in-use generally and as an important tool of organizational action. Power use implies a plan—that is, prethought, however informal. Unintentional results, even if desired, cannot be seen as power actions. Unless specific power use produces specific, intended, results in our targets, we cannot say that the leader or follower is using power. Perhaps the lack of prethought associated with much organizational politics accounts for its failure and therefore its negative image in the eyes of many group members.

A word about leadership and power is in order here. My experience is that all persons have and use power regularly in their relationships with others. When successful in applying power to get others to behave as we want, we are exercising leadership over those other people. Power is, therefore, a necessary and con- stituent part of leadership (Rost, 1991). All people use power. When they do, they are behaving in a leaderlike way. Leadership, of course, is not a synonym for management. Managers may—and often do—behave in a leaderlike capacity, but so may their employees. Whenever a manager acts to induce others to behave in ways they desire, power is in use. Similarly, employees also use power to impact the behavior of their managers or coworkers. Whenever either a manager or an employee induces others to behave in ways they would not otherwise have behaved, power *and* (potentially) leadership are being exercised. Leadership is therefore independent of rank or formal managerial position. It is an aspect of personal behavior that includes routine power use.

In any major effort such as writing a book, there are many people who give, often without knowing. My thanks to the scholars whose work I have studied and integrated into these pages. So implicit has been their impact (power) on me that I haven't always been able specifically to identify it. My thanks, too, to the myriad others—both leaders and followers—whose exercise of power has formed the basis for examples used. Special thanks to my family for being patient with my absences from the family circle and with a preoccupation that has excluded them at times. Much of my understanding of power and leadership comes as I see leadership operate in their behavior toward me and each other. I love them and all that I do is also for them and in their name.

Introduction

The study of power as part of organizational political action by all stakeholders is an emerging field of interest aimed at improving individual leadership and overall organizational effectiveness. All participants in the group—regardless of kind of organization—have and use power; men and women, superiors, peers, and subordinates. Men and women emphasize somewhat different ways to use power, as do subordinates when compared to superiors or peers. Group member success regardless of group is dependent on the appropriateness of the particular power tactic(s) used in their political dynamics with others in the group.

The perspective taken in this book is practical in the sense that the orientation is toward applied power use by individuals associated through organizational relationships. The locus is, of course, the group—an organization characterized by unique culture, values, and mores. The centerpiece of this book is a grouping of twenty-two specific power tactics people use in varying contexts to gain their objectives. These tactics are typical of internal political action seen in the social groups and organizational units—the interpersonal relationships—in which we all operate.

THE IMPORTANCE OF POWER IN ORGANIZATIONAL LIFE

Power is a part of all organized behavior. Organizational power politics permeates all organizational action. Using power is valuable to us as a means to achieve some desired future action in others. It is instrumental; that is, people use power as an aid to achieve their intended results. We use power to achieve other goals than power itself. Although we recognize that power can, and sometimes is, an end goal, its basic use is instrumental. Power has utility for the group member most often as an intermediary tool to achieve some personal desired end value. It does not have utility (or, some say, even being) as a "stored resource." In fact evidence supports the contention that power is not a "tangible," storable commodity (like information, or money, or raw materials). Rather its main value is in its use.

The idea of power has both emotional and ethical impact. For many it carries negative connotations. Some see power as "manipulation," "coercion," "control," "force." For many, power use has Machiavellian connotations. Of course, power is, or can be, manipulative. We see power at work in behaviors such as "brownnosing," "yesing" the boss, and similar sycophantic action. In fact, "Machiavellian" has come to epitomize the worst in manipulative, exploitative, self-serving power use.

A balanced perspective allows, however, for an alternative construction of the situation and a more positive view, one that sees power as ethically neutral. The ethics of power lies not in power itself, but in the motives and values of the user. As with any other tool, we can use power for "good," that is, for socially developmental purposes, or for "bad," that is, for personal aggrandizement. User goals and operational results achieved, not power application itself, are the ethical criteria (McClelland, 1975). One can use power without destructive result to either self or others. Results depend on the motives and skill of the power user. They are also a function of the power capabilities of all others involved in the particular power exchange.

Adolf Berle (1959) contends that power is a refuge from chaos in that it organizes and rationalizes human behavior. Accepting this perspective we also must accept the idea that power use becomes critical in understanding normal group life. All organization members use power to secure their goals; not just by the leaders, supervisors, and managers whom we traditionally view as powerful people. All people control scarce resources of some type in negotiating agreement among related individuals. We take independent action to direct organizational energies toward our predetermined goals, indeed, in setting those goals in the first instance. Effective power use secures both organizational and personal goals in most (if not all) organizational action. All of us most of the time engage in organizational politics as we negotiate our way through our careers.

Seen in this perspective, power is clearly a political activity. The literature supports this view. There is mounting support in current and traditional management writings that legitimizes power and defines power maintenance functions. Power is, of course, central to organizational impact processes such as leadership, planning, directing, controlling, and performance evaluation. It is in this sense that most leaders and other workers see power use. It is also in this context that power use has it most telling impact on personal and organizational success.

The task ahead is clear: develop a constructive way to think about and use power with a minimum amount of disruption, pain, and dysfunction. Before anyone can accomplish this there must exist a body of knowledge and a technology they can apply to the day-to-day situations. Until scholars and practitioners have these data at their disposal, it will be extremely difficult for either to be effective in making improvements. Until someone develops this knowledge both will have to get along on the basis of hunch, guess, and an individually ascertained, "cumulative wisdom." It is to this end that I dedicate this book.

NATURE AND SCOPE OF THIS BOOK

This book focuses on power use in organizations. Its scope extends to all those organizations in which we normally find ourselves: work, family, social groups. It develops a model of power-in-use, based largely on empirical evidence, which applies current power theory, knowledge, and technology. A secondary focus is on power use as a leadership function whether or not the leader also holds high position in the organizational hierarchy.

Conventional techniques of leadership such as, for example, participative management, decision making, or change or conflict management are no longer enough to explain fully organizational action. Seen in power terms, the behavioral changes leaders need to create organizations capable of adapting to the sometimes intense pressures placed on modern organizations become clear. New techniques and new thrusts—like power management—hold more promise of success. They can provide organizational leaders with new analytical tools and new skills, competence, and motivation to alter ineffective patterns of personal and group behavior.

There are many possible ways to use power successfully to get our way in the group. The methods used, and the skill applied in their use, will determine whether or not individual leaders and our organizations are effective. Working from a power perspective can increase the ability of organization members singly, and as a "whole," to respond to a constantly changing environment.

DESIGN AND METHODOLOGY

The aim of using power is individual (or group) goal attainment. This is true whether or not this achievement is in the full interest of the total organization or just of the individual. Power use leads to a program of action intended to produce success from the power user's point of view. This result may come from cooperative relationships, or can flow from terror, violence, force—or from anything between. Power use takes any of these forms or a variety of others—all intended to attain the users desires.

Much of the data upon which the power tactics described in this book are derived come from practitioners. The research methodology employed was statistical analysis of more than 100 detailed questionnaires completed by members of a variety of complex organizations. These data were coupled with in-depth analysis of case studies of specific instances of power use. Analysis of power-tactic use by individuals, the coworker targets of this usage, and the results reported form the basis for conclusions drawn. The research focus was on specific behaviors in which organizational members engaged to ensure achievement of their desired results through power action.

Analysis produced twenty-two separate power-use interventions that define specific behavior patterns—or tactics—individuals employ in securing their desired results. Other elements of the research probed specific use of these twenty-two discrete tactics. Respondents specified (a) which tactics they have used and (b) which ones were the most effective in achieving their desires. They also provided data about (c) the ethics of use of this power behavior and (d) the kind of relationships in which people employ specific tactics.

POWER TACTICS

This book will help in elaborating the idea of power as a positive tool individuals may use to attain their personal and organizational results. Its central contribution is in defining and applying twenty-two power tactics individuals may use in their organizational relationships. The tactics identified include behaviors easily recognized as power behaviors such as dispensing rewards, legitimizing control, or displaying charisma. Tactics identified and described in this book also include organizational political tactics like creating rituals, quid pro quo trade-offs, and brinkmanship.

As defined in Part II, the power tactics are specific, pragmatic interrelationship behavior patterns that individuals may use as tools to change their organizational relationships. The chapters in Parts III and IV provide detailed insight into how and when various kinds of individuals use specific power tactics for optimum results. ''Power tactics'' are discrete kinds of ways people use power in specific interpersonal situations. They define the technology of organizational politics. They are tools, tactics, not part of a grand conceptual scheme.

A certain level of abstraction is implicit in any analysis of power usage. The conceptual focus of this book concentrates on applied use, not theoretical niceties. It is about tactical power use and only incidentally about power strategies. Strategy, of course, refers to the planning and directing of overall operations; tactics, to more specific and direct application. Both aspects of power use involve alteration of the situational or resource elements of the decision issue. Strategies deal with the main forces and factors found in the overall situation. Strategy determines the general direction along which the power use intends to take the organizational unit or individuals dealt with.

This work avoids development of a grand strategy or encompassing theory of power. We need to know much more about the details and mechanics of power use before anyone can tackle this higher level of abstraction. Nevertheless, the information presented in these pages provides a helpful approach to others who may investigate the subject of an overall strategy of power. In this book the strategic orientation is on the target of our power use, either superiors, peers, or subordinates.

Of course, the analysis and use of power requires some sort of systematic structuring. In a broad sense, we can define power as a personal capacity, not an institutional grant. This personal capacity allows the individual to get his or her desired results from social interaction even in the face of opposition. It is a purposeful interaction of two or more individuals in interrelationship about the attainment of action or outcome goals.

Implicit in a power situation is the idea that individuals are in competition (or, even, conflict). This competition is over the use of materials, space, or energy in ways that if one participant attains his goals, the other(s) cannot. This is fully within the definition of politics accepted by most experts. We typically accept the idea that power use applies to the planning, selecting, and application of specific behavior (or sets of ritualized behaviors) in decision situations. We also must come to accept the idea that these activities involve us in organizational political activity. The particular power tactic used is a function of situational or personal factors in the decision situation and political contingencies present there.

Organizational politics—power use—will, of course, change the nature of the preexistent organizational relationships. Involved in the selection of a particular power tactic will be four factors. The first is the nature and composition of the parties in the relationship. Second, the decision issue under consideration. Third, the tactics available to the actors by virtue of either their training or experience in power use will condition the specific tactic chosen. And, finally, the results intended by the power users.

Power is a relative concept. An individual may be relatively powerful in one circumstance and not so powerful in another. The energy expended in any given power-use situation is a function of importance, the presence of needed resources, and skill in power-tactic use. Its use is a direct consequence of the intensity of interaction. Described as we have done so, power is a ubiquitous part of all group life. It demands our attention not only to ensure organizational success, but to ensure our own as well.

ORGANIZATION OF THIS BOOK

This book is not necessarily intended to be read sequentially—from the first page to the last. The reader with some background in power theory may want to focus primarily on Part II, which identifies specific power interventions, or tactics, used in group relationships by both leaders and followers. While each of the five parts of this book has value in delineating organizational politic and power in its various dimensions, each intends to convey a discrete aspect of the idea of power in late twentieth-century America. The reader may select which portion to read first, or even to skip portions entirely. The person just beginning to study power may find the Part I chapters instructive in defining power in organizational life and placing it in perspective. The beginner also may find Part V useful in getting a working handle on the forms power takes in working life and possible sources of power he or she might pursue. The student may find Part V chapters helpful in surrounding the concept of power as a theoretical and ethical challenge.

The experienced power user may find the Parts II, III, and IV chapters most instructive in describing alternative power tactics that may be useful in specific day-to-day leadership relationships. I trust all will find the twenty-two power tactics discussed and dissected in these parts helpful in defining power as it is applied in today's world as well as useful in helping to define the nature of power in our leader–follower relationships in life.

Part II presents an overall model of the applied power process. It presents a composite model of power use taken from a variety of current sources, identifies specific power interventions—applied behavioral tactics—and begins a discussion about power-use strategies. The focus of Part II, however, is not on strategic power use, but on tactical usage. Drawing on original research and that of others, it identifies twenty-two specific clusters of power behavior—called power tactics. These tactics describe various kinds of behavior we use to get others to conform their behavior to our desires.

Parts III and IV focus more fully on power-tactic-use aspects. Chapters in Part III describe power tactics used by superiors (Chapter 6), peers (Chapter 7), and subordinates (Chapter 8) in organizational hierarchies. They describe how each level of participant uses specific (and different) tactics in his or her work. These chapters provide details of frequency of use, effectiveness, and the ethical orientation most people take toward specific tactic use.

Finally, Part IV compares the extent of use of various tactics by men and women on these dimensions. It also compares other personal and organizational characteristics of the persons who use power to sway other's behavior in desired ways. Chapter 9 compares tactic usage by members of business, higher education, not-for-profit, and government leaders and followers. It notes both similarities in tactic use and important differences and implications.

Chapter 10 compares the use of power tactics by those in supervisory positions to power-use interventions by nonsupervisory people. Importantly, nonsupervisors use power, not just supervisors. And, there is much similarity in both frequency of use and in the kinds of tactics used by these two kinds of organizational participants.

Of special note is the material (Chapter 11) that compares power use by sex of the user. It appears that men and women in the organization use power differently. Data suggest that group members may emphasize specific tactics or concentrate their power use around specific tactics in ways that are sex-specific. Since women are just beginning to represent a large portion of leaders, we need much more research and analysis in context of their job. Available information may support a contention that women and men use power differently. That is, the sexes may behave in definably different ways as they employ power tactics.

Part V traces the historical importance of power ideas. It tries to pull together a growing body of information about power. The intent of Part V is to describe power use in operational terms and to summarize elements of history and theory that support an applied perspective. Part V chapters also make a case for the importance and range of scope of power in organizational life. This is the theoretical part of the book, and is intended to be helpful to the serious practitioner of power. Part V also focuses on the sources—bases—of power available to the active participant in organizational life today.

The Appendix integrates recent literature and the author's own research findings about power—its definition, forms, processes, uses, and sources. The Appendix focuses in on delimiting the various manifestations of power in statistical terms.

Part I

Defining Power
in Work Group
Operations

Contemporary society demands results from its organizations. While this is a commonly sought goal, we really know relatively little about the mechanisms needed to achieve needed results in organizations. Applied power theory may be one such a mechanism since it focuses on political relationships among the various organizational participants. Given this fact, the importance of the study of power is obvious. Unfortunately, research and theory building in power use is in its infancy. Definitional elements are ambiguous. Systematic and quantitative definition and measurement of power use in complex organizations is still rudimentary at best.

Scholars have amassed an impressive body of literature on organization behavior theory. It is interesting, however, how skillfully most writers have avoided discussion of power and its routine use in organization situations as members negotiate advantage vis-à-vis their coworkers. There exists almost no applied theory or theories about power outside sociology or political science. A few attractive concepts have evolved that have been described and in a few rare cases tried out in practice. Thus, in the last decade, especially, a spate of studies has been written on power use in organizational situations and in leadership studies (Fairholm, 1985). Some even provide specific strategies governing its use. Few, if any of these, have a theoretical cast. On the other hand, model making has been common in collateral disciplines. It may be that some of this collateral work will lead to power theory making on a sophisticated scale.

The gap between the scholar and the practitioner is also significant in understanding power usage. Scholars are spending relatively little time in learning about power and how people actually use power in organizations. Practitioners, however, are continuously and actively engaged in this kind of interaction. They need definitional and application models to help guide their practice.

There needs to be a closer relationship between the leader and other group-member practitioners engaged in day-to-day use of power and the scholar involved in power research. The role of the scholar is not only to observe, record, and interpret power use. Scholars also must develop and apply theoretical models to affect and effect organizational action. Until scholars and practitioners share information derived from their separate involvements in the organization little useful knowledge is likely to result. Our understanding of how people use power tactics must languish until both understand the needs and perspective of the other's role.

Many theorists are coming to realize that the truly effective organization is one in which the organization, its leaders, and individual members can grow and develop. Such an environment produces situations conducive to personal and organizational goal accomplishment. These organizations openly foster power use.

Too frequently the typical response to problems is to ignore power as a factor in their management. Alternatively, participants talk about it rather than act. One of the important conditions for initiation of response to this kind of situation is a felt tension arising from a need for change among those involved. This tension or awareness may arise in several different ways. Usually the awareness emerges from some problem condition that can no longer be ignored. This state of tension may result from internal growth or decline. It also may result from competitive, technological, or social changes in the external environment.

The demands of contemporary life leave practitioners little alternative but to engage broadly in power use. However, most practitioners have available to them too little theoretical or conceptual understanding of power dynamics. They go about the task of using power intuitively. And, importantly, the language of power is simplistic. There are too few ideas, models, and, even, words to describe power use. The result is that frequently they, and the organizations they serve, suffer social disorder, pain, and frustration. There are, of course, positive, helpful ways to use power. This book will describe some of them.

Chapter 1 will begin this elaboration with definitional dimensions of applied power usage in today's organizations by both leaders and their followers. This part lays out and elaborates a working definition of power. We can think of power as a personal capacity allowing individuals to get their desired results in the face of possible opposition from others. Chapter 1 identifies and describes eight dimensions of this definition. These dimensions comprehensively define power as it is used in modern organizations and groups.

Chapter 2 introduces the idea of power as a process in organizational life. It also places this concept in context of our self-perceptions, our views on organization and leadership, and our relationships in these formal and informal situations.

Elements of a Definition

Power continues to be a difficult subject to surround. Disciplinary foci have helped, but have left about as much confusion as they have added insight into the subject. Recent analytical studies, while relatively few, have helped to clarify elements of power, its sources, and constituent parts. This work has added needed insights into specific dimensions of power, but has not delimited the central essence of power. Indeed, most work on power adds to the ambiguity rather than diminishes it.

Any summary of research directions in operational uses of power points up this variety and breadth. For example, writers have defined power variously as a potential for social action and as a predictor and conditioner of behavior. They have described power as an ethical element of freedom, as a tool for analysis of influence, and as a basis of violence. Some see power as a possession in a zero-sum game. Others see it as a shared (or sharable) commodity, as a resource we can monopolize. And others view it as a general capacity of personality. All of these perspectives help somewhat in delimiting power. Individually, they elaborate salient dimensions of this complex social phenomenon. Together, however, they garble succinct distinctions and create confusion. Many specific power definitions overlap or even contradict each other.

Notwithstanding this confusion, power is attractive—if illusive. Socrates, Plato, Aristotle, and other philosophers have dealt with this subject. And, since Machiavelli, power theory has caused concern and some degree of discomfort for the serious student and for the generalists in human behavior. The essential nature of power has eluded us. Its dimensions are troublesome. Its meaning in practice enigmatic. Its theory is inconclusive and imprecise. Its ethical status ambiguous, and its use in regular and crisis operations suspect. Perhaps no other concept in social science is more confusing and troublesome. We may say about power what Saint Augustine said about time: We all know perfectly well what it is—until someone asks us.

The idea of power use to gain organizational (political) advantage has strong ethical overtones. Many writers view it negatively, especially those publishing before the 1970s. Archbishop Fenelon reflected many perceptions when he described power as "poison." The famous statement by Lord Acton, "Power corrupts; absolute power corrupts absolutely," is typical of much of the feeling and tone of power literature. Recently, some (McClelland, 1975; Winter, 1973; Follett, 1942; Nyberg, 1981; and others) have contended that power can be liberating, enhancing of the individual and those dealt with. This positive face of power is receiving much more attention now. It gives "research" support for activity, much maligned, but frequently engaged in by us all.

Power is a part of life. It is manifestly a part of interpersonal behavior in most social situations. People are always interacting in group settings to secure goals and desired results. All interactive communication is purposeful, and to achieve this purpose, the individual engages in power activity. Because of the ambiguity of the power concept in life, it is not hard to understand its multiple definitions. But, as Bierstadt (1950) noted, the more ideas one can apply to a term, the less precise is its meaning in a given context.

DEFINING POWER

Concern with differences between power and related concepts such as authority, influence, domination, force, or control is clear in the literature. Some writers use these terms interchangeably. Others make painstaking distinctions that, while useful to their particular discussion, have little value when we compare different writers and different theories (Yukl, 1981). We need a definition of power sufficiently broad to provide what Gardner (1964) called semantic space.

This kind of definition will allow the analyst to apply personally particular examples of possible power relationships. Such a definition would encompass the overall idea that power is the ability to do. Individual personality as well as control over material and psychological resources are part of power-use study. Its study incorporates both analysis of control over desired or needed resources as well as personal characteristics of people who use power regularly.

There is little agreement about what power is, where or when the individual gets it, or how to use it successfully. What is clear is that power is pervasive, interesting, and central to success in functioning in organizational settings. We experience the effects of power use at every level of human interaction. Perhaps its most significant arena is that of the complex organization. Power, as much as any single issue, helps us understand the inner working of the modern organization. It can give us help in analyzing current performance, measuring impact, and predicting future success.

Power defies succinct definition. It is, like many other terms, a universal idea: one not easily classified and specified. Reviewing the power literature quickly points up the ubiquity of the concept as an explicit and (more often) implicit element of managerial and organizational behavior. Power has occupied the attention of scholars from a wide range of disciplines, but even casual perusal confirms that they differ in their degree of rigor, specificity, and scope. Nevertheless, the increasing interest it draws is from both academic and practicing professionals in widely diverse disciplines. Writers in politics, religion, anthropology, psychology, sociology, and management and leadership confirm its importance.

The definition I used here is operational. Power is simply *the individual capacity to gain your own aims in interrelationship with others, even in the face of their opposition*. Implicit in this definition is the idea that power is the individual capacity of one person to get their way, even in the face of opposition. This is implicitly a political idea. This chapter attempts to elaborate that definition. Here we introduce and explain briefly several characteristics of power. These characteristics elaborate power as a personal tool leaders as well as followers use in interpersonal relations. These characteristics add depth to the definition of power and reveal something of its scope, extent, and domain.

The word (power) and the underlying concept have been the subject of extensive analysis. The result is there is much more confusion and distinction than harmony and synthesis in available definition. Some convergence centers around the ideas of power as a personal capacity. Many see power in use as a way to activate us so we can get our desired results even in the face of opposition or indifference. Implicit in this definition are several ideas important to the systematic use of power. Each of these ideas connote a specific characteristic of the concept called power. Thus power is a special kind of a social relationship characterized by the following ideas:

Power is intentional. It involves volitional, not random action.

Power is instrumental. It is a means to desired ends.

Power is finite. It is measured and compared in a given situation or occurrence.

Power involves dependency. There is a freedom or dependency–independency factor inherent in any power use.

Power is an action idea. It is apparent in use, not in mere possession.

Power is defined in results terms. Results determine our power.

Power is situational. Specific power tactics are effective in specific relationships and not necessarily in others.

Power is based on opposition or difference. Parties must differ before they will use power.

The sections that follow elaborate on these eight definitional characteristics of operational power.

POWER CHARACTERISTICS

Intentionality

Power is intentional. It requires forethought. Power use is only successful when it is a part of an exchange that results in desired behavior in the person toward whom we direct power. Our behavior may cause another to do something they did not intend to do. But, unless we consciously intend for a follower to behave in that way, we cannot say that our power use was effective. The cause may have been happenstance. We can say power is in use anytime we *try* to alter the current relationship. But it is successful only if the desired behavior would probably not have occurred if we had not been involved. Siu (1979) suggests that a measure of a person's power is in exerting power over another so that he can exact compliance *as desired* (my emphasis). Power is operative to the degree that intended and foreseen results occur.

People exert mutual power and control over other's conduct in relationships. That is, both parties in a relationship have and use power. We can define all social control in terms of this mutuality of influence and control (Berle, 1959). The relative power of the participants must be different—one participant must perceive him/herself to be relatively more dominant than the other—otherwise there would be no point in employing energy in power behavior. In this situation, one person consents and in that consent transfers power to the other making that individual relatively more dominant in that situation.

Intended power is influence exhibited in any of several forms. Traditional authority is one manifestation, one common in all purposeful groups. Persuasion, manipulation, and force are other examples of intentional power use. (See Chapter 13 for a more specific discussion of power forms.) Each form of power use involves the influencer in exerting predetermined behavior toward another person with the intent of securing some desired outcome.

Power makes use of both means and needs. If we have both a need (for a specific service, information) and the means (resources) to get it and consciously apply these means to secure the need, then power is active. The exercise must, of course, be conscious, planned, premeditated. We cannot define an expenditure of energy without a plan as an exercise of power whether or not we desired the result secured. Similarly, an action that culminates in an unanticipated action, even though desired, likewise is not a use of power since an unintended result occurred.

Of course, power use that produces something other than what was intended can impact another person. We cannot say this is a use of our power, however, because the outcome cannot be predicted, nor controlled. Effective power use must result in desired behavior in others. Unintended results are, by definition, anti-intent. Whether we consciously ignore a potential power-use situation or unconsciously engage in power use, the result is fortuitous, not a power result.

Instrumentality

Power functions through control over organizational and other resources (including other people) and through that control over specific people, things, or events. It is, in this sense, instrumental to final goal attainment. We activate power through a chain of events that connects control over needed and scarce resources with control over individual behavior(s). Power is always instrumental in this way. It is a means-based phenomenon, not an ends-based one. That is, we use power to gain something else, not just more power.

Influential people use control over scarce skill, ideas, or resources to secure the compliance of those who desire those resources. In a very real sense, power use is a special process of effecting policies and program results through actual or threatened deprivations to the nonconforming. Control over these resources empowers; lack of such control results in relative powerlessness in attaining one's desires.

Situational

We cannot define power apart from the situation. It is situation-specific. Power is operative through specific actors in a definite relationship in time. It is operative in a given situation where others desire a resource we hold or control. They must desire it with enough intensity so these individuals will behave in ways they would not otherwise behave to satisfy that desire. If the situation changes, the power relationship may no longer obtain. That is, if the desire of the participant changes so he no longer wants the resource we control, there is no longer a power relation. Similarly, if we lose control over a desired resource, the other participants are no longer compelled to follow our lead. They need not follow because doing so may not achieve their desired results. As these factors in the situation change, power use is affected.

Analysis of the power relationship reveals at least four factors that define a power situation. People use power when the situation can be described in terms of the following factors.

First, there has to be some interdependence of the actors in the situation. Unless there is some reason for the parties to interact, a relationship—power or otherwise—cannot exist.

Second, the participants must differ as to their goals and methodology for proceeding. That is, the situation must be one in which the participants desire results that both cannot achieve. Or, they must approach the relationship with different technological or methodological preferences that again are mutually exclusive. That is, a power situation is one of opposition. If both goals or both methodologies can be accommodated, there is no need nor opportunity to exercise power. Given differences in one or both, we must employ power in order for action to take place.

A third criterion deals with scarcity of the resources needed to achieve desired results. Resources available must be limited enough so both parties cannot achieve their goals or approach the activity from their respective methodologies simultaneously. If resources are adequate to accommodate both, we need not employ power. Given a scarcity of resources, however, the participant with the most control over needed resources can exercise power.

Finally, the parties must view the potential results to be sufficiently valuable to them so that they are willing to engage in competition to achieve their desires. Unless there is enough interest, we cannot define the relationship as a power relationship.

Opposition

Opposition is a part of all life. It is essential in understanding power-use situations. Our power is a function of our ability to overcome the resistance of another person. Bierstadt (1950) defines power as present only in situations of social opposition. Weber (1968) suggests that power is the probability that one member within a social relationship will be in a position to carry out his/her own will despite resistance. Lasswell and Kaplan (1950) see power as participation in the making of decisions. For them, A has power over B with respect to the values of C if A participates in the making of decisions affecting the C policies of B. Etzioni, similarly, includes overcoming of resistance as an element in the analysis of power.

Seen in this light, power is a shared phenomenon between opponents. Both (all) parties in the power relationship have some power in the situation (Berle, 1959). One participant exerts power as he overcomes resistance or opposition interposed by the other participant. Introducing change in the face of opposition is a common thread of definition of power.

In a related vein, but one with a more altruistic tone, is the work of Mary Parker Follett (1942). She agrees that power is definable in terms similar to those stated above: as the power of some persons over other persons. She also sees the possibility of those two participants exercising their power capacities in joint use. Her concept of power with rather than power over has the aim of unification, while allowing for infinite difference. Power here is coactive, not coercive, but operating, nonetheless, in situations of difference/opposition.

An Action Idea

Power is apparent in action. As noted, many writers relate power to overt action. As a personal capacity, power has being only in action; in use. Whether physical, mental, or moral, power is a relationship in which we impact the behavior of another through action that the second individual wants, or needs, or wants to avoid, and therefore acts in specified ways.

We often exercise power through threats or promises as well as overt actions (Bell, 1975). Persons respond to this exercise of power rather than incur the dire results threatened. Or, they respond to secure a promised outcome. In this sense, power is latent force. Power is the prior capacity which, when applied, makes the application of force possible in a given action situation. The key to power is in its use.

Dependence/Independence

Power operates in dependency relationships. At one level, we see dependency in domination of the powerful over the relatively powerless. We can think of power—all of life, actually—as a series of one-on-one relationships reiterated continuously. At times, one member of the dyad predominates, and at other times, the other person may be in ascendancy. We constantly move from direction to being directed in our relationships. At times, we persuade others to do something we want them to do—to follow our orders, to get us something we want, to laugh at our jokes, to understand or respect us or our ideas or values. At other times—often in the same conversation—we are persuaded, made to laugh, or do something that the other person wants us to do. Independence–dependence relations of this dynamic, interactive sort comprise the power dynamic and the dynamics of life.

From the perspective of the target of power (the more common focus of power research), power is constraining. The dictionary is typical in defining power as the ability or authority to dominate people, to coerce, and to control them. Power begets obedience. It can interfere with others' freedom, compel their actions in particular ways. Mechanic (1962) defines power as any force that results in behavior that would not have occurred if the force had not been present. Emerson also describes the power relationship in dependence terms. That is, A's power over B becomes a function of B's dependence on A. Hence, B will be dependent upon A in a given situation to the degree that B cannot find alternate sources for the resource(s) that A controls and B desires (Pfeffer, 1981). We find similar ideas in the work of many sociological theorists.

When the power user is the focus of analysis, we see a different perspective. Power, for the user of power, is liberating. Seen from this vantage point, we can equate power with freedom. The more power we have to determine the course of events that we and others follow, the more freedom we have. Our capacity to act (a key definitional element of power) is a measure of the freedom we have.

Viewed in this light, power is liberating of the individual. It is a self-developing capacity. As power-using individuals, we have our way in the situation. Freedom, therefore, is, in a real sense, having adequate power in a given situation. It becomes a desirable commodity. People seek power to enhance their freedom of action. It is not merely a negative element of some group situations.

Finite

Power is a finite resource. More accurately, it is control over specific physical or psychological resources needed by others and in short supply. That is, all parties wanting or needing the specific resource cannot be supplied. Handy (1976) distinguishes between influence and power. He points out that power is a resource that allows us to engage in a process of influencing the behavior of others. People often want a resource we control sufficiently enough to do something we want them to do to receive this scarce resource. In this discussion Handy, as do others, confuses the concept of power. Power is generic; influence is one form power takes in getting others to comply. His insight that power is a definite resource, however, is relevant to this discussion. Much of this book's later discussion about power sources confirms and elaborates this concept.

Kaplan (1964) talks about the domain of power. He concludes that as the amount of power increases, our domain of power expands. He defines the scope of power as the range of stimuli and the range of corresponding responses the power user affects. For Kaplin, one can define power in measurable terms based on the scope of impact over either people, material, or other resources held or controlled. For example, a chief executive leading an organization of 3,000 people has a measurably greater amount of power than one leading a group of 30 people. Similarly, a person who controls the time, money, tools, and equipment you need exercises more potential power over you than does the person who only controls tools. Kaplin refers to power as a specific capacity in a given situation, as a finite element of the situation.

To assume that power is concrete, however, is to overemphasize its resource character. Power is not, strictly speaking, a commodity. We cannot say we own power in the same way that we own money or property. Power is one of the factors of the situation and the dynamics of the interpersonal relationship. The targets of our power uses can have impact on our total power capacity to the degree that they desire or ignore a power resource we control.

Given appropriate situations, we may dissipate our power through use, or we can enlarge it through use. For example, organization leaders (powerful people) give power to others as an alternative (or supplement) to salary. Often power is transferable more easily and less expensively than monetary raises. Power is often a substitute for pay. We give power to encourage and motivate employees when their performance does not warrant salary increases, or money is unavailable or inappropriate.

The organization often functions as a kind of power broker. It dispenses power in the form of suzerainty over employees or resources or programs to those who want or need it to fulfill their individual goals. In this sense, we increase power by use. When we grant control over a portion of our work force to another, that new manager gets power. We also keep our power and, often, that power base is enhanced by the addition of another level of control (hierarchy). As the dispenser of power, we have enlarged our own locus of control as we create added loci of power in our newly empowered subordinates.

Power use can, of course, reduce our power. Consider the case of the individual who threatens another person with dire results if that other person fails to perform in a desired way. If the target of power fails to behave in the desired way and no dire results result, the power of the threatener dissipates and will not be as effective in future relationships. We lose power through this kind of use.

Measured by Results Attained

As a rule, we exercise power only when we achieve our desired results as opposed to results desired by another. When both parties in a relationship can and do gain their desired results independently, power is not operative. When one person gains power and the other does not, power is, by definition, a part of the power relationship. Succinctly put, we use power when we exert human energy to produce desired results.

The measure of effective power use, therefore, is achievement of our desired results. Power, in this sense, is a function of our ability to affect the behavior of others to further our desired results (Howard, 1982). Pursuit of individual goals requires the use of power (a personal capacity). So does pursuit of group goals. The power user may use personal power capacities or group power capacities, that is, authority (Grimes, 1978). Both are examples of power use since they focus on results.

tangible results

SUMMARY

Power admits to no simple definition. It is a part of the complex nature of human relations. It is central to life as we know it. It is critical to organized interactions. The ideas and issues raised thus far serve to introduce the idea of power in use in social groups by all participants to get their way. Chapter 1 focused more directly on the pure definition of power. Chapter 2 explores in some detail the use of power in organized contexts. Chapter 2 applies power use to the essentially political process of securing advantage over competitors. Power leadership engages the leader (all stakeholders) in using power politically, that is, to gain personal and/or institutional goals in competition with others.

Of course, we all exercise power within the context of our institutional and personal history and ethics. The historical and ethical foundations discussed in Part V chapters may help round out the definitional elements of the field of power action as a basis for the applied discussion on the issues of power in routine organizational life that constitutes the essence of the chapters in Parts II, III, and IV.

Power Politics in Organizational Life

In many ways power is a unifying thread by which we can connect and rationalize the history of mankind. Of course other, more traditional perspectives like economic events, wars, ideology, and religion provide important and needed perspectives on our evolution as a society. But, certainly understanding how leaders as well as followers used power will help in understanding our history. It will be equally useful in helping us determine how people will relate to each other in the twenty-first century.

Viewing our leaders, our literature, our government, our philosophy, and our religion in power terms helps us understand each other better. These social systems record our history of competition, conflict, struggle, violence, and war. In a word, they record our fascination with power (Winter, 1973) and the politics of power use. Perhaps there is no single concept of human relationship of more gut importance than how we get our way in the group. It is central to both who and what we are as individuals and as group members.

We engage in power activity in group (that is, political) settings. It is logical, therefore, that psychology, political science, anthropology, and the rest of the social disciplines should have interest in power. Each has something to add to our understanding of power and its use. Each discipline, almost each writer, has added specific definitions to the lexicon of power. The resulting confusion has done little to clarify concepts, or to reduce the trauma many feel when someone introduces the word power into a discussion.

The study of power dates from the earliest efforts to define a social science.

However, most of the modern work on power in organizational contexts had its beginnings in the 1930s. Since then, the focus of research has varied widely. Some focus on sociological underpinnings (Russell, 1938; Cartright, 1965; Follett, 1942; May, 1972; and Crozier, 1964). Some see power as political (Mills, 1957; Dahl, 1957; and Hunter, 1959). Others give it a behavioral twist (Weber, 1968; Homans, 1950; French and Raven, 1959; Cartright, 1965; Thibaut and Kelley, 1959; and many others). A few researchers give power a psychological thrust (McClelland, 1975; and Winter, 1973). And finally, some discuss power in organizational and structural terms (Etzioni, 1961; Smith and Tannenbaum, 1963; Crozier, 1964; McKinney, 1979; and Pfeffer, 1981).

Power continues to be a difficult subject to surround. Disciplinary foci have helped, but have left about as much confusion as they have added insight into the subject. Analytical studies, while relatively few, have helped to clarify elements of power, its sources, and constituent parts. This work has added needed insights into specific dimensions of power, but has not delimited the central essence of power. Indeed, most work on power adds to the ambiguity rather than diminishes it.

Power is a part of life. It is manifestly a part of interpersonal behavior in most social situations. People are always interacting in group settings to secure goals and desired results. All interactive communication is purposeful, and to achieve this purpose, the individual engages in power activity. Because of the ambiguity of the power concept in life, it is not hard to understand the existence of its multiple definitions.

For the purposes of this book I define power as the individual capacity to gain your own aims in interrelationship with others, even in the face of their opposition. I believe this definition captures the essence of power as we use it in group and organizational life. It becomes the foundation for the following discussion about power in formal organizations and in other issues raised hereafter.

POWER IN FORMAL ORGANIZATIONS

When analyzed from the perspective of the individual in a structured organizational setting, we see some interesting insights on power. Achieving desired organizational results is dependent on our capacity to influence others to our point of view. The mechanism often is one of offering desired rewards to followers as inducement to desired behavior. In effect, we say, if you do what I want (i.e., behave in a manner useful to me), I will provide you with physical or psychological results that will meet your needs or be instrumental in achieving one or more of your desires. In this sense power use is a kind of political exchange transaction. It is instrumental to task accomplishment.

Power is also a process by which we induce change in another's behavior or attitudes (Grimes, 1978). It is in this sense, then, that one can define power as the basis of all organized action. As a social structure of human interrelationships (Gouldner, 1960), the organization controls the action of individuals; and control over others is power. We organize for power (Follett, 1942). Control in the organization rests on power. Delegation is a power relationship. Negotiation is an exercise in power. Leadership is power in action (Zaleznik, 1963).

Organizationally, we can describe power as the ability to make something happen—the essence of the causal relationship. Power defined in these terms becomes the basis of the "power relationship." Power relationships are interactive, interpersonal processes where one gets power from and uses it in interaction with others in the group.

POWER AND FORMAL AUTHORITY

The literature equates the opportunity to progress within the group with a getting of more authority (position power) than other group members. We see it in action when the group places more of the total so-called "group power" on one individual (a formal manager or informal leader). Authority (only one of several forms of power) is a divisible commodity that managers ration among themselves via the process of delegation. In this sense it is the basis for organizational order, logic, and control. It is the basis of status and hierarchy in the organization (Barnard, 1948). → TJi STD - set of people w/ diftt. frameworks

A view of power in authority terms connotes a system of dependencies, and, in this situation, distribution is the key issue. Each member of the organization relates to others in a power role relationship that constrains each member (Molm, 1990). If one gains power, it is at the expense of others in the group. If one gains, others lose. Mary Parker Follett (1942) defined this "face" of power as "power over" others (as opposed to "power with" others).

POWER AND SELF-ESTEEM

Power is central to defining individual self-esteem within the organization. It is part of the pursuit of personal goals (Grimes, 1978). Gaining power allows the individual to place himself in the group context in specific terms, in a specific relationship to others. Adler says that power does much to explain the behavior of exceptional people. He claims that it, more than the sex drive propounded by Freud, is the dominant determinant of personality (1956). Weber also ascribes to power a dominant role in social organization (1968).

The word "power" derives from the same root as the word possibility. The Roman root "possess" literally means "I can." The Latin verb "potere" means "to be able." Both words connote the central function of affecting something or someone. The word power entered the English language from this Roman/Latin foundation at the time of the Norman conquest of England (Hunter, 1959). Over time, power has come to connote personal capacity in our English heritage. Power is a capacity, a talent, a skill resident in all of us, but held in larger quantities by specific individuals.

Power is the ability or capacity to induce others to behave in desired ways

(McKinney, 1979) in human interaction. All individuals can control or influence other people and, in turn, can be under another's influence. Power is part of all organized group activity that results in enhancement or limitation of our ability to do. Thus, power is a part of concepts like organization, authority, control direction, competition, conflict, coordination, planning, budgeting, staffing, or other administrative functions.

POWER IN LEADERSHIP

Power is the essence of leadership. It is the extra element in interpersonal relations that allows the leader to effect others and secure their willing compliance. Rollo May (1972) defines power as the ability to cause or prevent change. Kaplin (1964) calls it the process of effecting the policies of others. Bertrand Russell (1938) defines it as the "production of intended effects." Power allows people to alter the behavior of others in ways they—the power users—want. Power lets anyone be a leader. The source may (and does) vary but the object appears universal. Power allows the individual to effect, to sway, others' behavior in desired ways; in a word, to lead them.

At one level, all interpersonal relationships are leader–follower relationships. We are constantly moving from a directive position to a follower one in our contacts with others. At times we engage in persuading others to do something we want them to do. It may be to follow our orders, to get us something, to laugh at our jokes, or to understand and respect our ideas and values. At other times—often in the same conversation—we persuade them to laugh, or induce them to do something that we want them to do. We see power in leadership contexts in a much larger dimension. It is a personal, rather than merely a positional, concept. The operative characteristic of leadership is its intimacy. It is a personal power relationship between one leader and one follower reiterated in a series of one-to-one relationships. These power relationships are constituent parts of organizational (and all) life.

POWER IN USE IN ORGANIZATIONAL CONTEXTS

Few ideas are more basic to the study of organizations than power. It is an important and active reality in all dimensions of organizational life. Indeed, power interactivity is, perhaps, humankind's most pervasive dimension. We experience the result of power use at all levels in the organization and by all participants. It is a constituent part of informal as well as formal organization. As Dahl (1961) said, it is as "ancient and ubiquitous as any (concept) that social theory can boast." Power is central to both leadership theory and practice. It is a core element of human interaction.

Organization and management of the environment predate recorded history (Hodgkinson, 1978). It is a primary activity of human organization. Administration and the desire to order our immediate situation have inspired the classics in literature. Certainly, we must count Machiavelli's *The Prince* and Plato's *Republic* among those classics. They typify a literature that carry our search for order and organization of our immediate environment into everyday life.

Power is central to man's continuing concern for administration and organization. How people organize and relate to each other to get planned goals accomplished is central to organization and administrative theory. The overreaching problem of organization life is securing follower compliance. This compliance, however, must come without losing the long-term amicable relationship between the person desiring compliance and the person whose behavior change we seek. And this must be done with an eye on conserving scarce resources.

Machiavelli's *The Prince* provides extensive advice to rulers (read, ''leaders'') on how to extend and combine their power and capacity to direct compliance. Similarly the libraries of the world are full of books to help us to influence subordinates, raise our children, make friends, and influence others.

Few concepts are more crucial or more central to the understanding of behavior in organizations. We may treat it as a prime aim or as instrumental to other, strategic aims. Nevertheless, power is a necessary part of the interaction of people. Power is a cornerstone of both leadership and management theory and practice. It is the essence of leader behavior. It is central to subordinate-to-superior interaction. It helps explain the myriad relationships we experience with the many peers and external contacts that make up the fabric of organizational interaction.

On another dimension, most organization members influence others and are, in turn, influenced by them. Power use dominates not only management and leadership perspectives, but those of ordinary workers, suppliers, consumers, and other stakeholders also. People in all kinds of work or in any social or hierarchical relationship share the goal of getting others to behave in ways they want them to. We want others to like us, to work for us, to think the way we want them to think. We want them to go where we think they ought to go, to be what we think they ought to be. Seen in this light, power is a political transaction process.

In agrarian societies our power usage was more personal, immediate, and limited in scope and domain. In industrial societies, complexity has affected power use as well as other elements of life. Power use now is more impersonal, anonymous, and institutionalized. In real ways it is the primary measure of our value to the group—be it the work organization or the social group. Hobbes, as early as the seventeenth century, listed power as the measure of our social status. Today, power is in many ways the measure of position. Money or possessions, while instrumental, are less significant in assessing social position than is power. We are a power-oriented society: one particularized by institutions (i.e., organizational, hierarchical representations).

Using these ideas, we can see that many managerial and leadership concepts have power connotations. For example, we can define authority as a manifestation of power characterized by position and relationship within the formal, hierarchical system. Authority connotes the legitimate right of the holder to command, decide, or determine the way the organization will go. It is an obvious manifestation of power, one connoting the formally granted rights inherent in the organizational position held.

authority is given - a socially accepted position

Personal influence, an integral part of leadership, is a form power takes. Influence is a form of power, often subtle and indirect, by which we impact the situations and behaviors of others. We can understand influence best as a mechanism of attitude change. It uses esteem and respect to accomplish the task of changing the behavior of another.

Using a power connotation helps us interpret competition and its companion concept, conflict. In competition settings both participants exercise power in trying to achieve their purpose at the expense of the other person. Competition becomes conflict when we include emotions. Conflict, too, is a power relationship.

Power has a direct connection to many of the underlying functions of management. For example, power is a constituent part of organizational control systems. As individuals exert energy toward activating others to behave in organizationally useful ways (that is, to achieve organizational goals), they are exercising power. Direction, control, planning, coordination, and correlation are all manifestations of power used in organizations to accomplish intended results. The process is an impact one; the capacity is power (Handy, 1976).

In fact, we can understand all of a manager's tasks—execution of authority, personal interaction, control, direction, planning, conflict resolution, and so on—better from a power perspective. While often masked, ignored, and even denied, power is central in understanding organizational participant behavior. In budgeting, planning, staffing, controlling, and directing, individuals constantly engage in power relationships and power exchanges. They negotiate schedules, compromise goals, marshal support, and compete for available resources. Implicit in each of these traditionally accepted managerial activities is an element of power use, of producing intended behaviors in others. Every act of interpersonal behavior directed toward goal accomplishment results in actual or potential power use.

Using power allows us to affect another's behavior in ways we want. This effect can result regardless of the will of the target of power. Leadership implies the inducement of followers to do something that the follower would not do without the leader's intervention. At some levels, at some times, for some leaders, the operative words may be persuasion, opening of opportunity, or facilitation of the work of followers. At other times the focus may be on coercion, force, or control. Whether the connotation is positive or negative, we are in the business of getting others to do what they would not done if left alone.

ORGANIZATIONAL POLITICS

An obvious conclusion from this analysis is that management is a political (power-centered) activity. It involves us in all interactions aimed at reserving resources to our special needs. Much of existing literature on management and organizations, in fact, describes aspects of power acquisition, legitimization, and maintenance functions (Rubinoff, 1968). Even limited experience in organizational life will leave us with a realization of the importance of political negotiation in organizational systems. Our organizational laws, rules, standards, policy, and regulations are manifestations of political influence—that is, power. Power is at the heart of what Mayes and Allen (1977) call the "management of influence" throughout the organization.

Organizational politics has been a largely undiscussed phenomenon in organization and management theory and practice. It has only recently found its way into the formal literature of organizational behavior (Allen and Porter, 1983). Earlier writers also have made significant contributions to our understanding. Hobbes, over 300 years ago, helped distinguish political power (Kaplin, 1964). He pointed out that the power of the subject impacts the sovereign as well. Since then, the debate has ranged from concern with the instrumental nature of power to its resource qualities to its operating impacts in group situations.

Definitions of organizational politics typically include several factors. Organizational politics involve (a) actions taken by individuals throughout the organization (Mayes and Allen, 1977) and (b) any influence of one actor toward another (Gandz and Murray, 1980). It includes (c) effort by one party to promote self-interest over that of another and, therefore, threaten the second party's self-interest (Rosen and Lippitt, 1961). It also includes (d) actions typically not sanctioned by the host organization or results sought that it does not sanction (Plott and Levine, 1978). That is, organizational politics involve (e) some kind of exchange process with a zero-sum outcome (Frost and Hayes, 1979). Much of the literature suggests that organizational politics concerns itself with influence and control relationships of this kind.

Many definitions place organizational politics in this kind of control-of-others light. Pfeffer (1981) suggests that many definitions ascribe "sinfulness" or "illegality" to this social phenomenon. Porter, Allen, and Angle (1981) see organizational politics in self-interest terms (also negatively connoted). Martin and Sims (1974) tie organizational politics to control.

We also can see another construction of organizational politics. Operationally, organizational politics is a ubiquitous fact of organizational life. Allen, Madison, Porter, Renwick, and Mayes (1979) suggest that it is an important social influence process. It has a potential of being both functional and dysfunctional to organizations and individuals. Organizational politics is a solid part of organizational life. Its use conforms with current research suggesting that all group interaction has specific change purposes. Organizational politics is, therefore, a part of social interaction. Its positive or negative face is dependent on factors other than the mere fact of interaction for influence purposes. Our experience with power places it in the center of all social intercourse. Organizational politics is merely a structured, purposeful, organized group version of this universal social practice.

An operationally useful definition of organization politics may include elements that Mayes and Allen (1977) called the management of influence. For them, organizational politics is a process that involves formulating political goals, decision strategies, and tactics. It entails executing those tactics and setting up feedback loops to ensure effective results. Organizational power politics is also defined in terms of a process of change (Coenen and Hofstra, 1988). Defined in this way we can say that organizational politics is the essence of leadership. Organizational politics therefore includes actions taken to gain and use power to control organizational resources to achieve our preferred results instead of those of others. This definition places organizational politics in the classroom when a teacher "teaches." It is in the home as a father asks his child to do something. It is in the office as the subordinate "manages" his or her boss by couching interaction upward in ways calculated to induce the boss to respond favorably. And it is present when the manager orders employees to adopt a new procedure.

David Bell emphasizes the "talk" aspect of organizational politics (1975). He says traditional definitions of politics as who gets what, when, where, and how is not helpful. Getting control over needed resources can be, and often is, an intensely personal and private (even solitary) affair, not a public one. Talk, on the other hand, always involves others and more consistently conforms to the definition of politics. Talk effects others (Duke, 1976), and to that extent it is power. To the widest extent possible, organizational politics concerns how people affect each other.

Political Behavior

Given our definition of organizational politics, it is a commonplace activity in organizations. Research by Madison (1980) and others supports the idea that organizational politics is fully a part of organizational life. Sixty percent of managers he surveyed averred that it was "frequently" or "very frequently" a part of organizational life. Most managers see organizational politics as a part of work life at the middle and upper management levels and less so at the lower levels.

Engaging in the politics of the organization may be helpful to the individual. Madison's research report that 95 percent of respondents agreed that office politics is necessary in achieving individual goals. They also were unanimous in saying that it could harm them. For Madison, engaging in organizational politics is a "crucial path" to success in the organization (Madison, 1980).

We use political action in the organization in situations of uncertainty, importance, and salience to either the individual or the unit concerned (Madison, 1980). It is an old and hoary behavior pattern in groups. People in groups interact in a power struggle and to limit the exercise of power in others (Frost, Mitchell, and Nord, 1982).

Individuals behave politically in all facets of organizational life. They use power to secure promotion, salary increases, or job transfers. It is part of the interplay of activity involved in resource allocation and delegation of authority and responsibility. It is intrinsic to policy development and policy change, performance appraisal, grievances, and intraorganizational coordination. Politics is part of the process of rule making and decision making in all aspects of organizational activity.

Gandz and Murray (1980) ranked perceptions of political action of various common organizational activities and concluded that politics was instrumental in determining interdepartmental harmony. Other areas of organizational activity where politics was a significant factor included promotions and transfers, delegation of authority, facilities and equipment allocation, and work appraisals. Less significant arenas for the exercise of organizational politics were such activities as assessing penalties, hiring, employee development, policymaking, setting pay rates, and budgeting. Analysis of these data suggests that people use organizational politics most often in areas where individuals have some discretion in the actions open to them. We see less political behavior in those activity areas where formalized rules and systems are commonly in place.

Madison and others (1980) explored the positive or negative impacts of the use of organizational politics. His research illustrates that organizational politics can be useful in helping the organization reach its goals and cope with survival and organizational health concerns. It confirms also that organizational politics is helpful in coordinating staff and units, developing esprit de corps, and decision making. It is useful in organizational goal achievement. It can result in inappropriate use of scarce resources, cause divisiveness, create tension, allow less fully qualified people to advance, and reduce communication flows. And, finally, it can damage the image of the organization and sully its reputation.

Madison also assessed the positive and negative impacts of the use of organizational politics on the individuals concerned. Engaging in organizational politics can aid significantly in career advancement, getting recognition, and status in the organization, and increasing our power position. It also helps us accomplish personal goals and is helpful in allowing us to get our jobs done. Engaging in organizational politics can help individuals feel positive about their achievement and their ability to be in control of their organizational life.

There are risks involved, however. Engaging in political activity may result in reducing perceived or actual power in the group. It can result in removal from the organization (that is, loss of job). It can accentuate negative feelings about us by others. And, political activity can result in loss of promotion or increased feelings of guilt and interference with job performance.

Political activity can have both positive and negative results. Its use, however, is not in doubt. It is a ubiquitous part of organizational life. Older group members use it more than those newly inducted into the organization. This is the case also with middle and upper levels of the organization. They engage in organizational politics more than do those in lower-level positions. It is beyond doubt an instrument for securing organizational rewards.

Allen, Madison, Porter, Renwick, and Mayes (1979) assessed personal skills and traits common to politically active people in organizations. They conclude that effective political actors (be they chief executive officers, staff managers, or workers), all share some common characteristics. They are articulate, sensitive, and socially adept. They are competent, popular, extroverted, and self-confident. They exhibit aggressive tendencies, are ambitious, can be devious, and are clearly "organization men." They are also "highly intelligent and logical people." The politically adept individual in the organization is outgoing, competent, and effective in interacting with others. They are seeking, energetic advocates of their desired results. They are willing to engage others in competition for available resources and for the dominance of their ideas and ideologies.

Political Behavior versus Administrative Behavior

We can distinguish organizational politics from administrative behavior in several significant dimensions. Most view administrative behavior by organizational participants as consensus behavior (Frost, Mitchell, and Nord, 1982). Group members agree that the behavior in question is legitimate, that it flows from recognized "right," and that it fits the terms of the exchange. On the other hand, people resist political action and behaviors, if power targets recognize their intent. There is a consensus feeling that such behavior is illegitimate.

All members of the organization participate in power use. Senior executives, middle managers, informal leaders, and rank and file employees all use power. Madison's work shows that politics is more in the superior's mind and actions than in that of lower-level employees. While this may be true, it does not lessen the fact that all employees have some power. No one is powerless, even if it is only the power to withhold talent or energy. They use power to secure their desired results in the same ways that higher-level participants use their capacities.

It is a thesis of this book that power politics is a central activity of life. We can define much of life activity as the exercise of power (Krech and Crutchfield, 1948). Our success, in part, is a function of our ability to use power in our interrelationships. Success requires that we develop power skills along with, or perhaps in preference to, functional and task skills. Power is basic to effective living in the same way that energy is basic to physics (Mueller, 1970). It is a foundation element of human interaction. Power is the ability to activate human and material resources to get work done (Homans, 1950).

Part II

Power Use: Tactical and Strategic Models

People negotiate their desires via power use in a variety of circumstances and in a variety of ways. The exact method employed is, probably, a function of the personality of the power user. Simple observation of individuals in group interaction, however, suggests that many people use power in definable, predictable ways. The chapters in Part II define some of the most common tactical approaches and suggest some strategic orientations present in the workplace. They also provide some insight into the nature of the situation that lends itself to the effective use of political power in organizations.

Chapter 3 outlines a model of power use. This model describes conditions and situational factors important in the application and successful use of power in our normal structured group relationships. The power model identifies six elements of a situation conducive to power use in organizational political situations. Persons involved in power must come to the power-use situation with three capacities. The first is feelings that the event is important. They also must feel sense of freedom and independence in their use of power. Finally, they must feel in some ways competent in the situation. The situation itself must be one where choice is possible and, indeed, required. And the participants must be interdependent and the goals or processes of interaction and the resources necessary to goal realization scarce.

Chapter 3 presents an analytic model of power in use. The model described here tries to abstract essential factors in the interactive process of power use in social groupings. It highlights factors resident in the people involved, in the situation in which they find themselves, in the essence of the decision issues that relates both situational and personal factors into a coordinated action process that achieves the results desired by the powerful at the expense of the less powerful. This is, in essence, an organizational politics model.

In Chapter 4 the reader is introduced to twenty-two specific behavioral tactics useful in attaining organizational objectives through the application of power. These twenty-two tactics sum up the range of power behaviors observed in the workplace and in other interpersonal group situations. They define the operational scope of power use in organizational and group situations. The findings summarized there reflect real-world applications of power in formal situations by a variety of organizational participants. Chapter 4 also defines and illustrates the situations in which people use power in these three kinds of relationship. They provide some hint of the ways we use power in our relationships with those people superior to us in the organization, our peers, and our subordinates.

Chapter 5 concludes this part by identifying critical factors associated with the use of any of the individual power tactics. While power is, indeed, a part of most organizational life, its use is capable of analysis and, at least, partial predictability. This chapter identifies some of the parameters of power use that constrain and direct its use and provide the underlying rationale for its analysis. These factors also represent essential elements to be considered in planning power use.

Chapter 5 also presents a brief historical review of some of the strategic perspectives within which power might be employed as we strive to get our way in our relationships. The specific strategic orientation proposed for the reader's use here is one that focuses on the target of our power use. Tactics identified in this book can be effectively rationalized in terms of who we intend to effect by their use.

3

A Power-Use Model: Using Power in the Organization

We have shown that power use is a part of an organizational dynamic that is, at heart, political. This political process is an ingredient of planning, organizing, staffing, budgeting, goal setting, and program management. However, texts on management often ignore (and as a result mask) the political power dimension of these functions. In budgeting, to use only one example, guidelines concentrate on goals methods, steps, and criteria of the budget cycle; elements of the budget process; implementation; and control. They assume that producing a budget is as mechanical as, say, manufacturing an automobile.

The organizational reality is that participants influence each other during each phase of the budget process. They negotiate schedules, they compromise goals, they marshal support, they compete for limited resources. Budgeting and all of these other activities are power tasks. Organization members accomplish them via use of power tactics implicit in a political action process many call organizational politics.

We all continually find ourselves in situations where power negotiation is a legitimate part of our working lives. Organization members are continually in situations where they are competing with other people for dominance (Pfeffer, 1981, 1992). They compete for the capacity to get their own way in the face of competing action by others in their intimate work group. We can describe this situation in five sentences:

1. Organizational participants react continually with other people who are in interdependent relationship with them.

2. The participant's goals or methods (or both) differ with those of others in the relationship. This difference is such that if one person achieves his goals, the other is thwarted from accomplishing his goals or methods.

3. The participants are in competition with each other as to who will achieve desired goals.

4. There is scarcity present in the situation to some extent.

5. The participants attach enough importance to the situation, goals, or approach that they are willing to engage their energy in this relationship.

These five aspects of the power relationship also define typical organizational life. That is, most situations in which we find ourselves in organizations are situations where our understanding of what is happening increases by viewing the relationship in political power terms.

A POWER-USE MODEL

Power use is an action concept precipitated by a situation as defined above. It is operationalized in overt action by one or more of the parties in the relationship. It requires an interdependent relationship where there is some difference as to what or how participants take action. A model of the power process can be described using several key elements of the interpersonal relationship situation defined.

First, there must be a decision (choice) potential present. Some problem or situation of alternative courses of action must be obvious. Power use is a problem-solving action process.

Second, the situation must be characterized by two factors. One, an interdependency relationship must exist among the participants such that they cannot easily attain their goal(s) outside of the relationship. Two, the situation in which the interdependent persons find themselves must involve scarce resources, skills, ideas, creativity, or other parameters. That is, the resources situation must be such that it cannot easily accommodate both participants' goals economically, given available resources.

A third essential factor in modeling the power situation deals with the participants themselves. The two or more people who come to the choice situation must display three characteristics. First, at least one (and often all) have sufficient competence to function in this environment. Second, each attaches enough importance to the goals, the methods used, or the relationship that they will expend necessary energy to engage in required interaction. Finally, each (or at minimum one participant) must be in a relative position of freedom vis-à-vis others in the relationship. That is, one or more participants should feel they have the personal capacity to achieve their desired outcome.

Given these factors, the fourth element of power, action to effect other participants in the situation, will result. We use power to deal with the choice

Figure 3.1
Power-Use Model

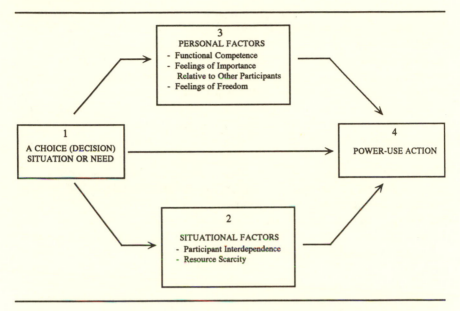

(decision) situation in relationships where these factors are present. Figure 3.1 pictures this condition.

Figure 3.1 depicts the four essential power factors: decision, situational factors, personal factors, and power-use action in dynamic relation. All of these factors must be present in the situation for someone to exercise power. A discussion of each of these four elements follows.

Power Requires a Decision Situation

Power is the ability to mobilize energy, resources, and information to support a preferred outcome. It is used in decision situations: situations in which participants make choices, the purpose of which is to maximize ensuing trade-offs of energy, resources, and results. People use power in these decision situations to secure desired results or to ensure the use of specific means to agreed-upon results. Decision situations imply any difference either of outcome desired or of means to results, whether mutually desired or not. Power operates in these situations of opposition—of conflict of results or means (Duke, 1976).

In this sense, conflict is merely a difference between participants. Nyberg (1981) correctly relates conflict to the whole gamut of behavior from mutual hostility, through acquiescence under threat, to commitment through informed judgment. Conflict not only refers to hostile encounters, it can also mean mere difference of opinion or of goal or of technology preferred. We can say two people are in conflict with each another when one person's desires are in opposition to those of the other person.

Conflict is a result of asymmetries of power, values, or status. It occurs out of ambiguity of jurisdiction (Madison, Allen, Porter, Renwick, and Mayes, 1980), scarce resources (Russell, 1938), or interdependence (Russell, 1938). We ameliorate these asymmetries through power behavior. Viewed in this light, difference (i.e., choice options) is a routine part of organizational life. Organizations consist of people who are competing for resources, information, status, or differing results (Cialdini, 1984). Power is the currency through which people resolve this kind of difference (Pfeffer, 1981; and Coenen and Hofstra, 1988). Difference, then, is basic to power use. Unless there is some opposition, some difference, some uncertainty, some choice among competing alternatives that interdependent people in the relationship must make, there is no need to use power. Powerful people reduce uncertainty in decision situations (Bass, 1960). Their position (Mechanic, 1962), personality (Winter, 1973), or expertise (Pfeffer, 1981) gives them the necessary resources to resolve differences and ambiguity. They can exercise discretion in assigning duties, can open previously closed doors to opportunity, and clarify paths to desired goals of those dependent upon them.

Situational Factors Implicit in the Power Dynamic Model

Power use depends on two situational factors. First, a social relationship in which participants are in some ways interdependent must be present. That is, a situation must obtain where action by one party impacts the behavior or choices of the others. And a condition of scarcity of items of resource critical in achieving the group (or and individual's) purpose must be present. That is, there must be present in the situation some limits on available and needed supplies of information, skills, materials, ideas, creativity, and so forth. We use power in situations where these factors are present:

Power Is a Part of Interdependent Relationships

Power is always found in relationships between individuals (O'Day, 1974). It manifests itself in the behavior of following (Ng, 1980). Power is tied in many ways to the personality of the individual participants. It is not solely, or even, in some cases, directly related to formal structural systems. One form of the power relationship—authority, or hierarchical power—is, of course, related to social position and role. Other forms center their power on the inner capacity or characteristics of individuals. It is from these personality factors that the informal organization phenomenon gets its genesis (Bachrach and Baratz, 1970).

Power relationships are recurring patterns of action that relate people in a hierarchy of independence–dependence. These relationships may be formed for essentially one-time exercise of power, or they can be of a relatively long-term duration spanning many situations and decision events (Bell, 1975). We can define this relationship in three characteristics: (a) the scope or comprehensiveness of the relationship among participants in the group; (b) the scope of decision events in which a particular person is powerful; and (c) the degree of compliance one can exact from subjects (Zald, 1970). Seen in this way—as a relationship, not a process or event—power becomes a central factor in most interpersonal relationships where we try to induce another to desired action, attitude, or orientation (Harward, 1982).

Bachrach and Baratz (1970) make a strong case for the relational character of power. They define three dimensions of this relationship. First is the idea of conflict or competition of values, ideas, or interests. A power relation exists only if one or more of these characteristics of competition are present. Second, a power relation exists if one person in the relationship actually conforms his behavior to that desired by the other person. Mere conflict of interest (or of ideas) is not enough for a power relation to occur. And, finally, a power relationship is present in the situation if one or more of the parties can invoke or threaten to invoke sanctions.

Power relationships are asymmetrical (Homans, 1950). One party must be more dependent upon the other or power is not in play. This dependence can include values or status factors. Either situation results in conflict and conflict leads to power use. These factors define the modern large-scale organization. The organization is purposely structured in a system of nonsymmetrical roles—a structured system of superior–subordinate (or independent–dependent) relationship. The tactical use of power in organizations is, therefore, inevitable. People in organizations are in relationships that call for the exercise of power in most, if not all, of their contacts.

Interestingly, the power relationship is one of interdependence in a situation in which the circumstances in one person's life will impact what happens to that of another. It is therefore relationship-specific. Our ability to influence another is not defined merely as proximity over time. It is the potential focus to dominate the other person through control of resources desired by that person (Szilagyl and Wallace, 1983).

This domination often is diffused as a result of two factors. First, other people in the relationship can determine factors in the situation that define importance or criticality (Schermerhorn, 1961). To the degree that we define our contributions as important or critical, to that degree our control over these contributions comprise power potential. As these controlled resources are defined as marginal or useless, our power diminishes or vanishes. A second factor of importance is that others in the relationship can disparage the uniqueness of our contribution. When the power targets see others as also being able to provide critical resources needed by the group, it diminishes our power. If the situation changes so once-valued resources are no longer valued by the group, or resources uniquely controlled become generally held by group members, our power (again) diminishes or is lost. The power relationship is interdependent, fragile, temporary, and difficult to maintain over time. Changes in the situation change the nature of the power relationship and the strength (utility) of the power we hold. We both control and are controlled by others in our relationship and these relationships shift over time and circumstance.

Power Comes with Control over Scarcity

Power operates to control scarce resources, ideas, or instrumentalities. It is exercised in situations where scarce elements of the situation are needed to achieve of desired results (Allen and Porter, 1979). The quality of scarcity may be real or only perceived to have the recipients respond in power terms. Power does not concentrate around abundance.

Those people who control the more scarce or critical aspects of the organization's work dominate. They have a natural advantage in developing and exercising power. Power accrues to those with information, skills, and resources especially as other alternatives or alternate sources of supply are lacking. Frequently, difficult people to replace will have more power than those easily replaced (Hoffer, 1969). And a subordinate with needed skill or energy will be able to exercise more influence in the organization than those without these resources (Kanter, 1979).

Scarcity promotes the use of power in those organizations that need a particular scarce item. Salancik and Pfeffer (1977) suggest that critical contingencies—also defined in scarcity terms—determine the sources and extent of power used. Critical contingencies determine the available needed resources and thus determine the choice situations. Their critical contingencies theory suggests that individuals and subgroups who can effectively control these critical contingencies will gain relative power. Those who cannot will suffer domination by the more powerful. While obvious, it is a critical factor in power use. People (and departments) differ in the strength of their capacity to provide needed, scarce resources appropriate to the critical contingencies (i.e., important elements) of the organization's life.

In many ways power, itself, has an inherent scarcity value. When one person has more power in a relationship, another has less. Indeed in situations where there is an absolute equality of power, people do not use it (Szilagyl and Wallace, 1983). In this sense we use power only when there is a relative scarcity of power held by all participants except one or a few.

Personal Factors of the Power Dynamics Model

We use power in situations where we must choose among alternatives. The participants themselves must partake of certain characteristics to ensure that the situation is truly one of power and not some other social phenomenon. First, a power situation must include people who are free to act to achieve desired results. Second, people engaged in power use must think the situation is sufficiently important, or value the potential result or the potential interaction sufficiently, to expend energy to engage in relationships on this issue. And finally, a power situation includes people who are competent enough to have some potential to succeed. When these factors are present we engage in power behavior. The power dynamic, while commonly found in most organized groups, nevertheless is defined in terms of these factors (along with the decision issue and situational factors alluded to above). The paragraphs below elaborate each of these personal factors.

Power Is the Freedom to Move (to Act)

Power and freedom are related concepts. Freedom to act, to move, to achieve defines power (O'Brian and Banech, 1969). A dynamic model of power must include the capacity of at least one actor to move (at least relatively) freely. That is, power use requires individuals to act in ways that achieves their will in the face of opposing wills of other people. Unless this freedom is present, power is not a part of the relationship. Richard M. Emerson (1962) characterizes power use in any relationship in relative independence terms. Independence empowers us. Being dependent upon another person, he says, gives that other person power over us. Power exists only in this kind of asymmetrical relationship.

Freedom, independence, dominance, and dependence are all power-tinted ideas. They are ideas, however, that are also implicit in the structure of organized groups. Life is a continuing series of attempts to make real our own agenda for action. This is a power process and power is the resource most used to accomplish our goals. Whenever we bring individuals together to accomplish some planned activity, the power process is active. In our formal organizations—the firm, the agency, or the informal social group—we can characterize these relationships by hierarchy. We each occupy a role, a set place in the hierarchy. That place is one that places us in a relatively independent–dependent status vis-à-vis others in the group.

Emerson (1962) confirms that power is present in any relationship in which one person depends on another. Being dependent gives the person toward whom we are dependent power over us. This is consistent with part of French and Raven's (1959) work on bases of power. This research defines power sources in terms of relative control (dominance) over certain fundamental materials or relationships. Those who control these scarce and needed materials have power because they command resources others desire, including friendship, rewards, experience, information, et cetera (Bachrach and Baratz, 1970).

Much of current leadership literature discusses the relative power of individuals who are prominently placed in the hierarchy over those lower in the pecking order. Mechanic (1962) cautions that not only the leaders, but lower-level employees can hold and use power. They also can dominate in a given situation. While leaders may get and use power due to their place in the organization (and the concomitant control they can exercise over needed desired resources), so, too, can lower-level members. Kotter (1977) confirms that it is primarily because of the dependence leaders have on employees for work, for information, and so on, that employees can have and use power. Much of the underlying basis for informal organization rests in power exercised by these lower-level people who can dominate others above them in the hierarchy through their control over resources the leaders need (Krupp, 1961).

Dominance equates to leadership and leadership with ability to get your own way—that is, with freedom. Stogdill (Bass, 1981) reviewed many power and leadership studies. He points out that, in several empirical studies, dominant members of a group were chosen to lead more often than other, more submissive, members. His abstract of the research also concludes that groups are more satisfied when led by people who are dominant. Dominant people are confident, aggressive, outgoing. Much of Abraham Maslow's (1971) work, especially the earlier experiments with animals and later, the development of self-esteem and self-actualization motives, has relevance here. He suggests by his life's work that dominance is an attitude set involving such things as confidence, self-respect, pride, sureness, masterfulness. Sik Hung Ng's (1980) comprehensive analysis of power in social psychology reviews Maslow's work on dominance. He concludes that the "dominance feeling" (Maslow's term) means "an assured sense of self-power."

Power Operates in Situations of Importance to Participants

Power implies commitment to the desired result enough to spend needed energy to achieve it. The exercise of energy in action comes for us all only as we desire something more strongly than we value repose. We move because we desire to be in some other state more than to be at rest. Similarly, we employ power only in those circumstances where our desire for a particular outcome is stronger than for other results. Commitment is a state of being in which we become bound to a particular action(s) by a belief system that sustains those actions and our own involvement (Rubinoff, 1968). In this sense, we activate power as we commit to a belief system and a course of action consistent with achievement of that belief goal.

Unless we feel a particular outcome is important to us—more important than other germane alternative results—we will not engage in power activity (Bacharach and Lawler, 1986). Patchen (1974) researched salience as a factor in power usage. He concluded that the degree of involvement in a decision process relates to the salience of the decision issue to the individual. Power is a part of a relationship only when one or more parties have a reason for engaging in interaction. At least one person in the relationship must have a plan, an agenda, a reason for using energy (Berle, 1959). Nyberg (1981) says power is instrumental to the individual in achieving his desired results, of realizing his plan.

Power is, in this sense, important as an instrument to achieve some preconceived state or desire. It arises out of a felt need (important enough to cause use of energy) and a mechanism (the control over resources needed by others) that allows for possible amelioration of that need (Kipnis, 1980). Power is intentional and instrumental in its use. We activate it only as we value the possible outcome sufficiently to expend needed energy in power action.

Power Flows Out of Competence

A final personal factor in the power dynamic deals with participant skills. All competition is fundamentally a struggle for domination and the most astute individual usually wins the struggle. Competence, or the ability to respond appropriately in a situation, is an aspect of power. It is a part of the power model in organized groups. It is instrumental in the power struggle situation that typifies modern life.

Competence implies expertise in the task or process areas of value to the group. Competence also means facility in functioning in power terms. Competence involves ability to function in interpersonal situations, successfully using skills of communication, persuasion, manipulation, and others implicit in human interaction or power use.

Power Use Is an Action Process

Power is visible only in action. It derives from our ability to take needed actions to achieve desired results or to withhold such action. It is a dynamic, interactive phenomenon. It is manifest in the unusual. The individual who can take dramatic, visible, and appropriate action has power (Kanter, 1979). Above-average or excellent performance alone is not power. Rather, we see power in the exceptional, the unusual, or the nonroutine. And others in the group must know the action and recognize it as germane to whatever situation the group feels to be significant.

SUMMARY

A descriptive model, such as the one proposed here, must make some compromise with total accuracy. Power, like any other social interactive process is complex and multifaceted. The political power process in our organizations is a dynamic, interactive, perishable process that is effective in the moment of use and not so much in its mere potential. It is a part of all organizational life. It is implicit in the idea of division of labor and in hierarchical structure. It permeates social intercourse where people interact in more or less intimate relationships to influence others to behave in desired ways. It is, therefore, a common element of organizational action. Leaders will find continual opportunity to sharpen their power-use skills in every contact they make in the group and with relevant stakeholders.

4

Power-Use Tactics: Application of Power on the Job

Power has little direct utility as an abstract concept. We think about power only in terms of its use in specific relationships and in specific politically charged situations. It is a concrete, not an abstract, phenomenon. Yet this tactical aspect of analysis has received little attention. Some recent work seeks to begin this tactical phase of analysis. To date it is spotty and suffers from lack of a specific language of power.

On balance working, tactical power use may be the most fruitful line of inquiry into power use and theory building. It also holds promise of illuminating many of the quandaries of organizational life and its development toward organizational health. It also has the potential to legitimize organizational politics as an additional tool all organization members can use openly. The power process involves a collaborative relationship between an individual and a target. Power users enjoy differing styles, philosophies, and approaches. In general, however, they perform a discrete set of functions toward the target. These functions include intervening in the relationship to promote desired action by the target. That is, they promote change from the current level to some ideal or desired level of action.

A study of specific tactics used today points to a wide range of power tactics operating in our groups and organizations. (See the Appendix.) Using survey techniques coupled with interview and observational data, the author surveyed a variety of individuals in several types of organization. The focus was to explore the kinds of operational (tactical) behavior they engaged in routinely on the job.

Details of this study and detailed summaries of findings are found in the Appendix. A summary review of some specific findings about the tactical use of power by these respondents follows in this and later chapters.

Study subjects illustrated sufficiently broad-based characteristics to form a sound platform from which to describe power use in organizations and in specific work situations. Data collected were subjected to several statistical procedures, the results of which show that specific power behavior interventions (tactics) are discreet. That is, the twenty-two power tactics produced do not duplicate each other. Neither are any tactics related to each other in statistically significant ways. The power-use tactics shown in Table 4.1 reflect real-world behaviors. These twenty-two tactics describe a wide variety of behaviors that have as their main purpose getting others to behave in ways we desire; that is, in ways that the target of these tactics probably would not have behaved if left alone.

The focus of attention on the employment of power in organized group contexts has important potential significance. This work may help in efforts to determine specific methods and approaches for directing power to the accomplishment of desired organizational and personal results. These studies and others have confirmed observation of people in the workplace. They help verify the twenty-two specific behavior sets—or tactics—that delimit the range of power behaviors displayed by persons to attain their desires. These power tactics form a useful paradigm within which we can view power use. They define its impact and results. The tactics prescribe its effect on personal goal attainment and the personal relationships present in the organization (Pfeffer, 1992; see also Fairholm, 1985).

Identification of these tactics also provides a needed and useful addition to our "power language" and a new perspective from which to view organizational behavior. This perspective is one that can add insight not now available.

The tactics represent approaches to personal goal attainment available to us in specific organizational situations. Each tactic defines the parameters of a set of specific actions we can take to get others to behave in ways we desire. That is, in ways in which the target of power would not otherwise have behaved. Together they represent alternative patterns of behavior from which we may select to increase the likelihood of success in personal goal attainment. Table 4.1 displays these twenty-two tactics in alphabetical order based on the key idea of each.

EXTENT OF USE OF POWER TACTICS

Power is beginning to receive serious attention from transactional perspectives as distinct from political, sociological, and psychological viewpoints (Pfeffer, 1992). This tactical focus is important. It portends help for us in determining specific approaches we can take to direct available power to the accomplishment of our organizational and personal desires.

Involved in the development of a particular use of a power tactic will be four

Table 4.1
Twenty-two Power Tactics

Controlling the Agenda	Determining beforehand the issues, subjects, or concerns for group action or decision.
Using Ambiguity	Keeping communications unclear and subject to multiple meanings.
Brinkmanship	Disturbing the equilibrium of the organization to control choice options.
Displaying Charisma	Using the respect that others have for our character traits, presence, or method of operation to effect another's behavior in desired ways.
Forming Coalitions	Securing allies--both employees and other stakeholders in the organization or associated with it.
Co-opting Opposition Members	Placing a representative of the opposition group on our decision making body to induce the representative to favor, rather than oppose, our interests.
Controlling Decision Criteria	Selecting of the criteria by which decisions are made so that desired decisions result regardless of who decides.
Developing Others	Increasing the capacities of others, thereby increasing overall power.
Using Outside Experts	Involving congenial experts in organizational decisions, thus allowing us to effect results without personally deciding.
Building a Favorable Image	Creating a persona of skills, capacities, values, or attitudes to which others defer.
Legitimizing Control	Formalizing our right to decide through appeals to hierarchy or legal precedent.
Incurring Obligation	Placing others under obligation to us so they do what we desire.
Organizational Placement	Placing allies in strategic positions or isolating potential opponents.
Proactivity	Unilateral action to secure desired results.
Quid Pro Quo	Negotiating trade-offs with others to secure our desired results.
Rationalization	Conscious engineering of reality to secure desired decision results.
Allocating Resources	Distributing resources under our control in ways that will increase our power in relationships to others.
Dispensing Rewards	Rewarding or punishing others to win their support.
Ritualism	Inducing institutionalized patterns of behavior in others or in the organization.
Using a Surrogate	Using an intermediary to secure compliance in others.
Using Symbols	Reinforcing control through symbolic objects, ideas, or actions.
Training and Orienting Others	Transmitting skills, values, or specific behavior to others to instill in them our goals, values, philosophy, or desired behaviors.

factors: the nature and composition of the parties in the relationship, the decision issue under consideration, the tactics employed, and, finally, the results intended by the power user(s). People in organizations may and do use the full range of power tactics in attaining their desired results. It is important to note that both parties in the relationship exercise power. Sometimes we control material resources, but always we control our attention energy and our ideas and attitudes. Power use is another way to view organizational behavior. This perspective may add insight on how we behave in group settings and how we drive organizational performance.

The power user often intervenes through direct means, that is, by direct interaction. He may also intervene in indirect or covert ways or through others who act as surrogates for the power user in certain circumstances. Often power use in a relationship is from the top down, from someone higher in the group hierarchy than the target. It is also common that the power user acts in the situation toward someone equal or superior in formal status.

The facts suggest that we relate to other people in three different sets of group settings. The first setting is toward those superior to us in the hierarchy. Second to those on a more or less equal or peer level. Organizationally, we also relate to those subordinate to us in the formal or informal pecking order. How we get our desired results made real in each of these settings differs. That is, we use different behavior sets, different power tactics, to achieve our desired results in each kind of relationship. Some interesting findings are clear from research that sheds light on the question of how we get our way in each of these group settings. Chapters in Part III elaborate on these three directions for power use.

The power user must face many different types of situations when intervening in an organization and with individuals. One may classify them as targets of support. In the most favorable type of situation all interested parties—superiors, peers, and subordinates—recognize the need for power use. They support it, the specific tactic technology employed, and the results sought. In another type of situation, top management recognizes the need for specific power use to attain a desired goal and provides needed support. In this situation, peer or subordinate levels are nonsupportive or ignorant of the power application tried. Still another type of situation occurs when lower levels of the organization are supportive while top management resists its use.

Some writers have begun to focus specific attention on these power tactics. (See, for example: Allen, Porter, Renwick, and Mayes, 1979; Allen and Porter, 1983; Fairholm, 1984, 1985; Merrell, 1979; and Pfeffer, 1981.) They suggest that tactic choice is a function of place in the group hierarchy. The higher the status in the formal or informal hierarchy, the more direct the exercise of power is. That is the higher the position, the more the power user selects tactics that use direct power forms like force, authority, and threat. The lower the status, the more the user makes use of indirect forms such as manipulation, persuasion, and influence.

The higher the role, the more rational, aggressive, and open are the tactics used. Those closer to the bottom of the hierarchy use the more indirect and persuasive tactics. We determine tactic choice by a variety of factors. Among them must be relative role position, scope of power base, and skill in using available tactics.

TARGETS OF POWER USAGE

One can use any of the twenty-two power tactics in any relationship with either superiors, peers, or subordinates. Most often, however, people use a specific tactic in relations with one type of organizational coworker. The data

Table 4.2
Targeted Tactics Ranked by Frequency of Use

Toward Superiors	Toward Peers	Toward Subordinates
Proactivity	Quid Pro Quo	Training and Orienting Others
Using Outside Experts	Allocating Resources	Developing Others
Displaying Charisma	Forming Coalitions	Dispensing Rewards
Rationalization	Co-opting Opposition Members	Controlling Decision Criteria
Using Ambiguity	Incurring Obligation	Legitimizing Control
Building a Favorable Image	Using a Surrogate	Organizational Placement
	Controlling the Agenda	Ritualism
	Brinkmanship	Incurring Obligation
	Building a Favorable Image	

summarized in Table 4.2 reflect statistically meaningful uses of individual tactics toward each of the three target groups. These data summarize research findings about typical applied use of power tactics in each of these three settings. The tactics shown in Table 4.2 have a statistical likelihood of use with the appropriate group of at least .001.

As shown, respondents typically concentrate use of each tactic toward one target group to the general exclusion of the others. It is thus realistic to say that the three lists of tactics shown are accurate. They reflect the preferences of power users in securing compliance from each group of coworkers. Table 4.2 includes two exceptions. People find some success in using the tactics of building a favorable image and incurring obligation in others toward more than one classification or target. We use building a favorable image toward both superiors and peers. We also use incurring obligation toward both peers and subordinates. In all other cases people use specific tactics toward the specific group shown. The reader should note that, in research supporting this data, respondents say they used each tactic toward colleagues of all three types. The Table 4.2 listings show the statistically significant frequency of use (see Appendix for statistical rationale).

In selecting a specific power tactic, the user must consider several factors. Among them are the nature of the problem situation, the goals of the change effort, the cultural norms of the client target, and the expected degree of resistance. Selecting a specific tactic involves us in comparing and testing possible tactics against some criteria. Three broad factors are of concern to power users in selecting the right power tactic to secure their organizational goals. The first is the potential results of the technique. That is, will it solve the problem? Will it produce positive results in the organization and the intimate relationship? And are there potential negative results likely to occur in its use?

A second factor is the potential for successful implementation. Can the proposed tactic really work in practical application? What are the reasonably forecastable costs in dollar and human terms? And how do these costs compare with alternative tactics? The acceptance potential of the tactic is the third factor. Is the technique acceptable to the targets? Is it tested in this kind of application, in this kind of situation, and with these kinds of targets?

Users should consider these important factors before making a final decision about the selection of an intervention. The final selection is usually a trade-off between advantages and disadvantages because there is no precise way to answer all the questions in advance. After comparing the advantages and disadvantages, the user selects a specific intervention technique for action.

Since power use in office politics is a dynamic interactive process, the boundaries of what is or is not power usage are ambiguous and evolving. The tactics included here provide examples of the diverse techniques that exist. However, the list is not all-inclusive.

These planned activities or tactics are aimed specifically at correcting inefficiencies in the relationship of which the power user is a part. A basic assumption underlying the intervention activity is that the target has the resources—personal capacities or organizational resources—for change. It also assumes that the role of the power user is to energize these forces by helping the target in behaving in appropriate ways.

Using power tactics makes things happen. It causes changes in the behavior of people, the allocation of resources, and the systems of which the tactics are a part. These power tactics include techniques focusing on several organization levels ranging from subordinate contacts to peers and superiors. All are proper environments within which to use power and to plan and carry out power tactics.

People design organizations to use the energy and ability of individuals to perform work and achieve goals. Members bring to the organization their own values, assumptions, and behaviors. The effectiveness of the organization then is a function of how effectively we integrate the needs of the individual members with overall goals. There are a range of power activities aimed at enhancing the development and functioning of the individual organization member. Essentially the underlying assumption of these approaches is simple: If the individual becomes more effectively responsive to our needs and more skilled, we increase the potential for success.

In a general sense, such interventions aim at improving communication ability, interpersonal skill, and managerial or technical behavior of organization members. If we increase interpersonal competence, we also should improve organizational performance or relationship results. As a result, several power intervention activities aim at enhancing the attitude and behavior patterns within the organizational environment. We apply these basic power techniques in all organization changes. The presentation following is systematic. It relates power forms to the primary—or most significant—target of use, either toward superiors, peers, or subordinates.

5

Using Power in the Organization

Power permeates our lives. We are often in situations with others where we are controlling some people or being controlled by them. We cannot choose whether power will be used in our internal organizational political relationships. We can only determine whether we will think about it and act on the basis of an understanding of its use. Facility in its use can help both the practitioner and the analyst in understanding what takes place in organizational life. Power is an essential element of resource allocation, conflict, competition, decision making, planning, staff selection, and the whole range of management, supervisory, and leadership tasks. In a very real sense, power in use is merely organizational dynamics—the action of people in relationships.

Obviously we all use power routinely. It is a central activity of mankind. For Plato, power was "being." In *The Sophist*, he argues that anything that possesses any sort of power to affect another or to be affected by another, if only for a single moment, however trifling the cause or however slight the effect, has real existence. Writers such as Hobbes, Machiavelli, May, Berle, Russell, and scores of others have viewed the question of power as one of the central issues of society. Power use resolves itself into the question of who is contending for what result and with what resources? These are, at heart, political questions. Our power behavior determines their answers.

Power is omnipresent in organizational decision making. It is critical in selection of key staff. It is a part of all resource allocation. Promotion actions, reorganization decisions, and the development, flow, and use of information needed by organizational members all involve power use. It is the medium of leadership. Gellerman puts the issue in motivational terms. For him, power is the critical difference between the person who seeks to control the conduct of the individual and the group and the leader who exercises control over the results they achieve. Power use earns us the right to lead (Goodstadt and Hjelle, 1973).

Effective leadership today must depend on power use for success. Skill in its use is central to accomplishment in organizations. Basic to the act of organization (creating a homogeneous unit from the collective whole) is the need to control, direct, and focus subdivisions toward planned goals that give purpose and coherence to the organization. The behavior in which people engage to accomplish these ends necessitates using power. No one group or individual has exclusive rights to exercise power; it is a part of the behaviors of all of us. It is especially significant to those who place themselves at the head of others and of our social organizations.

REASONS FOR POWER USE

People seek to exercise power for a variety of reasons. They use it to obtain their desires in situations where all participants compete for available resources. On one level, according to Plato, power use defines "self." Some use power for the sheer enjoyment of it. Mueller (1970) said the "sheer love" of power drives some people. Russell (1938) saw power and glory as synonymous. For these people, power use is a desirable end in and of itself. Others see it as instrumental in achieving other, more valuable results, whether psychological or material (Kipnis, 1980).

David Kipnis produced a list of reasons why people exercise power in organizations. His list included the following kinds of reasons:

1. to receive help in our job.
2. to assign work to a target of power.
3. to acquire benefits from the target of power.
4. to aid in improving the target's performance.
5. to initiate change.

Others have added additional reasons, including:

6. for the fun of it (Mueller, 1970).
7. to meet ego needs (Adler, 1956).

LIMITS OF POWER USE

While power is, by definition, a part of joint action, it is constrained by a variety of factors in the situation and the character of participants. One factor constraining power use is the perspective from which we view it. We are constrained whether we see it as an end or only as instrumental to other ends. There are always constraining factors that limit its use and effect. For example, personal characteristics or physical appearance impacts our power use. Those with attractive physical or personality characteristics find it easier to exercise power than those not so well endowed. Height, intelligence, relative comeliness, and similar factors help or hinder our effectiveness as power users (Kotter, 1977). These factors are seen as symbols of our power.

Similarly, factors in the situation surrounding power use can impact effectiveness. Position held in the hierarchy is significant, as is socioeconomic status, the size of the group, and the nature of the task dealt with. All of these factors, individually or combined, can impact our ability to use power productively. The central factor in power use is will and resources. Unless there is enough of both, we cannot exercise power. Success in achieving desired results in the face of opposition is a function of individual will and control and the imaginative use of available resources.

RESISTANCE TO POWER USE

By definition, power is not in use unless at least two participants in the relationship are at odds with each other on some issue. Resistance, therefore, is a common reaction to our use of power. People resist the power we use against them by (a) using a countervailing power, (b) striving to destroy or limit the base or bases of power we control, (c) seeking to wrest from us power bases that we hold, (d) trying to disengage from the relationship, thereby destroying not only our power, but also the underlying relationship itself.

Resistance can result from inability to respond appropriately. That is, others fail to respond to our power use because they do not have the resources necessary to effect compliance even though they want to comply. They do not have the requisite skills, time, materials, or the information needed to effect our outcome desires. Resistance also can result from an unwillingness to comply. That is, the target can, but chooses not to, comply with our desires. In both cases, the resistance is real, and the impact on our use of power is similar: We must increase the force or scope of the power use or give up.

Several reasons present themselves as to why we cannot bring to bear enough power to overcome resistance. Obviously, we may not have the means available to us, as in the case when a supervisor cannot promise a promotion (or other reward) for needed performance. And, too, when we employ one means of power use we often cannot thereafter employ some other form of power in the same situation. For example, a decision to use force precludes the later use of, say, persuasion by us in that situation. A supervisor whose strategy of power is authoritarian cannot easily employ within that context the power form of persuasion or influence. Once we employ authority, targets will not easily respond in ways appropriate to other forms because of the force of the authoritarian style dominating the relationship between the two participants.

RESULTS OF POWER USE

The goal of power use is realization of desired behavior, attitudes, or characteristics in others or in groups. We use power in situations where goals are to be formed, resources allocated, information disseminated, assignments of staff made, performance improved or altered. In short, we use power when we require any choice. Its use impacts the user as well as the target of power. For example, Kipnis (1976) concludes that, psychologically, using power empowers the power holder and devalues the target of power in the power holder's eye. This situation sets up a relationship that can lead to abuse of the relatively powerless persons.

Goodstadt and Hjelle (1973) also studied this relationship and confirm Kipnis's results. They also looked at the impacts of power use on group members previously seen as relatively powerless. When given power, these people resort typically to coercive power forms. Goodstadt and Hjelle found that the impact on personal and target self-esteem follows the Kipnis research results. Kotter's (1977) work suggests that power use increases the speed of results attainment. Power use speeds up action in the group and hastens goal accomplishment for the power holder. Kipnis also found that power use increased the assertiveness of power users. Power use has the potential for great good. Its use also allows the user to impact people adversely.

Power is both an offensive and a defensive tool. Most research deals with the effectiveness of power use in getting our way in the organizational relationship. There is, however, a growing body of information discussing the ways people use power to forestall someone else getting his way. People use power to prevent someone from doing something we do not like or that will hurt us. It can be effective in either offensive or defensive modes.

IMPORTANT FACTORS IN SUCCESSFUL POWER USE

The ubiquitousness of power in social interaction presents a problem as we try to identify the critical factors essential to successful power use. Because it is so much a part of all (most) social intercourse, it is difficult to isolate situational factors essential to its use. In one very real sense, power use is possible in any circumstance. We see it in situations that facilitate its successful use and in situations where the chances for success are marginal to say the least. The nine situational factors listed below facilitate its successful use. Readers must recognize that they also can successfully use power in other situations.

Discretion

Kantor (1977) says that people most easily use power in situations that allow us discretion and flexibility. Nonroutine tasks that permit adaptation in method and outcome and allow us to exercise some creativity also provide an environment where we can use power.

Centrality

Kantor also identifies the critical nature of the factor of relevance. Her research suggests that being close to the center of activity enhances power use. Korda (1975) and others confirm this.

Exchange

Several writers identify the power situation as being one of exchange. A social exchange is one where both parties have something to give and some expectation of potential attractive results from the interaction (Michner and Schwartfeger, 1972; and Molm, 1990).

Status with Supervisors

Pety found that individuals in intimate contact with people superior in the hierarchy were more effective in getting their way than those less well connected. Contact and influence with superiors is a useful factor and is effective in power use (Bass, 1981).

Conformance to Group Norms

People who personify the underlying group norms are more powerful in that group than those who do not (Cavanaugh, Moberg, and Velasquez, 1981).

Legitimacy

Much research supports the idea that those people we accept as legitimate or rightful authorities are more powerful than those who are not (Falbo, New, and Gaines, 1987). Congruence with rightful authority, traditional activities, or with accepted figures endows us with credibility, and power use from that foundation can be effective.

Association

Power use can be more effective if our power targets see us as being associated with other like-minded people.

Personal Status

People with high personal standing in the group, according to Kipnis (1976), have more influence. Others see those people held in high esteem as powerful and will accept their desires more readily than those with lower status (Bachrach and Lawler, 1986).

Personal Characteristics

Some research (summarized by Mechanic, 1962) suggests that some personal attributes are factors in successful power use. We associate commitment, high energy use, interest, skill, attractiveness, and similar characteristics with successful exercise of power.

EXPECTATIONS AND POWER USE

An organization has certain expectations of its members. Especially in business organizations, leaders spell out member behavior very clearly. The organization undoubtedly expects its members to be on the job during certain hours of the day. It expects a level of quality and quantity of work, loyalty, appearance, and various other behavior unique to the organization. To satisfy the organization, the individual member will need to comply with group expectations, at least to some degree. Organizations place requirements on members if there is to be a lasting and healthy relationship. These organizational cultural constraints may be friendly or unfriendly to participants (White, 1990).

Similarly, the individual has certain expectations of the organization. An individual may expect to gain work experience, security, and advancement. He probably expects to meet people, make friends, and form social relationships. He undoubtedly expects pay from the organization. The organization will have to meet these or similar expectations to satisfy the individual for long. When either the organization's or the individual's expectations are not satisfied adequately by the other party, friction and difficulties may develop. Failure to resolve these problems may culminate in separation of the individual from the organization. All too often, the problem is solved by not solving it. It takes too much effort sometimes to deal directly with the underlying issues, so nothing is done. Both parties continue with a tenuous and unproductive relationship.

Sometimes the relationship between the individual and the organization does not even address key expectations. One or both of these parties may assume that the other party agrees to some unstated expectations. Such unstated or assumed expectations can lead to an organization peopled by individuals who feel cheated or leaders who feel disappointed in their subordinates. Power is in action both in the behaviors that lead to this kind of relationship and in the actions both parties take to remediate the unhealthy relationship.

Our organizations must maintain a stable identity and operations to accomplish their primary goals. Consequently, organizations involved in managing growth find that the way members use power is critical. There is a need for the use of a systematic approach, discriminating between those features that are healthy and effective and those that are not. Erratic, short-term, unplanned, or haphazard use of power may well introduce problems that did not exist before. At least they may produce side effects that may be worse than the original problem necessitating power use in the first place. We should be aware that stability, equilibrium, aids a healthy organization. Power use just for the sake of power use is not necessarily effective and can be dysfunctional.

The important issue is whether or not we can deal effectively with power and the use of power. Organization members, whether they be in business, governmental, educational, or nonprofit settings, rely upon power. The individuals in positions of influence constitute the power structure and frequently are power-motivated people. Leaders compete for promotion, and department and division staff conflict over resource allocations. But, importantly, all members of our organizations have and use power for their own personal or institutional political purposes. Political infighting is a reality (even though sometimes a dysfunctional factor) in most organizations. Here the issue is whether the individual can deal effectively with the power issues and situations that, in truth, make up organizational life.

STRATEGIES OF POWER USE

We can look at power research on two levels. First, we can analyze power as a series of separate and legally isolated empirical events that show it in use in organizations, but in specific and discrete situations, using limited forms, bases, and directed to specific targets. A second level of research, characterized as universal in scope, tries to integrate power theory with socio-organizational theory and practice. Power use at this level of inquiry becomes part of the larger picture of human motivation and leadership. Some of these attempts have resulted in perspectives that can help us understand the overall power-use context. These studies also can be helpful in clarifying the strategic dimensions of power use.

Historically the use of power has been antithetical to open, participative management systems and admitted, but deplored, in authoritarian systems. The common orientation is to be sure you have necessary power and people know it, but to take every opportunity not to use it directly. But, the fact is, most organizations operate within some type of system that sanctions and uses power. The organization's members are motivated to some extent by the perceived power they command within the organization or the power their part of the organization commands vis-à-vis other units of competitors in the external environment. It is useful to make more explicit the nature of the extent of power systems in organizations and of the many various power interventions used.

Coping with power use in both the internal and external environment requires increased sensitivity to changing conditions. It also asks for improved knowledge of ways to incorporate adaptive mechanisms within the organizational system. Such flexibility may mean the difference between the successful institution of corrective action and worsening of the problem conditions. To meet these challenges, organizations and individuals are developing strategies of coping that employ power in all of its forms and using various specific power tactics.

The starting point for engaging in power usage as organizational politics is the definition of an overall power strategy. The specific relationship with the target, as well as the organization climate, will influence the selection of specific power tactics. The overall strategies aimed at improving individual and organizational effectiveness are also relationship-specific.

Strategy involves the planning and direction of power action programs. Tactics are techniques, or the specific means, by which people attain their power goals. Before we can implement power techniques or tactics, the power user needs to develop a strategy to guide future actions. For the power strategies to be successful, the power user must consider the interdependencies that exist among the various subelements of the organization. A power-induced change in one will have some impact upon other elements of the system. The user must be alert to the special factors in the situation and select a strategy appropriate to the situation, not rely on a "favorite" strategy.

Another factor to consider in strategy selection is the second-order consequences. This refers to the indirect or deferred results coming from the immediate impact of power use on individuals, organizations, and situations. A change in one aspect of the situation resulting from power use can impact other, not directly of concern, parts of the organization. This can create new problems of other situations where power must be employed.

Typically, attempts to collapse power use into a few discrete strategies have used resources or bases of power as the desideratum. They group power tactics into categories depending on the resources or bases that are most critical to its exercise. Perhaps the best known of these are in the work of Max Weber and Amitai Etzioni. Weber's (1968) classification of power exercised in organizations includes three groupings: traditional, charismatic, and rational–legal. Weber's synthesis proposed that one exercises traditional power against others, in one set of circumstances, because people accept our commands as legitimate and justified when they conform to traditionally accepted patterns of behavior. A simple example is in the routine orders leaders give to employees who follow them because it is expected of someone in their position to do so. Power use is effective in this case because the leader controls either the definition of what becomes "traditional" or the means to activate traditional methods.

Weber's second class of power use centers around force of personality. He suggests that persons who have attractive personality characteristics, charisma, or special "calling" attract a cadre of people to them. They are often willing to accept their commands as justified on the basis of those personality factors. Possession of these attractive, charismatic qualities facilitates effective power use.

Finally, Weber suggests that people accept another's commands as authoritative because the action conforms to known law, rule, or policy. That is, they view the rules on which the specific command is based as legal, rational, legitimate, and acceptable. Control over, or conformance to, the legitimate rules governing organizational life empowers the controller with effective assets in interpersonal relationships. The ubiquity and effectiveness of standard operating procedures is a simple example of this form of power use. Powerful people create procedures that perpetuate their power and others follow them because they feel it is the legal or appropriate thing to do. Weber's work has had a profound impact on the study of power as well as on organization and management theory.

Subsequently Etzioni (1961) formulated a strategic typology (also in three parts) using bases of power as his foundation. He distinguished between coercive, remunerative, and normative power. Each corresponds to power resources of force, material reward for desired behavior, and conformance to group-recognized standards of acceptability (legitimacy, prestige, love). Power-use behaviors are, for Etzioni, founded on one or the other (or combinations of two or more) of these types of resource control.

For Etzioni, power use is a transaction in which compliance is given in exchange for desired resources classified in organizational terms. His three-part typology adds to our understanding of power use.

1. *Coercive power* helps us get compliance when we have control over sanctions important to the target. The ability to punish noncompliance is central to the use of this strategy. We must be able to control sanctions important to the target. And, importantly, the target must perceive this situation accurately in order for this strategy of power use to be effective.

2. *Remunerative power* is illustrated when we control important and needed resources and use them as rewards for compliance. Again, the exchange is compliance for reward in the same way that we exact compliance from the target under threat of punishment as noted above.

3. *Normative power* describes a situation where one controls resources having high symbolic value. Control over ideas, ideals, values, goals, or approaches that have emotional appeal to others places us in a power position vis-à-vis them. Those in the organization who want to identify with these abstract (symbolic) ideas submit to those who espouse them.

The wide appeal of Weber's and Etzioni's strategic typologies lies in part, at least, in their universality. These strategies can help us understand the workings of power in organizations. They also can help us select from available resources a coherent, consistent, and predictable range of specific behaviors intended to impact others' actions. However, they are somewhat artificial. They fail in some real ways to rationalize power use fully and to provide a true strategic basis for its use. Seldom can one isolate a pure example of a typology. They are most often seen in combination. And, the typologies do not relate to any found in a natural or pure state such as up/down or superior/subordinate.

Benne and Chin's (1961) strategic model is also in three parts and is similar to Etzioni's. The first, Empirical–Rational Strategies involve direct proposal of change with reasons to the affected people. Normative–Reeducative Strategies modify the problem-solving capabilities of a system or foster the growth of the people making up the system. This strategy assumes a direct connection between the people making up the system and the system itself. Finally, Power–Coercive Strategies assume compliance of those with less power in the situation to the will of those with more power. This typology is, perhaps, more useful. It, too, suffers from lack of purity. They are seen most often in combination, not in their pure forms.

Each of these strategies of change implies a specific kind of power use. We see power in use in all human relationships. We see it applied in all three kinds of relationships. The Empirical–Rational kinds use power based on knowledge. The flow of power is from those who know to those who do not, through a process of education. Normative–Reeducative Strategies share power—that is, their knowledge of human behavior—with the client system. Both of these strategies avoid coercive tactics on both moral and practical grounds. Power–Coercive Strategies, however, use both legitimate and illegitimate power—that is, moral and unethical dimensions of power.

Benne and Chin also identify three Power–Coercive Strategies: nonviolent, invocation of political institutions, and manipulation of power groups. We see nonviolent strategies used in the behaviors of Mohandas "Mahatma" Gandhi and Martin Luther King. Achieving desired results by using political institutions is traditionally apposed in our society. Political power is widespread through all types of organizations. Nonviolent power is also a form of office/organizational politics. This form has some shortcomings as a method of achieving desired results. Users of power under this strategy often overestimate its effectiveness. Getting a law (or policy) passed does not guarantee compliance. Finally, manipulation means that power is taken from one group and redistributed to another group, often unobtrusively. Karl Marx is this method's most famous proponent. Marx advocated bringing about change through recomposing power groups and used three strategies of manipulation as a plan for fundamental social change.

Other strategic orientations also have been identified. Power can be reactive; that is, we can employ it as a response to some actually or assumed initial power play begun by another. It also can be proactive, employed as an initial ploy in a relationship. Power-use tactics can be rationalized within a strategy of openness or, conversely, it can be used unobtrusively. That is, power can be exercised within overt or covert strategies. We can classify tactic use also according to our intention to block undesired behavior of others or to extend our own power domain. Similarly, power can be exercised overall according to our desire to persuade, induce, or constrain our target.

Pfeffer (1977), Kipnis (1976), and others have suggested that power exercised unobtrusively or even covertly may be preferable in some circumstances and for some people. It is clear that much organizational power use is of this type. At least some of the negative feeling people have is traceable to its covert application. Covert tactics may include manipulation. It also includes any activity that structures reality in specific ways to meet our explicit goals. Covert tactics operate without cooperation or knowledge of the target of power.

Unobtrusive power use is common in organizational life but need not carry negative connotations. In fact, much routine organizational activity requires us to comply without explicit explanation or understanding of the reasons for the instructions. This situation need not cause hurt to the organizational group members. Nevertheless, this strategy causes many of us ethical and moral concern.

Michner and Schwartfeger (1972) summarize some significant power strategy literature in developing their classification scheme. For them, a significant strategic orientation in power use is blocking. Use of many power tactics results in blocking the target from attainment of his results. This negatively connoted strategy implies a restriction or constraining of access to desired results. It is clear as an underlying strategy in much power use. They also suggest that a common strategy in power use revolved around attempts to expand our power domain, scope, and range.

Creating a need that only we can supply, widening the network of information and communication contacts, building additional support for our programs and policies—all suggest an enlargement of our power base, and all are viable and common organizational strategies.

Persuasion is another strategy seen commonly in routine uses of power. Many specific tactics have as their purpose the persuasion of another to our point of view, behavior, attitude, or values. This strategy relies on another value system (logical argument) and another range of resources (ideas, values, and ideology) than those mentioned to this point.

A final strategic orientation, the one adopted here, can be identified that focuses on the targets of our power politics. The strategic orientation chosen as the foundation for this book, power use, can be directed at any of three specific targets: those superior to us in the organizational hierarchy, those on an equal or peer level, and those subordinate to us. This three-part strategy emphasized that organizational politics can be directed toward any participant in the organization, bosses, colleagues, as well as subordinates. Managing the boss and peers is no less frequent than managing subordinates. Exercising power politics to get these several targets to comply with our wishes is all part of organizational politics and asks us to become experts in using different power strategies for each target.

SUMMARY

These brief descriptions of strategic orientations within which power use takes place must be illustrative only. There is a wide variety of strategies we may follow in exercising power in working contexts. Prior consideration of strategic factors is prudent in predicting ultimate success in exercising power in just the same way that planning and consistency in any endeavor is usually more effective than random behavior.

Our level of understanding of power, as a central factor in organizational life, at this stage is too rudimentary to develop much precision about power strategies. Indeed, there is some logic to the proposition that too much specificity in early stages of understanding will hamper, not help, deeper analysis. Settling too soon on one strategy may limit wider experimentation and hamper full understanding of this critical element of group dynamics.

Of course, strategic orientation is a significant factor in applying power use. It is an evolving, creative dimension of the power dynamic. It is one we should not prescribe too closely too quickly. The several types of power-use strategies reviewed here offer useful insights into the ways people use power in contemporary organizational life. They do not offer definitive guidance as to which strategy will be absolutely effective in a given situation. Neither do they offer significant insights into specific behaviors people use to securing their desires in competition with others in the group.

Few of the older, more traditional strategies described above make explicit the ways we use power in relations with our superiors, subordinates, or peers. Nevertheless, these are the critical organizational relationships most people have. They are the real focus of power use in group settings. Some strategy must be developed to rationalize power use in these three important contexts. The strategies available to us treat only implicitly this context.

A focus of this book is on power use from the strategic position of the director of power action toward superiors, peers, or subordinates. The chapters in Part III present a rationale and examples of how people use power to affect the behavior of people in these three levels of the hierarchy. This organization of power use by the hierarchical rank of the user may be another strategic orientation. Hopefully, at least, some helpful insight on the question of the working uses of power in our relationships will be found there.

Part III

Power Interventions
That Work in the
Organization

It is one thing to know that power exists and is a part of a political dynamic in organizations. It is quite another to be able to make power work for you. Part III examines ways we can become effective participants in the power processes. It lays the foundation for successful power use and applies the tactics to goal attainment within various groups. The chapters in Part III focus the application of power tactics toward three strategic targets: our superiors, our peers, and our subordinates.

We organize to get work done. But, the focus of this action is personal. We behave in organizations in ways that we intend to achieve *our* goals. That we also achieve those of the organization as a result of our action is, while important, secondary. Theory supports this perspective. So does observation in the field of motivational dynamics. We behave in relationships with others to achieve our desires. Sometimes achieving our desires also obliges us to work to achieve the goals of the organization. At other times our goal attainment actions hinder group goal attainment.

The prime motivation for action is personal needs satisfaction—that is, satisfaction of *my* needs. This basic purpose of organizational action is entirely consistent with the ideas implicit in organizational politics and attendant power behavior. Analysis of organizational power behavior, its use, theory, and ethics takes on meaning as we see it applied in work situations that help us to achieve our goals. Part III examines the three traditional hierarchical levels of organizational action—superior, peer, and subordinate action.

Each chapter in Part III examines the power tactics favored by members in each organizational level and identifies characteristics of that use. These chapters enlarge upon the general descriptions of the twenty-two power tactics developed in Chapter 4 and relate them to various strategic targets. They provide context and application information about how each tactic is used by group members toward their organizational associates in each strategic level. These chapters explore the relative success organizational participants enjoy in using each tactic. Part III also provides some information about the ethical perspectives group members have about the appropriate use of each tactic.

Chapter 6 discusses the use of power tactics toward those superior to us in the organization. This chapter is interesting in that it makes explicit the fact that subordinates are powerful and engage in power-use behavior regularly to secure their desired results from those in authority over them. Subordinates make particular use of six tactics routinely in working within this strategy to impact their superiors. They are proactivity, use of outside experts, displaying charisma, using ambiguity, rationalization, and building a favorable image.

Chapter 7 describes the nine tactics organization members frequently use in their power strategy toward their peers. They include quid pro quo, allocating resources, forming coalitions, co-opting opposition members, incurring obligation, using surrogates, controlling the agenda, brinkmanship, and building a favorable image. Image building is a common tactic also used by group members to get superiors to conform. These tactics reflect logical kinds of power behavior given the role peers play toward their peers in our organizations.

Finally, Chapter 8 discusses a subordinate power strategy. It develops and elaborates on those tactics people subordinate in the hierarchy use toward their superior officers. It appears that superiors also make most frequent use of nine of the twenty-two power tactics. The use of these nine is largely unique to superiors. These tactics include training and orienting others, developing others, dispensing rewards, controlling decision criteria, legitimizing control, organizational placement, using symbols, ritualism, and incurring obligation. As in the case of the tactics used toward the other target, those used toward subordinates are logical. They center on application of resources subordinates need and are typically under the control of superiors.

The conclusion of the analyses in Part III chapters is that, regardless of strategic orientation, power is a routine part of organizational life. These chapters specify what tactics are most often used with each kind of organization colleague we interact with. They also spell out details of frequency of use, ethicality, and overall style of use of the power tactics commonly used toward each class of target. The implications of the data contained in Part III for organizational participants as they begin to, first, recognize the importance of power-skill in their organizational success and, second, plan a strategic approach to their power use to maximize their impact are significant. The conclusions of these chapters provide an effective, practical outline for our present and future power-use experiences. They also provide a strategy for planning power use to maximize our effectiveness in securing our agenda in the group.

6

Tactics Used with Superiors

Conventional wisdom leads us to believe that power is directed downward. The fact is that it flows in both directions. Some of the most important of our power relationships are those we have with our superiors. These relationships often constitute critical relations in the sense that success here determines our overall success in the group. They define much of what conventional wisdom calls office (organizational) politics.

These superior-directed contacts constitute some of the critical contingencies in our overall association with the organization (Pfeffer, 1992). Our power behaviors toward superiors are central to attainment of our formal agendas. Indications are that our uses of power in these situations are somewhat less specific, less direct, and less overt than are the tactics we use toward other organizational targets (Porter, Allen, and Angle, 1981). Nevertheless, this power-use strategy constitutes a critical element of organizational politics.

Porter, Allen, and Angle (1981) suggest that while every relationship between subordinates and superiors may not be power-related, the probability is that most are (Bacherach and Lawler, 1986). Obviously, normal downward-directed relationships between superiors and subordinates are power-tinged. Issuing orders, giving instructions, evaluating the work of subordinates all have power aspects. These uses of power are understandable to most. But power is, or can be seen, in most reverse relationships. That is, power is a part of the relationships from subordinates upward as well as from superiors downward. Both participants in this kind of relationship have and use power routinely (Mechanic, 1962).

How much power use is implicit in normal business relationships with superiors? Any attempt to secure a favorable decision from a superior is a potential power relationship. Getting a travel authorization, securing approval to buy needed items of supply or equipment all have power connotations. Getting agreement on a course of action, program change, or budget decision also constitutes a typical context within which power tactics may be and often are used by subordinate to secure superior compliance (Coenen and Hofstra, 1988). The results may satisfy a personal or an organizational need. The key factor is the subordinate's desire to attain a superior's action relevant to that outcome desire.

The notion held by some that subordinates are powerless—or even significantly less powerful than superiors—does not stand up to experience. Leader or supervisors cannot be successful without the energy, skill, talent, information, and willingness of their subordinates. This fact places the subordinate in a favorable power position vis-à-vis the superior. Too often superiors find themselves in thrall of the subordinate expert or specialist. And always they are dependent on subordinates to do the actual work of the organization both serve. This dependence relationship can account for some of the behavior we see in organizations where subordinates seem to direct organization affairs in ways not explainable by their role and official prerogatives.

Subordinates are as powerful as superiors in that both can control scarce resources needed by the other. The scarce resources controlled may differ, but the relationship is similar. The exact balance seems to be a function of the situation and the personal capacities of the individuals involved as much as it is a function of the formal organization structure and work systems. Organizational life is a series of intentional acts by both superiors and subordinates aimed at securing individual needs satisfaction or goal attainment. The action is in both directions. Downward-directed actions by superiors to subordinates are common, but so, too, are upward-directed actions intentionally made by subordinates to secure superior compliance. Power perspectives such as these add significant insights into the nature and purposes of organizational activity. This perspective may be as helpful as some more common perspectives on organizational behavior such as communication, competition, decision making, or conflict resolution.

A subordinate trying to "direct" the behavior of a superior is faced with a situational context that differs in some real ways from other relationships (Kanter, 1979) Typically the conventional wisdom suggests that the subordinate is less powerful than the superior and is, as a result, limited in the behavior options open to him. This research suggests that this may not be fully true. It is true that there is a statistically significant leaning toward a relatively few power tactics in these relationships. But, importantly, the data confirm that, by and large, all subordinates can—and many do—make use of all twenty-two of the power tactics in their contacts with superiors.

In dealing with superiors, we tend to concentrate on more personal kinds of power tactics (those based on personality) more than, say, material resources (Pfeffer, 1992). In these relations we tend to concentrate on using personal skills, characteristics, and capacities to attract superiors to our point of view and to change their behavior. This is understandable since subordinates normally do not control as many organizational sanctions mechanisms or legitimizing mechanisms. Interestingly, neither do they use coalitions with others to concentrate available power in much of their power interaction with superiors.

Subordinate power users rely less on force and authority power forms and more on manipulation, persuasion, threat–promise, and influence forms. Indeed, the six tactics used most toward superiors are, in order of frequency of use, proactivity, use of outside experts, displaying charisma, rationalization, using ambiguity, and building a favorable image. These tactics rely significantly on aspects of personal character rather than prerequisites of position. They often are employed in indirect, unobtrusive, even covert ways. The superior-officer target of this power use is often unaware that power is in play.

POWER TACTICS SUBORDINATES USE TOWARD THEIR SUPERIORS

It is important to note that subordinates use all of the twenty-two tactics listed in Chapter 4 (see Tables 4.1 and 4.2) in their behaviors toward superiors. Analysis of respondent choices, however, indicates that only six are commonly selected for frequent use within the superior strategy. Each of the six tactics used toward superiors are defined below and some illustrative examples are given to place each tactic in context of normal operational behavior in organizations. A short analysis of the nature and character of that use is provided in the next following section. (See Appendix for more detail.)

Proactivity

Proactivity is the single most often-used power tactic subordinates use toward superiors. Seventy-eight percent of respondents selected this tactic as an often-used behavior pattern in superior relations. Proactive behavior is dynamic. It concerns actions we take within our personal capacity, not necessarily within our legitimate authority. It is a process of doing something first and of seeking permission afterward. It can be formally defined as taking innovative action to secure our desired results. Proactivity appears to be statistically significant in subordinates' relationships toward their superiors. While we may use this tactic in relations with either peers or, occasionally, with subordinates, the predominant target of use is toward those in superior roles in the organization.

Proactivity is a tactic of major innovation that tends to bypass official system constraints as well as psychological resistance, aggression, or hostility. It reorders internal relationships by changing the environment, usually before most participants are aware that a change is occurring. It often is seen as a fait accompli, a situation in which we present our colleagues with a completed decision or action and seek support after the fact. But it also can be seen when projects or actions are promulgated in situations where no other solutions are readily identifiable—that is, suggesting ideas in a vacuum. The proactive individual acts rather than reacts.

Proactive behavior takes many forms. An example is seen when a branch manager who does not have the authority to staff a key position, say, personnel assistant, makes internal staff changes so that the person she wants for the position begins to function in an acting capacity. The manager then requests validation from headquarters. Proactivity also may be seen in purchasing actions taken without prior authorization, internal reorganizations, initiation of new programs, and similar actions.

It also is seen in blaming or attacking behaviors directed toward other persons in the organization in an effort to reduce competition for scarce resources (promotions, status, budgets, space, etc.). It often includes action taken "outside" the normal organization structures or channels of action. Since many organizations are in some ways obsolete, proactive power users may operate outside accepted authority parameters in securing their desired results. Thus proactive action can be productive of significant accomplishment. Both McMurray (1973) and Merrell (1979) propound the virtues of proactive behavior for, in the one case, the maverick executive and, in the other, the successful huddler. Merrell (1979) describes the proactive individual in terms of assertiveness. Those with assertive authority, he contends, assume a dynamic posture—one involving initiation of action to cause something to happen.

Using Outside Experts

Subordinates use outside experts to help them secure their objectives with superiors. Using outside experts is a power tactic of support. It uses respected "significant others" to help convince superiors that a choice alternative is the correct one. Using outside experts is an open tactic, one easily recognized by superiors and other observers. Nevertheless, while the fact of use is easily known, the expert's professional bias or philosophical leaning may not be. Hence, use of this tactic is felt by many to be unethical.

The using outside experts tactic is the second most often-used power tactic in relationships with superiors. Over 61 percent of those responding use this tactic toward superiors rather than any other target group. But, importantly, only about 30 percent of those queried use this tactic at all. Most of us do not select this behavior option when considering approaches to impacting superiors' actions. Four reasons can be cited: First, use of this tactic is often expensive. Second, appropriate experts may not always be readily available. Third, timing is often a factor and arrangements to employ experts take time that is sometimes not available. Finally, many of us appear to regard using outside experts to be unethical. People may not use it too often for these reasons, even though they find it to be relatively more effective than most other power options open to them. Indeed, using outside experts is the third most effective tactic used with superiors.

Involving experts in organizational choice determinations allows the powerful person to indirectly impact choices made in specific ways. Selection of the right expert—one whose recommendations will correspond with our objectives—can have great influence on superiors. Judicious selection of the expert that will provide the "right" recommendation is an effective way to predetermined decision results.

Expertise connotes an ability to take action and action is a foundation of power use. The expert acquires and maintains power so long as others in the organization depend on that expertise (Mechanic, 1962). But expertise does not have to reside in the individual officer. It can be held by the individual seeking to exercise power or it can be located in a particular outside expert whom we engage to serve our needs. Teachers are respected, obeyed, and deferred to by students (and the society at large) because of the feelings others have that they know something the others do not know yet (McKeachie, 1969). Their power in any group is a function of the respect and difference others have for their special expertise.

To be useful as a power tactic, using outside experts must respond to a felt need. That is, the expert's special capacities must be relevant to the needs of the individuals or group members toward whom it is directed. It must be visible among the members of the target population and must be seen as contributory to problem solutions. Given these criteria, the outside expert can be effective in directing the group toward results desired by the person who brings the expert into the situation. Modern organizations are complex, multidisciplinary structures requiring many special skills and knowledge. Judicious selection of the right expert for the right problem can add to the benefit of the power user. Selection of an expert who is known to favor a given approach, philosophy, or technology can ensure that that perspective will be reflected in the recommendations ultimately given.

Experts can be regularly established consultants, persons with expert status within the larger organization, or experts from any of the various organizations in the contextual environment of the host organization. Control over the expert is helpful in power terms when the expertise is specific to the problem at hand. It is also often helpful when an expert in another field of specialty is employed to endorse our desired results. Regardless of the specialty of the expert, if his or her expertise is recognized as legitimate, the members of the group will be influenced by his or her recommendations. It is, for example, a common occurrence for people to perceive an individual who is powerful in one context, say, the theater, to be powerful in another, say, politics. Although the influence of the expert may vary over time, while she is recognized as an expert, she represents a power base and we can enhance compliance in others, by involving outside experts.

Displaying Charisma

Many of us make use of our special attributes and characteristics of personality in relations with others. We employ this power tactic mostly in superior relations, but find it also of use in peer contacts. Only a few people employ displaying charisma as a power tactic toward subordinates. It apparently is not needed in these organizational relationships since other approaches are available and are more sure.

Displaying charisma relies on our personal traits of character, our special presence, attractiveness, idiosyncratic approaches, or methods of dealing with personnel or program elements of our relationships. Displaying charisma is based in conceptual forms of power, like persuasion, threat–promise, and influence. Other forms (force, authority, and manipulation) are not typically a part of this system of power relationships. Table 6.1 shows that displaying charisma is rated as the most effective power tactic in superior relations. It is felt to be positive ethically and is most often used in initial power contacts with others.

Sometimes we can garner power by fostering an almost unconscious identification in others with our ideas. A Freudian concept, this behavior set is most clearly seen in the way people look up to charismatic people. Max Weber introduced Western civilization to the concept of charisma. Charismatic people, for him, are those who have a mysterious "gift of grace" that irresistibly attracts followers. Charisma originally had a sense of the supernatural or the superhuman: followers recognizing this characteristic feel empowered, loyal, devoted, and obedient.

While probably relatively uncommon in the population, displaying charisma is, nevertheless, a useful tactic to foster to help us get others to help in achievement of a desired result. This tactic involves us in attracting follower support because they (followers) are attracted to something about our personality or about our ideas or ideals. That something may be a magnetic personality, or a gift for persuasion, or it may be based on the fact that we arouse confidence in followers to the extent that they want to comply. Some charismatic people attract followers because they make them feel stronger about themselves. Charismatic people inspire us to do our best. They define a situation in which followers are presented with a goal or task and feelings that they are capable of being successful in its performance.

There is some logic to the proposition that power use based on charisma is inborn, that you either have it or you do not. Others suggest that individuals can develop power based on other's idealized views of them (Kotter, 1977). Much of the self-help literature deals with "how to" behave in ways that others respect, become visible in the organization, improve communications skills and persuasiveness, identify with and shape organization goals, and similar skills. Yukl (1981) lists several factors that, he says, can be used to assess leader charisma. The following listing incorporates his ideas and can be used to describe behavior objectives we can adopt to exert power in our cultural situations. If we would be powerful, we should:

1. behave in ways that develop follower trust in us.
2. show followers how their goals can become congruent with ours.
3. foster unquestioned obedience to our instructions.
4. foster affection for us personally.
5. challenge followers to high performance.
6. relate task accomplishment with the follower's own ideals, values, aspirations.
7. show followers how doing what we want will contribute to group goals accomplishment.
8. develop emotional attachments between followers and us.
9. recruit people over whom we can exert emotional impact.
10. develop communications and persuasive skills—including storytelling skills (O'Day, 1974).
11. personify group goals.
12. dramatize ourselves.
13. be assertive.
14. articulate and live an acceptable moral standard.

Charismatic uses of power are based on emotional appeal—an almost visceral connection between the powerful and the relatively powerless. This tactic is based on our personality and character, and involves us in any of a wide variety of behaviors that elicit follower compliance. Those listed above illustrate only some of the range of options open to us in using this tactic.

Rationalization

This tactic involves the conscious engineering of reality to justify decision results or specific points of view. Often, in using rationalization, we mask the real purposes of the action or appeal to "higher" values, motives, norms, or customary modes of thinking. Subordinates use this power behavior cluster frequently in swaying superiors to their desires. It appears to be primarily used when superiors evidence initial resistance. Most power users find this tactic to be effective, although it is the least effective of those tactics used mostly in superior relations. And, rationalization is felt to be ethically negative.

The rationalization tactic uses language or symbols to construct a particularized view of reality that legitimizes our decisions. We "engineer" consent (Pelz, 1952) by manipulating the process by which our action is given meaning and purpose. In using this power tactic we make our point by projecting a desired perspective, one that assumes our desired orientation or actions are accepted and valued (Nyberg, 1981).

The rationalization tactic runs the gamut from education to propaganda to outright deception. Even such lofty activities as theory building involve describing reality from new perspectives and/or introducing new constructs of reality that emphasize one or a few elements over other possibilities. This activity is as much a rationalization process as chauvinistic patriotism.

Our construction of actions or events or facts can define the effective parameters of the analytical processes others use and keep them from raising undesirable alternatives (Pfeffer, 1981). In an organizational management or leadership context, this tactic is seen when individuals use words to give a particular sense of meaning and focus to events or facts. Misrepresenting reality can be part of this tactic, but so can motivation and inspiration (Pfeffer, 1977). Budget justifications and program planning rationales are examples of using language to inculcate ideals, values, and overall points of view among decision makers that foreclose alternative constructions of reality.

The rationalization tactic is frequently seen in labor negotiations. Both sides attempt to construct a definition of reality that favors their position and close off consideration of alternatives. The decision constraints are couched in terms (e.g., demands) that forestall argument. And, obviously, rationalization is common in politics.

Description of some of the forms the rationalization tactic takes in operational use may help illustrate the impact of this set of power behaviors.

Persuasion

Persuasion is perhaps the most common form of the rationalization tactic. Persuasion can be effective in situations where there is a mutuality of interest, where both parties care about the result in similar ways. Persuasion is an egalitarian technique that leaves intact the free choice of the person persuaded. Because of this fact, some have not defined persuasion as a part of power. In fact, it is both a major form of power and a strong technique in securing compliance to our point of view. It must be included under a definition of power (Wrong, 1979). Persuasion is effective, requires little expenditure of resources, and, given a skillful orator, involves little risk. It is therefore a reliable technique of the rationalization tactic.

Structuring Reality

Rationalization, as a tactic of power use, can include action to selectively present factual material and/or physical objects to emphasize one perspective over other possible perspectives. This technique may run the gamut from selective emphasis to distortion to presentation of false material. At one level, it is logical to say that all people, all of the time, select from available "information" those items they favor and present them to the world as true. Certainly there is an element of selectivity and decision in any action we take. More to the point is the action we sometimes take to consciously structure reality to make our case to the world. Editing out "relevant" materials is one form; another is selective use of statistics, directing only some information to targets or outright lying.

Emotional Appeal

The rationalization tactic also is used when we present information in a way to appeal to the emotions and sentiments of our targets. Inspirational appeal occurs when we induce the target of power to do something that appears to be a necessary expression of his values or ideals (Wrong, 1979). The key to this technique is linking desired performance to a target's value system or emotional makeup.

Humor

This technique involves any action we take to cause the proposals, ideas, or values of another to be rejected in favor of our own by getting group members to laugh at, ridicule, or scorn the other person's proposals (Duncan, 1990). Rationalization is founded on trust and respect, and if respect is lost, so too is much of our power. While power may abhor a vacuum, it equally abhors scorn. Without respect, dominance cannot be maintained. Getting others to laugh at or denigrate in any way the proposals of others that we oppose is another way to exercise power in the organization.

Perhaps the ultimate in withdrawal of consent is laughter. Nyberg (1981) proposes that laughter, not revolution, is more common in overthrowing a regime. Authority fears rejection more than any other threat to its legitimacy. Especially in informal organizations, if we lose the respect of our fellows we are incapable of securing their compliance in even nominal organizational transactions.

Using Ambiguity

Keeping the situation ambiguous allows us to maintain a central position in the communications systems and flexibility in negotiation and decision making. By keeping communications unclear we often can find ways to attain our desired objectives in the face of opposition from others. The tactic, using ambiguity, is the fifth most often-used tactic toward superiors. Fully half of those responding to a questionnaire rate this behavior cluster as a frequent approach to deal with superiors.

Sometimes keeping information, instructions, and policy ambiguous and vague can be used to ensure that our personal alternative has a chance of being achieved. Using ambiguity allows for several alternative constructions of a particular situation or decision event. In effect, it keeps open a choice that would be closed off were the problem, situation, or language made more explicit. We are limited in the results we can achieve by the "rules" under which we work. The vaguer we can keep those rules, the more options we have. Whenever we can do something and then say, in effect, "You didn't tell me I couldn't do it," we are using the ambiguity tactic.

In power terms, then, it is to our advantage to have instructions from above made explicit when we want to do what others want us to do. It is also to our advantage to attempt to keep them vague when others are opposed to our preferred course of action. Ambiguous goals, jurisdictions, performance criteria, or instructions tend to break down formal rules and procedures that govern interaction and allow us to function independently. While conflict may be a part of this relatively unstructured environment, it is a precondition of power use and can be instrumental in increasing the power-use options open to us. Using ambiguity allows us to expand or maintain maneuverability in the organization (Yukl, 1981). It contributes to the flexibility in responding that Kanter (1979) and others suggest is important in the environment if power is to be used effectively.

By definition, ambiguous situations are situations of multiple, chaotic interactions where understood norms of human interaction are broken down and new standards have not been solidified. It is difficult in these situations for us to exert control over others. But, they are times of power vacuum when anyone with a strong desire and a plan has an opportunity to advance his position, accumulate power bases, and otherwise take action to enhance his power position vis-à-vis others.

From a power perspective, ambiguity is opportunity. It may be difficult to assign credit for good work in ambiguous situations. But it is also a time that allows us viability and opportunity for doing good work. And ambiguous situations, while masking specific responsibilities, allow us to assume power and authority for accomplishment in ways and to degrees not possible in a routine, highly structured environment. Indeed, one explanation for why leaders emerge in newly created organizations may be in part ascribed to their ability to function in situations in flux. The capacity to operate in ambiguous, changing situations is a commonly accepted mark of leadership capacity. It is directly related to power use and the opportunity that ambiguous situations allow for innovation in method, policy, program, or in individual leadership.

Building a Favorable Image

The building a favorable image tactic refers to attempts we make to change the perception others have of our skills, capacities, values, or attitudes in order to enhance our power among followers. Akin to displaying charisma, it builds power through augmentation of the personal resources we bring to our relationships (Bass, 1981). This is the sixth most frequently used tactic toward superiors and the fourth most effective of the superior-oriented power tactics. Persons using this tactic find it useful in superior-directed power uses as well as toward peers. It is a statistically significant pattern of use in both of these organizational relationships.

Effective use of power presupposes that we have some control over a resource needed by others. One such basis for power use is image, a structured perception fostered in others of ourself. When we enjoy the prestige, regard, or respect of our associates we are powerful to the degree of that deference. Prestige can come from talent, position, control over key information, or other sources; but the result is that people with prestige are listened to first and their message is considered more fully than those without prestige in the group.

People using this tactic may project a particularized image ranging from the honest, upright, "nice guy" to the ruthless, scheming tyrant; they may appear confident, develop a flair for the dramatic, or acquire a persuasive approach. On another level, they may adopt methods of interaction that include such things as giving and taking advice, maintaining aloofness, keeping secrets, and being flexible (judiciously bending the rules). The methods are as varied as the individuals involved, but they all have in common the aim of substituting an emotional response to our personality for rational action on the part of the follower.

In effect this tactic involves attempts to attract follower support based on our perceived qualities of personality rather our authentic personality or on the quality of our decisions. Any attempt to induce another to accept decision or a position on an issue because we ask, as an alternative to independent analysis, is an example of this tactic. It involves the use of charisma, but goes further than the commonly accepted implication of that word.

Any of a wide variety of techniques to change others' perceptions qualifies as a use of the building a favorable image tactic. One lower-level bureau manager attempted to improve her image as a hard worker and creative system designer by requiring all bureau reports and systems change recommendations to be distributed only over her signature regardless of who did the work. Her image among higher managers, at least, was enhanced by this move. Similarly, another leader ensured that external reports including news items reporting agency action always included his name as the "announcer" of the innovation, implying a direct role in creating the changes reported. Both built an image of power that differed from real power held.

Building a favorable image also includes efforts to enhance our organization as an effective (influential, innovative, or hard-working) unit. Publicity programs that advertise the accomplishments of one unit over other units in the organization imply more power is resident in that unit and its key people. The individual who effectively places his/her unit in the forefront of action enhances both his/her image and that of the unit.

ANALYSIS OF THE USE OF SUPERIOR-DIRECTED POWER TACTICS

Frequency of Use

The six power tactics described as most often used by people to impact their superiors in the organization are shown in Table 6.1. While all of the other

Table 6.1
Frequency of Use Toward Superiors

Tactic	Rank
Proactivity	1
Using Outside Experts	2
Displaying Charisma	3
Rationalization	4
Using Ambiguity	5
Building a Favorable Image	6

tactics are used on occasion in power activity with superiors, these six are the most significantly used. Each is described and elaborated on briefly below.

Proactivity

Proactivity is the power tactic most frequently used by businesspeople, government workers, and those in nonprofit organizations. People in both larger and smaller organizations and those in service, product-oriented, and professional and technical–clerical occupations find this tactic of frequent use. Employees in higher education and persons in professional–technical–clerical occupations also find this a useful tactic in peer relations.

Many people also use proactivity in relationship with their peers. A few people use proactivity toward subordinates; none in remarkable ways, although older employees will sometimes use this tactic with subordinates. Those with less than a year of service in their work unit also employ this tactic. Proactivity appears to be in the tactic of choice for most kinds of people. Men and women use proactivity more or less equally. Both older and younger group members rate this tactic as most often used, as do supervisors (toward their bosses). Non-supervisors use two other tactics more often, but also make great use of proactivity. Length of service does not appear to be a factor either; people with both short and long tenure in their organizations use proactivity most frequently. And, finally, relative boredom or excitement with our work is not a factor in frequency of use. Both kinds of employees use this power tactic often.

Using Outside Experts

Using outside experts is the second most popular tactic with persons using power toward superiors. Women use this tactic next often only to proactivity in dealing with superiors. On the other hand, men find displaying charisma to be a little more useful; rating both proactivity and displaying charisma above using outside experts in terms of frequency of use. Age differences do not effect frequency of use. Both older and younger members see this tactic as useful.

Supervisors use outside experts a little more often than nonsupervisors, who place this tactic fourth among tactics used with their bosses. Supervisors rank it second in frequency of use. Those who find their work exciting use this tactic more than those whose work is seen as boring. Those with exciting work rank using outside experts second in frequency of use, while bored workers rate it as fifth most used.

Workers in smaller work units and organizations find this tactic more useful than those in larger units. People in higher educational institutions find using outside experts to be the most used tactic, with proactivity rated third. Government workers rate it as second most useful, but business and nonprofit organization members rate it as fourth and fifth, respectively. Members of product-oriented organizations find this tactic to be the least useful tactic of those significantly related to relationship with superiors. And service-oriented organization workers see it as second most successful.

Displaying Charisma

Overall, displaying charisma is the third most often-used tactic employed by subordinates toward superiors. Interestingly, men see displaying charisma as their second most often-used tactic. Women use this power tactic relatively infrequently; they rate it as seventh most frequently used. Women use displaying charisma more as a power tactic toward peers. They rate this tactic as eighth in frequency of use toward peers. Older employees use displaying charisma more than those under 40 (second versus fifth most frequently used power tactic). Both supervisors and nonsupervisors use displaying charisma significantly in relations with supervisors. It is an often-used tactic for those who find their work exciting. It is not a statistically significant use for those who are bored with their work. Bored workers, rather, use this tactic more in their peer relationships.

Displaying charisma is used with superiors in statistically significant ways by people in higher educational institutions, government, business, and nonprofit organizations. Government workers seem to rely on this tactic a little less frequently than do those in other kinds of organizations. Those in their immediate organization less than one year appear not to rely on displaying charisma very much. Rather, they use this tactic in behavior toward peers. Those with longer service and in either large or small organizations find this tactic usable. Displaying charisma is used frequently toward superiors by service, product, and clerical–professional–technical organizations.

Rationalization

Rationalization is the fourth most often-used tactic in relationships with superiors. Regardless of personal characteristics—male–female; older–younger; bored–excited by work; supervisor–nonsupervisors—all use rationalization toward superiors in statistically significant amounts. Rationalization is a part of the behavior of people in dealing with superiors in government, higher education, and nonprofit organizations, but it is not a statistically significant means of securing compliance in business settings. It is used by people in product-oriented, service, and clerical–technical–professional organizations. It is also a part of routine behavior toward superiors in organizations regardless of overall size or the size of the worker's immediate work system.

Ambiguity

Ambiguity is the fifth most frequently used power tactic favored by workers toward their superiors. It is used frequently by both men and women, by older and younger group members, by those who find their work boring and those who find it exciting, and by supervisors. Nonsupervisors also find this tactic effective. It is the most often-used power tactic of any used by nonsupervisors. Those who find their work boring use this tactic more often than those excited about their work. Ambiguity is also a part of the behavior of people in all kinds of organization members.

Building a Favorable Image

Building a favorable image is the sixth most often-used power tactic toward superiors. In fact, men do not use this as much toward superiors as women do. Men do not find this a statistically significant power-use tactic. Both older and younger workers use this tactic in their relations with superiors. Nonsupervisors use it frequently; supervisors do not use it in a statistically significant way. Those who find their work exciting use building a favorable image; those finding their work boring do not.

Building a favorable image is not a frequently used tactic (statistically) for workers in higher education, government, and nonprofit organizations. It is often used by business organization workers. Time in the organization work team is not a distinguishing factor; people use building a favorable image regardless of time in service. Those in product-oriented organizations use building a favorable image; those in service or clerical–technical–professional units do not.

Effectiveness of Use

Each of the six power tactics people use in their relationships with their superiors in the organization are effective. Data compiled suggest that these tactics are generally used by all group members with success. Table 6.2 presents these tactics in the order of their perception of effectiveness by respondents. Each tactic is analyzed briefly below. Emphasis is given here to special deviations from perceived effectiveness shown by various actors. Nothing is presented to challenge the overall effectiveness of these power behaviors.

Overall, displaying charisma is the most effective of those tactics related to

Table 6.2
Effectiveness of Tactics Toward Superiors

Tactic	Rank Among Supervisors
Displaying Charisma	1
Proactivity	2
Using Outside Experts	3
Building a Favorable Image	4
Using Ambiguity	5
Rationalization	6

superior relationships. Women power users are the only exception to this statement. They find this tactic more effective when used toward peers rather than superiors. It is not a significant power behavior in superior relations for women. They rate displaying charisma as the most effective of all of the power tactics, however. Men find this tactic to be the most effective of those directed toward superiors—fourth overall below allocating resources, developing others, and training and orienting others.

Those under age 40 see displaying charisma as the most effective of all power behavior sets. Those over 40 rate it about average in terms of overall effectiveness. Both supervisors and nonsupervisors rate this tactic as effective as do those who define their jobs as either boring and routine or exciting and varied. People in both large and small organizations see this tactic as effective. Indeed, most people in most kinds of organizations rate displaying charisma as effective and as a significant power-use tactic.

Proactivity is generally as helpful as displaying charisma in securing our desired results. Among the organizational participants who rate proactivity as relatively less effective in relations with superiors are those who find their work routine and boring. This is also the case with persons in higher education work and those in nonprofit organizations. Nevertheless, these workers and all others find proactivity an effective power tactic.

The power tactic of using outside experts is the third most effective tactic in power action toward superiors. Most categories of worker rate this tactic in the middle of all tactics in terms of effectiveness. Nonsupervisors find this tactic less effective than do supervisors (thirteenth and seventh, respectively). Perhaps the cause is in the resources and experience differences in these two types of organizational coworkers. Those working in smaller (fewer than one hundred employees) units find using outside experts a less effective tactic than workers in larger organizations.

Higher education workers find using outside experts to be the most used power tactic. These people find it only generally effective. Their ranking is about the same as the general population. Businesspeople find this tactic somewhat less effective than the average worker—sixteenth of twenty-two. Product-oriented workers find this tactic to be nineteenth most useful while service-oriented workers rate it as fifth most effective. On balance employment of outside experts to assist in getting our way is a useful, effective tactic, if one that is not used too often.

Rationalization is an effective power-use tactic. It ranks thirteenth overall and sixth in effectiveness among the six tactics most often used toward superiors. All categories of personnel studied—men and women, older and younger workers, and those who find their work boring or exciting—see this as an effective tactic. Supervisors also find this tactic to be effective in securing desired results. Nonsupervisors, however, disagree. They find rationalization statistically ineffective. On balance, however, rationalization is seen as effective by workers in all kinds and types of organizations studied.

Using ambiguity is also an effective power tactic. Without deviation, people in all kinds and types of organization find it works in getting their way. Understandably supervisors do not find ambiguity as effective as some other classes of worker. They rate it as the sixteenth most effective of the twenty-two power tactics on this measure. Neither do government workers (who rate it fifteenth of twenty-two), nonprofit (twentieth of twenty-two), or service-oriented (sixteenth of twenty-two).

Building a favorable image is the least effective of the power tactics we use in our attempts to get superiors to do what we want. It is, nevertheless, an effective power tactic. All persons in organizations surveyed rated building a favorable image as an effective tactic. No one found this tactic to be ineffective. Higher educational workers see building a favorable image as relatively more effective than most other tactics (They rank it fourth most effective of the twenty-two tactics). Those older than 40 see it as relatively less effective than most other tactics (eighteenth of twenty-two), as do those in business organizations (eighteenth of twenty-two), product-oriented organizations (sixteenth of twenty-two), and those working in organizational work teams of 50 or more people.

Ethics of Use

Four of the six power-use tactics are seen by users as ethically positive (see Table 6.3). That is, most people assume it is ethically alright to use ambiguity, displaying charisma, a constructed image, and proactive behavior to induce our superiors to behave in ways we desire. They feel that the other two, rationalization and use of outside experts, are ethically wrong. As we look at each tactic, some interesting variations are evident. For example, men find using ambiguity ethically neutral; women find it a positive approach. Those over 40 see it as positive; those under as neutral. Nonsuperiors see it as positive; supervisors as neutral. For those excited by their work using ambiguity is neutral; those bored with their job find it positive. Workers in higher educational institutions find using ambiguity positive, as do business and nonprofit workers. Government employees find this tactic ethically neutral. Product-oriented workers also see using ambi-

Table 6.3
Ethics of Tactics Used Toward Superiors

Ethically Positive Tactic	Ethically Negative Tactics
Proactivity	Using Outside Experts
Displaying Charisma	Rationalization
Using Ambiguity	
Building a Favorable Image	

guity as positive, as do clerical–technical–professional workers. Service-oriented workers see it as neutral. No one sees using ambiguity as negative.

Both men and women see displaying charisma as a power tactic toward superiors (or toward other coworkers) to be ethical, as do those of any age, both supervisors and nonsupervisors, and those who find their work either boring or exciting. Workers in government, business, higher education, and nonprofit institutions also feel displaying charisma is ethical. Both service- and product-oriented organization workers find this tactic to be ethically okay. People working in small work units (ten or fewer workers) do not rate displaying charisma as ethically positive, nor do those working in organizations of fewer than one hundred workers. Workers in all other organizations find displaying charisma an ethically positive power tactic.

Most people view building a favorable image as ethically positive. It ranks as the fourth most ethical of all tactics measured and the most positive of the six used toward superiors. No category of respondent ranked building a favorable image as unethical, or even as ethically neutral. Men find this tactic generally more positive than women (third to tenth). Nonsupervisors find this tactic more ethical than superiors (second to fifth). People working in all kinds of organizations rated building a favorable image as ethical at about the same level. Neither is size of organization nor size of work group indicative of a difference in ranking of the ethicality of this tactic.

Overall, the proactivity tactic is the most ethical tactic reported of this group. It ranks as the second most ethically okay (behind developing others) of all twenty-two tactics. No one rates proactivity as unethical.

Two tactics are seen as ethically negative: rationalization and using outside experts. Less than one-fourth of those responding found rationalization to be ethical. Men find this tactic to be neutral; women rate it as unethical. Both older and younger people see it as unethical. Other breakdowns of respondents personal characteristics see rationalization as ethically neutral. Only nonprofit organizations see rationalization as ethically positive. The others—business, government, higher education—rate it as neutral.

Less than one-third of those responding rated the using outside experts tactic as ethically positive. Indeed, statistically, the probability is that this tactic is seen as unethical by most people engaged in power use. Perhaps the reason for

Table 6.4
Tactics Used Toward Superiors as an Initial or as a Resistance Strategy

Tactics Used as an Initial Power Approach	Tactics Used upon Encountering Resistance
Proactivity	Using Outside Experts
Displaying Charisma	Using Ambiguity
Building a Favorable Image	

this negative feeling relates to the sometime use of consultants to validate a decision result that has not been successfully presented via normal relationships. For most respondents this tactic is used, but is considered ethically neutral or negative. Apparently its effectiveness dictates its use regardless of the moral overtones it carries. Only nonprofit organization members and people with more than five years of work experience in their immediate work unit find this tactic to be an ethical behavior pattern. In the nonprofit situation, the use of experts—often unpaid volunteers—is common and may account for this rating among these kinds of workers. Those people with relatively long-term connections with the same organization may also see past successes in using this tactic and other tactics as a basis for their ethical stand. In nonprofit organizations this tactic is used often and is felt to be effective. Success over time, indeed, may be a conditioning factor in determining ethicality.

Style Factors

Proactivity, displaying charisma, using ambiguity, and building a favorable image are all used typically in initial power contacts with superiors. (See Table 6.4.) It is interesting to note that these tactics are the same ones organization members identified as being ethically okay. We appear to use ethically acceptable tactics initially and move to those less ethical tactics when resistance is encountered.

People generally find these four tactics appropriate when no effective resistance is encountered from superiors. These are power tactics centered mostly in the personality of the power user. Most people surveyed followed this style of power tactic use in their relationships with superiors. Displaying charisma is almost uniformly used exclusively as an initial power ploy. This is also the case with using ambiguity.

Several classes of people find building a favorable image to be important in their initial contacts: females, nonsupervisors, people in larger organizations, those in service-oriented organizations, and those in work groups of fifty or more. Others find it generally useful as one of several initial behavior tactics.

There is also some deviation in style of use of the proactivity tactic. Most people employ this tactic in routine contacts. They do not employ it typically when the target of their power try resists their overtures. In two cases we see significant deviation. Those over 40 years of age typically do not use this tactic in those cases where there may be an exception. And, people in higher education and those with only a year or less of service in their organization use this power intervention about equally in initial power tries and as a response to resistance.

Two superior-oriented tactics—using outside experts and rationalization—are most used as a counter to resistance from their superiors to their use of power. The using outside experts often is used as a reaction behavior when other, initial compliance tactics have not proven successful. Most of us find this tactic to be appropriate when we have encountered resistance to earlier power-tactic use. Those over 40 years of age are an exception. They find using outside experts to be useful as an initial—not a resistance—power behavior pattern. So do those who find their work routine and boring, those who work in smaller organizations, those with less than one year of service in their immediate work team, and those working in product-oriented organizations. Business workers also use outside experts as an initial contact tactic as do nonprofit workers. Higher education and government workers do not; they employ this behavior pattern in resistance situations.

Rationalization is another tactic many of us use when we encounter resistance in applying some other power tactic. Those over 40 use it as an initial power behavior. No other category of organization member deviates from the general norm of use (that is, to use rationalization to counter resistance).

CONCLUDING COMMENTS

Generally speaking, these six behaviors characteristic of this superior strategy—with variation in specific ranking—are used in contacts with most superiors. Some preliminary conclusions can be elicited from the analysis above. These conclusions constitute possible guidelines on use of these power tactics in our efforts to get superiors to comply with our wishes.

- Proactivity is the most frequently used power tactic toward superiors.

- Both men and women find the proactivity tactic to be most often used toward superiors, as do all classifications of organizational workers in general.

- Education workers use outside experts more often than proactivity.

- Using outside experts to help validate our desired choice options is also a powerful tactic.

- Since using outside experts requires resources, only those persons who control relevant resources resort to its use.

- Displaying charisma is a very effective power tactic in superior relationships and in any other context in which it is used to secure target compliance.

- Displaying charisma is less risky than some other tactics.

• Rationalization encompasses a major cluster of power behaviors. It includes much normal communication behavior in which we engage. It is used primarily toward superiors in power situations.

• Using ambiguity sometimes found in the situation often makes it easier for subordinates to induce superiors to desired actions.

• Attempts to build a favorable image of us in the minds of superiors is an effective and frequently used power behavior in our contact with them.

7

Power Tactics Used with Peers

Much of our thinking about organizational interaction concerns hierarchical relationships. However, organizational interaction also occurs between peers; that is, between people in coordinate, or lateral, relationships. These contacts constitute another power-use strategic orientation. This strategy for engaging in organizational politics makes up a unique arena within which people exercise organizational power. When a manager tries to induce another manager at the same relative hierarchical level to do something, we have an example of peer power use. Similarly, when members of a group (either formal or informal) try to socialize a new member with habitual patterns of behavior, accepted mores, or group values, we have another example of peer power at work.

A peer relationship is one between persons who do not have a clear, unambiguous hierarchical relationship defining their association. That is, a peer does not report directly to another peer. Peers need not be equal in power or capacity or resources. All a peer relationship requires is a nonhierarchical formal or informal relationship (Szilagyl and Wallace, 1983).

As a result of this kind of relationship, power behavior in this strategy is not characterized by force or authority forms of power. Neither do peer power relationships typically use persuasion forms. They rely instead on more indirect and subtle forms. All the power tactics used by peers are potentially useful to those engaged in peer relationships. The fact is that power use among peers relies most often on interventions that show manipulation, threat, or influence forms of power. The peer strategy tactics described here fall generally into these categories of power.

Peers are interdependent and, given this fact, need to relate to other peers in

Table 7.1
Summary of Tactics Used Toward Peers

Tactics Ranked by Frequency	Tactics Ranked by Effectiveness	Tactics Ranked by Ethical Pattern		When Used	
		Positive	Negative	Initial	Resistance
Quid Pro Quo	6		N		R
Allocating Resources	1	P		I	
Forming Coalitions	2	P			R
Co-opting Opposition Members	3	P			R
Incurring Obligation	8		N		R
Use of Surrogates	5		N	I	
Controlling the Agenda	7		N		R
Brinkmanship	9*		N		R
Building a Favorable Image	4	P		I	

* Not effective
I   Used as an initial contact approach
R   Used upon encountering resistance

ways that recognize this interdependence. Therefore, they exert power through forming coalitions and co-optation of opposing peers. They also selectively allocate resources needed by others in exchange for desired behavior, and use brinkmanship. They also use control over factors in the environment that, properly used, help individual goal attainment. Peers use nine tactics most often in relationships with others. The nine are: quid pro quo, allocating resources, forming coalitions, co-opting opposition members, incurring obligation, using a surrogate, controlling the agenda, brinkmanship, and building a favorable image. They represent the prime tactics peers use toward peers to get them to conform their behavior to that desired. Only infrequently will peers employ these interventions toward superiors or subordinates.

Table 7.1 compares these tactics on several dimensions—frequency of use, effectiveness, ethicality, and style of use. The table rankings are significant. As a general statement, all respondents used the trade-off behaviors most often. However, various classes of group member used the others in unique ways. Men, for example, lean more toward the use of group-oriented behaviors such as building coalitions, co-opting others to their position, and similar behaviors. Women rely a little more on personal tactics like placing others under obligation to them, controlling the action agenda, and allocating resources.

Businesspeople also often use trade-off tactics. They then move to some of the riskier tactics such as co-optation, brinkmanship, and use of surrogates. Peers in government rely somewhat more on use of resources available to them to get their way. They also regularly use tactics such as coalitions, obligation, co-optation, and use of others as surrogates.

Peers do not use rational, logical tactics such as rationalization ritualism, legitimizing control, and setting of decision criteria as much as superiors or subordinates do. Peers in most kinds of organizations refrain from use of these kinds of tactics; higher educational institution members are the exception. These people find rationalization a viable behavior set while peers in other types of organizations do not. Maybe it is a function of the "mind-set" of the typical academic. The fact is, however, that university politics is as complex as reputed. Unfortunately members of these organizations routinely structure reality to suit their particular frame of reference.

Research supports the fact that peer power relations rely on power bases that ease exchange transactions. Peers engage in transactions that require control over and manipulation of material or psychological resources. They also identify with powerful others and control critical situational factors, or the ambiance of the situation of the social group. Peers also use power bases of solidarity, and centrality. Obviously, these bases of power are logically related to peers.

Peers do not make use of authority, legitimizing control, or force power forms since, typically, peers control these power bases in roughly equal measure. They must rely on material, informational, and psychological resources that they can hold in varying amounts. Interestingly, peers do not typically make use of power behavior that relies on personal characteristics, capacities, or qualities. This is an interesting finding; one not expected at the outset. Peers engage in power use to get other peers to behave in desired ways, by using "trade-off" techniques. Peers do not use personal qualities or capacities as much as superiors or subordinates for power purposes. The sections below describe and analyze each of the statistically significant peer power tactics.

QUID PRO QUO

We characterize peer power relations by transactions between powerful people. Peers spend much of their power-related time in exchange relationships, that is, where one person has comparably more of a desired resource and is willing to trade it for specified peer behavior or support. The quid pro quo tactic epitomizes this kind of power behavior. This tactic is the most frequently used tactic in peer relations and is seen as an initial approach in power contacts. It is similar to other tactics used in peer relations in that many of these tactics are covert in nature.

The quid pro quo tactic involves any of a wide variety of efforts to negotiate trade-offs with others to secure desired results from peers. The best example of quid pro quo is in the direct bargaining where individuals use needs and resources to negotiate a mutual agreement. Labor negotiations would be an example of this kind of behavior. Other examples include budget negotiations, policy development, and implementation and similar kinds of intraorganizational balancing of resources held by different parties at interest.

Analysis

The quid pro quo tactic is seen in straightforward bargaining for material resources, but it also uses nonmaterial, emotionally based resources. Accordingly, attention is a negotiable resource; as are time and skill. So, too, are association, recognition, and praise or blame usable in this approach. Quid pro quo is in play whenever we do a favor for another person in exchange for a specific action by that other person. Saying "you do this for me and I will help you with your (whatever)" is typical of this kind of trade-off of personal capacities for desired target behavior.

The quid pro quo power tactic is the single most frequently used cluster of power behaviors used toward peers. More than 78 percent of those responding to a power-use questionnaire reported using this tactic. Survey results showed little variation among respondents. Quid pro quo is the most often-used power tactic by both men and women, older and younger workers, and supervisors and nonsupervisors. Those who find their work exciting also use quid pro quo most frequently. People bored with their work prefer brinkmanship or using a surrogate more than quid pro quo.

When analyzed for the organizational environment in which people work, we find business, government, and higher educational institutions' leaders use this tactic. Leaders in nonprofit organizations use it less frequently. These workers rated quid pro quo as the sixth most frequently used tactic. Leaders in other kinds of organizations ranked it first. People with less than one year in their jobs also use this tactic less frequently than do those with longer tenure.

Quid pro quo is effective in achieving target compliance in most situations and for most kinds of worker. Leaders older than 40 appear to value its effectiveness higher than most other kinds of people surveyed. While a solidly effective tactic, quid pro quo is seen by respondents as less effective than more than half of the twenty-two tactics identified. Overall it ranks fifteenth of the total twenty-two tactics in effectiveness. And, when looked at in terms of the organizational situation within which people operate, it is the case that people with more than five years service favor this tactic more than other classes of people. They rank it fifth of the twenty-two tactics in effectiveness.

Summary

As a general statement most people who use quid pro quo find it ethically neutral—neither fully ethical nor unethical. Only workers in nonprofit organizations, those with work groups of more than fifty people, and professional–technical–clerical workers find this tactic to be ethical. People use quid pro quo most often in initial contacts with others. Most workers used this tactic in initial contacts rather than as a response to resistance. Of the organizations studied, only business leaders use this tactic as a typical response to resistance to earlier exercise of other power tactics.

Quid pro quo is the most frequently used power tactic in peer–peer relations. It is a trade-off tactic. It involves any of several material or personal resources or capacities we may hold and offer in exchange for desired peer performance. It is effective, ethically neutral, and, most often, used as an initial power behavior in our peer relations.

ALLOCATING RESOURCES

This tactic involves the conscious use of organizational resources (including information) to increase our power position vis-à-vis others. While used only third most frequently, this is the most effective cluster of power behaviors respondents reported. It is more effective in achievement of desired results than any other power tactic used in peer as well as other relations. People feel this approach is ethical and use it in initial contacts with those they wish to influence.

Control over resources needed by others is a prerequisite to power. Using this tactic involves allocation of needed resources to others in exchange for their compliance. Allocation of controlled resources is a common phenomenon in today's organizations. Indeed, this power tactic is implicit in routine assignment of duties and responsibilities, budgeting, information processing, networking, and similar organizational activities. Control over, and judicious allocation of needed resources (both psychological and material), makes up much of our work as peers. Resources may be institutional (controlled by virtue of position held in the organization) or personal (fashioned out of the unique qualities of each) (Kipnis, 1976). Providing or withholding of resources places the controller in a power position relative to those who need/desire the controlled resource.

Examples of use of this power tactic in peer contacts are common. They range from giving or withholding needed or desired space, material, information, financial resources, skills, cooperation, or work assignments to participation in decision or policy activity or access to powerful, influential, or attractive people. Any of these or similar resources can and are tactics routinely used to aid one peer gain compliance from another. Several kinds of resources are identifiable as they relate to power use. Each is described below:

Use of Information

The control of access to information is an especially effective integration of this tactic. The conscious impedance, acceleration, or frustration of the official flow of information to specific individuals or units can help or hinder achievement of their goals. This tactic can take any form. For example, delaying information without altering its form or content can disrupt achievement goals of the recipient of this delayed intelligence. Similarly, burying critical information in a mass of extraneous data may accomplish the same result. Intentional distortion (ranging from lying to judicious structuring of information to emphasize a given perspective) is also common to get desired results. So, also, is controlling the distribution of information a possible example of use of this tactic. This specific technique is also seen in the rationalization tactic behavior. Each example represents a particular form of control over the allocation of this resource with the intention of securing our desires over other possible results.

Use of Financial Resources

Control over financial resources is a common version of this tactic. The regular budget allocation procedure is one form of use of this power tactic. Other forms include such behavior as requiring individuals to submit to repeated and extended reviews, audits, and other controls over their use of monies to ensure compliance with our goals (as distinguished from goals of the peer or the overall organization both serve). Extensive approvals, audits, and sign-offs common in some budget offices also exemplify this tactic.

Also common is the requirement that program managers secure repeated approvals before they can pay out funds already allocated in the regular budget process. For example, requiring special treatment to authorize overtime payments (or any special handling) places the peer colleague requiring this extra work in a power position vis-à-vis those whom they ask to conform. Some cost accounting procedures fall into this grouping in that the procedures applied discriminate to force the individual peer to obey. Excessive security of monies procedures also arrogates power to the instigator or controller of these security measures.

Use of Physical Facilities

In using this tactic we may make use of items in the physical environment to emphasize or reduce our power. Items such as dress, furniture, office size and location, work-space layout, and other accoutrements of the physical workplace add or detract from others' perceptions of our power. They, therefore, bear on our ability to be effective. The physical structure of the environment is important, and as we control access to these physical facilities we gain power not otherwise available to us.

Use of Energy

Another resource helpful in gaining and maintaining power has to do with the personal energy we are willing or capable of bringing to bear. Expenditure of high energy levels on a task affects the perceptions of others and can help us achieve compliance from them. The allocation of personal or unit energy to a given task has a direct relationship to task accomplishment. Setting up of exchange relationships where we trade work effort for some desired benefit is an example of this tactic. Used in this way, allocation of energy for salary becomes a common power relationship in organizations.

Willingness to help peers in exchange for desired behavior is another way we can see this tactic to gain peer compliance. Leaders often offer a quid pro quo for desired performance to ensure task performance by those equal to the leader in the formal structure.

Analysis

People in all classes of personal characteristics often find this a useful tactic and make significant use of it in their peer contacts. There is no material deviation in frequency of use when we look at workers in terms of their organizational situation either. It is the second most frequently used peer tactic behind quid pro quo.

This tactic is the single most effective power tactic in both peer relationships and generally. Ninety-five percent of those responding find this tactic to be effective when used regardless of the target. Higher educational institution workers find this tactic a little less effective than three other tactics (developing others, training and orienting others, and using a surrogate). The allocating resources tactic is a highly effective power approach in securing power compliance.

People in organizations also find this tactic to be ethically okay. None find it to be an unethical application of power in peer relations. In only one case is this tactic seen as unethical. Persons employed in institutions of higher education do not see allocating resources as an ethical means of swaying peers to their desires.

Allocating resources is seen mostly as a proper cluster of behaviors to use on initial contact with peers rather than as a fall-back approach if one meets resistance. Those with less than a year of service in their work group use it more often as a counter to resistance. All other classifications of workers use it in initial peer contacts.

Summary

Allocating resources to peers to get them to behave in desired ways is an often-used and effective means of using our power. It is the most frequently used tactic behind quid pro quo and the most effective. It is an ethical tactic, one used primarily as an initial approach to peers. The resources used can include any material, data, or psychological resource a peer needs. It only requires that a peer desires a resource we control for us to be in a powerful position vis-à-vis the wanting peer.

FORMING COALITIONS

Organizations are clusters of interdependent people. This tactic involves allying ourself with certain members of the organization and, sometimes, with persons outside the organization to add to our perceived influence level. Coalition building is a commonly used power tactic in peer relations. It is the second most effective of all peer-oriented tactics and the third most frequently used power tactic in this kind of relationship. Coalitions combine the power that people with similar concerns on an issue have.

Examples of this power tactic include office cliques, informal associations of people, groups of people who belong to professional associations, and others. Coalitions unite independent, but interdependent, people on specific issues or actions. They are fragile. We often form coalitions specifically for each given power issue. Several variations of this tactic can be seen.

One approach involves conscious efforts by leaders to merit the support of followers for a decision or action (Rosen and Lippitt, 1961). It tries to integrate the follower core into a supportive force behind the leader's personal organizational goals (as distinct from or in terms of formal organizational goals). This can involve such disparate items as "being one of the boys," developing mentor–protégé relationships, or offering support in return for personal loyalty. Similarly, networks of peers or colleagues used to multiply power to achieve our aims are also common manifestations of the coalition tactic. Primarily, this involves creating a loose confederation of support among colleagues and from client groups that we can mobilize to help secure our goals.

Developing friendships with peers through research and contact to learn about their attitudes, values, and priorities is helpful in securing their support for our outcomes. Peers represent powerful potential support for our own power use. In this version of the coalition tactic we try to ingratiate ourselves with peers to gain their support. It is an effort to manipulate the peer to achieve our goals by becoming essential in a primarily personal, rather than organizational, way.

We also commonly form coalitions with individuals and groups outside the immediate organization. Establishment of good relations with persons in the larger organization can lead to increased power within the organization. These external contacts may enhance our prestige or provide innovative sources of information, ideas, or approaches. They are alliances that help us internally to cope with specific situations and induce other to our point of view. Others regard individuals who have contacts in other organizations who are useful in achieving the organization's tasks as more powerful. According to Stogdill's research, these multi-organization individuals are seen by coworkers as more influential on specific issues of interest to the organization. Coworkers list their names more often as social and business friends. The contact network is an important source of power (Bass, 1981).

Analysis

The third most frequently used power tactic is forming coalitions. Men use this tactic a little more frequently than women. However, both find it frequently useful. Interestingly, supervisors find this tactic helpful more frequently in their peer relations than nonsupervisors. They rank frequency of use of this tactic at second and seventh, respectively. All kinds of organizations—business, government, higher education, and nonprofit—find this a frequently useful power tactic in peer-to-peer situations. Those with little time in their work unit use coalitions more than any other tactic. This tactic is an often-used power behavior type.

Uniformly, persons surveyed confirm that forming coalitions is a very effective power-use tactic. All classifications of people find it so. Coalition formation is a positive power use in peer relations. This tactic is ethically positive. No classification of worker found this tactic to be unethical.

Coalition formation is useful most often in responding to resistance to other people. Nonprofit organization members differ from the norm here. They prefer to use coalition building as an initial power-use effort. Persons working in work groups of more than fifty people also use this tactic in initial peer contacts.

Summary

Forming coalitions of peers or other significant people in and around the organization is an effective power tactic. It is the second most effective tactic we employ in peer contacts. It is seen as ethical and found effective most often in reacting to resistance met in peers.

CO-OPTING OPPOSITION MEMBERS

This tactic involves giving a representative of the organization or subunit whose support we seek a position on our decision-making body. Co-opting opposition members involves an attempt to change the position of powerful actors so they favor, rather than oppose, our interests. Obviously this cluster of power behaviors presents a risk to the user. By co-opting another we may gain a powerful ally—and eliminate a powerful foe. The risk is there that the target of co-optation may sway us instead.

A form of coalition building, this tactic attempts to add key individuals from opposing forces or potentially powerful individuals whose support would aid in goal attainment, or whose opposition would hamper realization of goals, to the decision group. An example of co-opting opposition members would be to try to involve constituency group leaders in policy formation forums of an organization serving that constituency.

One state used co-opting opposition members to create an urban development unit to represent local elected officials in a governor's office. This example of co-opting opposition members involved a vocal local government association leader opposed to the governor's urban policy. The governor gave this local leader status and some sense of legitimacy in the administration. The municipal officer found his new status and power in the administration attractive and became wary of risking his new position by too vocal an opposition. He also became privy to the overall policy environment of the administration and came to see his one-issue concerns in a more balanced light. The policy rationale of the administration became a part of his value system. As a member of the governor's advisory staff, he came to accept some of it as reasonable.

Co-opting opposition members has the effect that the co-opted members become associated with the position and rationale of the former opposition and begin to defend it (or at least not oppose it) in public forums. Co-opted leaders have information, perspective, and logic that they otherwise would not have, and, therefore, would not be required to understand or defend. They also become a part of the new group. In this new role they are labeled as associated in formal ways with what might formerly have been the opposition point of view.

Co-opted individuals are subject to information and social and formal organizational pressures to conform to the perspectives of the co-opting agent. They are placed in a position where they must justify their position in an environment antagonistic to their former stand on the issues. And, it gives them a stake in the organization they join. It also motivates them to take an interest in that organization's survival and success as well as that of the parent organization. Co-opting opposition members is a bid to change the position of powerful social actors so they come to favor the position they formerly opposed. This is in an old and time-honored stratagem that occurs across organizational lines.

Analysis

Co-opting opposition members is the fourth most frequently used power behavior cluster in peer contacts. Women use this tactic, but less frequently than do men. Business workers find this especially useful, employing it more frequently than any other power tactic except quid pro quo. Other classifications of organization members conform to the overall ranking of this tactic as the fourth most often used in peer contacts.

Co-opting opposition members, like forming coalitions, is seen as effective in peer contacts. There are no special situations or kinds of organization participant that find co-opting opposition members either more effective than the average, or less so. Co-opting opposition members is the third most effective of those tactics used primarily in peer relations. It is the eighth most effective tactic of all those identified.

Co-opting opposition members is ethically acceptable to most people. No group of respondents found this tactic to be unethical, although workers in higher education see this tactic as ethically neutral. This tactic represents a range of specific behaviors people use most of the time to counter resistance in others. They seldom use it as an initial response.

Summary

A risk tactic of some significance, co-opting members of opposing groups nevertheless is seen as an effective method of power use with peers. It is seen as ethically appropriate or as neutral, but not as an unethical behavior pattern. People who use this cluster of specific power behaviors do so most often in situations where others have offered resistance to earlier overtures. Most people, regardless of their personal or organizational situation, frequently use this power tactic with some expectation of success.

INCURRING OBLIGATION

This tactic involves us in developing a sense of obligation in others to induce them to do what we want. This tactical approach to power is frequently a part of peer relations. It is the fifth most often-used tactic in peer relationships. However, people use it with other organizational power targets only infrequently. It ranks twentieth of twenty-two overall in frequency of use. When people do use it toward other targets in the organization, they most often use it toward subordinates, not superiors.

It is a common perception in management circles that participation in decision making increases the likelihood that participants will support the decision when executed. This idea is a version of a powerful, yet subtle, power tactic: obligation. We often can ensure compliance with our desires if we can make the target feel indebted to us. Bell (1975) identifies obligation as a specific base of power. It is more appropriate to classify obligation as a tactic in power use, however. It most often represents the nature of a relationship, not a resource in the classical sense.

We create obligation out of an unequal exchange between two or more people (Szilagyl and Wallace, 1983). The maxim, "There is no such thing as a free lunch," suggests the nature of the obligation tactic. Power users may provide information, money, materials, psychological support, friendship, or other needs to the target and then use the sense of obligation incurred to later induce compliance.

Several versions of obligation as a power tactic in peer relations are clear. We incur obligation when we promise another person specific action or reward for current cooperation. Obligation is a kind of conditioned compliance; compliance founded upon the specific or implied promise of expectation. It is similar in general to quid pro quo. The distinction is that in this trade-off, obligation (a psychological action) is the stock-in-trade, not some intrinsic commodity.

Friendship, too, can be a form of debt. Most people prefer to deal with friends. Friendship helps reduce tension, encourages trust, and eases communication and tension in social situations. As we develop friendships with others, they want to obey our wishes to maintain friendly relations. Peer friendships, of course, may be present without overt power implications. It is nevertheless a common form of power use in peer relations.

Self-sacrifice may seen altruistic and moral, but it also can be a power behavior. Peers use the superior moral position of having sacrificed self in some way to dominate the other person in direct ways. As an example: Ghandi's self-sacrificing acts produced a powerful need in millions of Indians to conform with his wishes in partial repayment.

And, finally, we incur obligation through praise. Most people want our good wishes. They will follow our orders as we continue to value their behavior and are willing to express that value in praise and compliment. This is a subtle, but powerful principle of action, one in which peers engage regularly.

Analysis

Incurring obligation is useful in relationships with all three target groups, but especially with peers and subordinates. In both latter uses, obligation is a statistically significant power behavior pattern. We can see several patterns in the use of this tactic in peer relationships. Women use it more than men, supervisors more than nonsupervisors, and government, business, and nonprofit organizations more than higher education workers. In some cases, however, it is seen as a useless tactic. People in small organizations (fewer than one hundred employees total) use this tactic only infrequently. Nor do workers in large work groups (more than 1,000 people) or service organization members use this tactic often.

Incurring obligation is uniformly seen as unethical. This is an interesting finding, given the ubiquity of use and the many innocuous situations in which we can envision it in operation. One reason for the negative moral valuation may lie in the use of friendship and the potential for manipulation. Many people use incurring obligation to get others to follow their wishes as a response to resistance more than as an initial tactic. However, considerable numbers of people used this tactic as an initial approach. For example, men use it as a resistance-countering tactic, women as an initial behavior approach. Similarly, those under 40 use it as a fall-back behavior approach and those older find it useful in initial contacts.

People in organizations with fewer than one hundred employees also use it more often as an initial approach to peers. So do workers with more than five years in their work unit. So do professional–clerical–technical workers and those in product-oriented organizations, higher education, and business organizations. Other groups of workers use it to respond to peers who offer resistance to initial power tactic use.

Summary

Incurring obligation is a frequently used power behavior toward both peers and subordinates. Few feel it to be ethical, however. There may be a manipulative element in this power tactic, one that puts people off. And, too, it is not too effective. As shown in Table 7.1, most people find it less effective than most of the tactics analyzed.

USING SURROGATES

This tactic describes those situations in which we make use of a third party (or parties) through which to exercise power. Anytime we substitute another person for ourselves to get others to do what we want is using a surrogate in the sense meant here. Surrogates "front" for the power user. They do the work of influencing others as an instrument of the powerful individual. Persons using this tactic find it comparatively effective. Users see it as ethically neutral. It is a second-level response to peers when earlier behavior fails to achieve desired results from them.

Sometimes we use other individuals to mask our use of power. While an indirect power tactic, it is common in most organizations. Often, we use others to represent us before constituency groups—sometimes without the knowledge of those constituents that we are even involved. Gaining compliance from others by having the proposal for action presented by a popular (or otherwise accepted) individual can help the accomplishment of our results.

The literature on community power illustrates this tactic of power use. Much of the early community power literature dealt with relatively unknown "powers behind the throne" in local communities. These individuals were most influential, yet largely unknown to the general population. These elites, nevertheless, exerted significant influence over community decisions through less powerful intermediaries (surrogates).

We can use surrogates to mask the real identity of powerful people to reduce opposition, or merely because we desire anonymity. Peers use surrogates as scapegoats also to dissipate negative energy in target groups and to allow real power holders to keep their power. Scapegoating is impersonal; the emphasis is on getting past a bad situation with power intact.

Analysis

Using a surrogate is the sixth most frequently used power tactic in peer relations. No unique difference in the overall frequent use of this tactic is evident. It is a covert power tactic, one some see as manipulative in its essence, although most of us use it often.

Most people surveyed find the using a surrogate tactic effective in attaining their desires from peers. It is the fifth most effective tactic in dealing with peers. Those more than 40 years of age find it more effective than younger workers. And, people working in higher education see it to be more effective than either their government, business, or nonprofit counterparts.

Using a surrogate through which to direct our power is seen as ethically neutral. Women find it ethically positive; men find it ethically neutral. Those more than 40 years old also value this tactic positively (i.e., find it ethical) on this dimension. So do supervisors and those people who find their work boring and routine.

Government workers and those in nonprofit organizations also see this cluster of power behaviors as ethical. Members of business and higher education organizations rate this tactic as neutral. Workers in product-oriented jobs find this tactic unethical.

People find most success in using surrogates to counter initial resistance of peers to our power actions. Interestingly, people in nonprofit organizations do not use this tactic in either initial or follow-up situations. Leaders in these kinds of organizations did not rank this tactic at all on this dimension.

Summary

Using intermediaries as substitutes to act for us is a common power behavior pattern. It is seen by most to be neutral in its application. They see it as effective in achieving desired results and as a fall-back tactic, most helpful in countering resistance from peer targets.

CONTROLLING THE AGENDA

An infrequently used power tactic, agenda control involves us in a priori determination of the issue context within which to conduct peer interaction. It is planned and structured behavior that allows us to control the topics for discussion, their timing, and their content. The purpose is to attain our desires in the face of possible opposition from peers.

Controlling the agenda for action is a basic power-use tactic. Power comes from controlling action alternatives (Pfeffer, 1981). Whether or not the action agenda we control is innocuous or critical, if we can determine issues for discussion or decision, we have power. This tactic involves us in setting agendas for action, determining the timing of consideration of specific items, and placing an item or items on the agenda. It also has a reverse image: keeping items off of action agendas. We frequently exercise power in determining that a particular issue should not reach the action stage and therefore not be considered for decision action. The ability to limit what goes on and what stays off the organization's action agenda is equally an element of power use (Bachrach and Baratz, 1972). If we can control agenda preparation (sometimes even the simple act of typing the agenda and setting the order of items for consideration), we control a potential for influence. Agenda control impacts not only decision effects but also the behavior of others in the total decision making system.

Selecting agenda items ensures that the issues discussed are those that we want and for which we have prepared. The issues that we are prepared to deal with become the action issues. Obviously, placing an item on the agenda when we are ready increases the likelihood that our arguments will, at the least, receive a hearing. Withholding an item until we are prepared or placing it on the agenda when others are not expecting it and, therefore, are not prepared to deal with it also enhances our relative power position.

Controlling the agenda includes taking control over the formal mechanism for accepting items for an action agenda. Making it difficult, complicated, and time-consuming to place an item on the agenda limits the number of items so placed. It also limits the number of people who will take the time to follow these procedures. This increases the power of those who know how to work the system and allows them to control the decision agenda in ways outlined above. Arbitrary deadlines, strict procedural steps, and similar requirements fall under this tactic or power use.

An interesting aspect of the mechanics of controlling the agenda has to do with the order of placement of items on the agenda (Salancik and Pfeffer, 1977). Apparently, when a decision body considers an item can influence results. Research shows that special placement of action items vis-à-vis other items impacts results (Plott and Levine, 1978). Available research data are spotty and specific, and recommendations are as yet inconclusive. Nevertheless, depending on local organizational customs and the nature of the issue under consideration, the specific location on the agenda may bear on power use and attendant results. Placing an item first, for example, implies that the group will make a decision on that item before a decision pattern is discernible. Thus location on the agenda may increase our risk of an unwanted decision. Alternatively, placement later on the agenda will allow us to assess voting patterns of the group and adjust persuasion strategies to suit.

Additionally, once we establish an agenda, it becomes a fixed political environment within which the power actors operate. The specific items on an agenda for decision make up the materials around which we determine our strategy for achieving desired results. It is only within this context that we decide which results we prefer and which we can trade off for advantage elsewhere. For example, those in control of agenda preparation can place unimportant items first on the agenda to build support for later, more critical items that we especially desire (Porter, Allen, and Angle, 1981).

Caution must be taken in using these data. Success in using item placement depends on the characteristics of the decision-making process routinely present in each organization. Precise guidelines about special placement must consider these local customs. In some organizations, customs and the characteristics of the people involved might dictate early placement of important items and later consideration of nonimportant ones. In other organizations, the reverse or some other arrangement of action items might yield advantage. Until others complete further research in a wide variety of circumstances, it is best to caution care in dealing with this aspect of controlling the agenda. This element of power, however, warrants our attention and may help achieve our results more often.

Analysis

The seventh most frequently used power tactic in peer contacts is controlling the agenda. Women use this tactic a little more than men do, as do persons older than 40. Several kinds of workers do not use this tactic in statistically significant ways. For example, workers in organizations with fewer than one-hundred employees fall into this class. So do people with more than five years of service in their immediate work group. Other kinds of organization leaders find this tactic frequently useful in their peer relations. Controlling the agenda is an effective power tactic. Only employees in units with more than 1,000 workers or in immediate work teams of more than 50 people rate this tactic as ineffective.

Most people do not consider this tactic to be ethically acceptable. They rank it as an unethical power tactic. We find exceptions to this position in nonsupervisors who rate it as neutral. Government workers and those in service-oriented organizations also find this tactic neither particularly ethical nor unethical. Finally, those in units with fewer than one-hundred employees and people with less than one year's service in their unit see the tactic as ethically neutral. Other kinds of leaders surveyed find this tactic to be ethical in peer usage.

We use controlling the agenda mostly in countering resistance from peers. Some people use it in initial contacts—for example, those people more than 40 years of age, people in smaller (less than one hundred employees) organizations, and those in product-oriented organizations. The rest of us continue to find this a helpful tactic when others resist us.

Summary

People use controlling the agenda for action mostly in their peer relations. It is effective, but not exceptionally so. Those who control access to or the content of the topics for decision action use it to aid in personal goal attainment. As power users we find this cluster of behaviors to be unethical, using it only when others resist initial influence overtures.

BRINKMANSHIP

This tactic includes any effort directed toward disturbing the equilibrium of the organization as a prelude to other action we might take to control choice. Of course, resources may include skills, capacities, values, attitudes, or actions of others. Brinkmanship behavior has the purpose of creating organizational crisis (even chaos) preparatory to direct action to attain our goal. It is a risk tactic of some magnitude and appears not to be very effective in most circumstances. When people use it, they use it as a fall-back behavior when targets resist other attempts to get their way.

It is possible to create or reinforce an intolerable situation so we can then step forward with a ready solution. Brinkmanship is a risk tactic that entails allowing the situation to deteriorate to a point where colleagues will favorably receive any positive action we suggest (Pelz, 1952). The key element for success lies in proper timing in introducing our preferred action to ameliorate the crisis that we have allowed to develop.

An example with which many will be familiar deals with system automation.

Sometimes program managers will resist full automation of manual systems because of initial costs and their fear of this technology. The computer system manager who wants to automate may allow excessive backlogs in the semiautomatic system to develop. The program manager then has no option but to purchase the specified computer system.

Brinkmanship is risky! We risk others perceiving us as incompetent and firing us. The risk for our peer targets is that failure to follow our recommendations will result in collapse of their system. Use of the brinkmanship tactic often can be seen in labor negotiations, structural reorganizations, and in budget implementation. Peers use it in many situations where the stakes are high enough and the calculation is that success may result.

Demanding stances; confrontation; forceful, assertive (even aggressive) argument; demands for our specific result in opposition to all other possible results; and shows of extreme confidence in risky situations are all examples of brinkmanship. It is a planned, considered introduction of stress in the situation that applies pressure to peers to conform their behavior in certain ways we desire. Any purposely created situational crisis that we intend to work to our advantage falls under this tactic's definition. Winter (1973) also includes purposeful violence and brigandage as examples of power behavior falling under the brinkmanship umbrella.

Analysis

People trying to effect their peers use the brinkmanship tactic infrequently. Both men and women use this tactic about equally often. Older workers seldom, if ever, use this tactic, although younger workers use it a little more often. Interestingly, superiors use brinkmanship very infrequently (not at a statistically significant level). Nonsupervisors, however, find this the most frequent form of power behavior used. There may be something in the lack of formal authority that induces us to use this risk tactic. Those of us in routine or boring work also use brinkmanship more frequently than any other tactic. People in exciting jobs rate its frequency as ninth most frequently used.

This tactic is seen as ineffective by those surveyed. Peers nevertheless use it frequently on many kinds and types of workers. This is an interesting finding of this research. In only two cases is this tactic found to be effective. Workers in organizations with one hundred or fewer total employees use it. And people in higher educational institutions use it. Both kinds of organizations contain situational elements that require risk tactics to achieve desired ends. Higher education peers do not have much formal authority and the opportunity for brinkmanship behavior is plentiful.

Most respondents see brinkmanship as the most unethical power tactic. Dispensing rewards runs a close second. In fact, dispensing rewards is the most unethical tactic for workers in work teams of more than fifty people and for professional–technical–clerical workers. Many regard brinkmanship as the most unethical power tactic studied for peers as well as for the other two classes of targets.

Peers use this tactic most often to counter resistance in the peer target. People with less than one year in their immediate work group find this tactic sometimes useful in initial power behavior toward peers. No other classification of worker uses it significantly except as a resistance-countering tactic.

Summary

Brinkmanship is a risk tactic. People find its use to be unethical. Nevertheless, we use it fairly often. People use it commonly in peer relationships. They also use it somewhat in superior relationships and to a more limited extent toward subordinates. It is a fall-back tactic, coming into play most often when another tactic did not produce the desired result. This tactic tries to trade off solution of a problem in exchange for acceptance of the power-user's plan.

BUILDING A FAVORABLE IMAGE

Many of us find it helpful in achieving our goals in peer relationships to use the tactic, building a favorable image. We use this tactic also in statistically significant levels in superior relations. (See Chapter 6 for a more complete definition of this tactic.) It is the fourth most effective power tactic used in peer relations. A carefully cultivated, directed reputation can attract peers to us and place them under our power. This is a frequent power ploy in peer relationships.

Any time we try to attract people to us or our point of view based on personal qualities we have—or appear to have—is an example of this tactic. When we induce others to follow us because it is "me" asking, we are using this cluster of power behaviors. Building an image as having superior knowledge, status, prestige, presence, or specialization allows us to influence peers' behavior and aids in personal goal attainment. Many examples are obvious in work situations that illustrate this power tactic.

Analysis

Building a favorable image is a tactic used frequently by people wanting to influence both superiors and peers. It is the ninth most frequently used power tactic toward peers. Men use this tactic frequently (statistically) but women do not. Supervisors find this tactic useful but nonsupervisors do not. Nor do workers under 40 find building a favorable image a frequently used tactic, although their older colleagues do. Building a favorable image behaviors are frequent in educational, government, and nonprofit organizations, but not in business organizations. Work tenure is not a factor in analyzing this tactic. People with short or longer-term tenure in their work team both find this tactic to be less than frequently used.

Building a favorable image is an effective tactic with peers (as it is with superiors). This tactic is seen to be ethically okay. Its use with peers follows the parameters outlined for superior target uses: All respondents find this tactic ethical. Men find it a little more ethical than do women. Nonsupervisors see it as more ethical than supervisors.

Building a favorable image is most often an initial power use tactic. Most people surveyed find it useful to open power relationships with peers. Peers use this tactic primarily as an initial behavior approach in working with peers. Women, nonsupervisors, service-oriented workers, and those working in immediate work groups of more than fifty people specially favor its use.

Summary

Our image is a power resource. Building a favorable image provides the individual with an entré with peers. It is effective, ethical, and used frequently by most organization members, often as an initial power-use try.

8

Tactics Used with Subordinates

Leaders rely most often on nine power tactics in employing their subordinate-oriented power strategy. These tactics are training and orienting others, developing others, dispensing rewards, controlling decision criteria, legitimacy, organizational placement, using symbols, ritualism, and obligation. They are separate from the tactics leaders use toward superiors or peers with only one exception. We use incurring obligation about equally with peers and with subordinates.

The subordinate-directed tactics are less risky than those used within other strategic target groups. They concentrate more on traditional organizational systems. Subordinates base the tactics used with peers and superiors somewhat more on system aspects of power than on personal aspects. That is, subordinate-oriented tactics rely more on power bases such as (a) legitimate position in the hierarchy, (b) routine patterns of behavior and relationships common in the specific organization environment, (c) control of resource-based rewards or the promise of reward, (d) control over decision parameters, (e) formal relationships, and (f) hierarchy and similar aspects of organizational life (see Barnard, 1948; Bell, 1975; Etzioni, 1961; and Winter, 1973).

Leaders using power in their downward-directed relationships rely more on traditional forms of power of force, authority, and manipulation. Interestingly, they also make limited use of the other power forms—persuasion, threat–promise, and influence. Individuals using these tactics behave in many ways that most of us would find common and acceptable. In two cases, however, the pattern is broken. Many organization members use developing others as well as training and orienting others tactics in their relations with subordinates. These two behavior sets, especially developing others, are on a different base. These tactics rely on psychological relationships and principles of human development to ensure compliance. They represent two ways of sharing of power, rather than of rationing it out to others to get what they want from them.

Developing others is a tactic of distribution of power from the powerful to the less powerful. The result is a real transfer of power, a change in the power equation existing between the parties involved. Training and orienting others also entails a sharing of facts, ideas, and attitudes with others. These power tactics (developing others and training and orienting others) are in use significantly more often than any of the others directed toward subordinates. Training and orienting others and developing others are the most effective tactics used with subordinates to get them to behave in desired ways. Then follows a series of "system-based" tactics (for example, ritualism, controlling decision criteria, use of legitimacy, organizational placement, and resort to symbols). It is only with incurring obligation that we return to personal tactics in relations with subordinates.

This chapter defines and delimits the tactics identified above. Table 8.1 summarizes cogent elements of data developed from research about uses of these nine clusters of power behavior directed toward those subordinate to us hierarchically.

Power directed downward in the hierarchy relies understandably on the formal authority implicit in participant roles. The terms superior and subordinate refer only to relative authority roles and not to relative power held by the parties. Typically the person in the superior role has more formal (authority) power. The subordinate may have more overall power in the particular situation by virtue of personal capacities developed. Or his or her power may be a result of skills, information, experience, or other critical resources controlled.

This analysis confirms that we base much power directed to subordinates on legitimate authority and takes forms of force, authority, and manipulation. It also points up that some (a statistically significant portion) power use is in nondirective, sharing forms. Superiors often use power by sharing their power, not husbanding it. They actively try to give power to subordinates so the subordinates can be more effective in achieving their individual goals. While we assume that the primary reason for this sharing is to enhance productivity, evidence marshaled here neither supports nor refutes that classical reason. Rather, from this data only we can conclude that superiors share with others to accomplish the subordinates personal goals.

Plott and Levine (1978) suggest that when we act in this sharing-of-power role we are in a leadership mode. When this element of power is absent we function in a managerial role.

Conventional wisdom suggests that subordinates are effectively powerless in relationships with superiors. This research refutes this view and confirms Mechanic's (1962) view that everyone in the organization is powerful. In power

Table 8.1
Summary of Tactics Used Toward Subordinates

Tactics Ranked by Frequency	Tactics Ranked by Effectiveness	Tactics Ranked by Ethical Pattern		When Used	
		Positive	Negative	Initial	Resistance
Training and Orienting Others	2	P		I	
Developing Others	1	P		I	
Use of Rewards	9*		N		R
Controlling Decision Criteria	5	P		I	
Legitimizing Control	4	P			R
Organizational Placement	7		N	I	
Using Symbols	6		N	I	
Ritualism	3	P			R
Incurring Obligation	8		N		R

* Not effective
P   Seen as ethically positive
N   Seen as ethically negative
I   Used as an initial contact approach
R   Used upon encountering resistance

terms the distinction between supervisor and subordinate is one of degree, not the absolute presence of absence of power. Surely subordinates are dependent on superiors. So, too, is the superior dependent on the subordinate in achieving individual and mutual goals.

Data collected suggest that we can describe downward power as system-based. It relies on formal systems more than on personal characteristics of capacities. Displaying charisma, for example, is not an important tactic in downward power use as some popular literature suggests. Rather, we suggest that strong leaders institutionalize operating and relationships systems that carry the organization. It is these institutionalized power tactics, such as ritualism, symbols, organizational placement, legitimacy, establishment of decision criteria, reward systems, and formal training, orientation, and development programs, that direct subordinate behavior more than personal charisma or a favorable image.

Discussion of each of the nine subordinate-directed tactics follow. These sections discuss significant findings about each tactic.

TRAINING AND ORIENTING OTHERS

This tactic involves transferring specific behavior, skills, or values to subordinates to inculcate our goals, value system, or philosophy. This is a frequently used, effective, and acceptable power tactic for those working in superior-to-subordinate relationships. It is a commonly used approach to get others to behave in desired ways.

Training and orienting others means the process of transferring desired skills, information, attitudes, or values to others to ensure specific results. Involved is knowledge transfer activities as well as specific skill or value transfers. Two separate versions of this tactic are seen in practice: (a) skills training and (b) value change education. In the first version, the emphasis is on changing the skills or knowledge of targets of power so they accept our result desires. In the second, the focus is on attitude change.

When our targets have the information and skills needed to do the job desired, they are likely to behave in desired ways. This is especially true if these are the only skills owned. To the degree that we can change another's attitude about a common goal, we exert more influence toward goal achievement than any other single action we can take.

The purposes of organizational training and orienting others programs are to acculturate and socialize the individual member to desired modes of thought and action. Extraneous education and training only dilutes the purity of our relationship with our targets. This, as much as any other factor, accounts for the general concern about employing overqualified people.

Specific techniques of training and orienting others cover the gamut of educational methodology. They include behavior modification, classroom lectures, coach–student systems, mentor–protégé systems, and selective dissemination of information within the organization. They also include gatekeeping into higher levels of power, displacement of values, role definition, integration, instruction, indoctrination programs, counseling systems, and many more. These activities are actions we might take to change a subordinate's knowledge, skills, or attitudes and, therefore, behavior to conform to our needs.

Analysis

Training and orienting others is the most often-used power tactic by superiors toward their subordinates to change their behavior. People also use training and orienting others infrequently in contacts with peers and only rarely with superiors. More than 77 percent of participants ranked this as a prime approach in using of power toward those lower in the hierarchy. And, significantly, most respondents reported use of this tactic.

When analyzed according to personal characteristics of persons using this tactic, we find that both men and women use this tactic. However, women report using dispensing rewards behaviors a little more often than they do training and orienting others. Age apparently makes little difference. Both older and younger workers rank this tactic as either the most frequent tactic used or the second most often used. Expectedly, this is a frequently used tactic by supervisors. Nonsupervisors report using both dispensing rewards and developing others tactics more often.

We would expect that training and orienting others is implicit in the prerogatives of authority. That those without this power base resort to other kinds of behavior to affect others more often than they do training and orienting others is logical. Their use of this tactic at all is a finding of some significance and interest. People excited about their work ranked training and orienting others the most often-used tactic. People bored with their work rate it as the fifth most often-used tactic.

Analyzed for the characteristics of the organization worked for, we see that leaders in business organizations use this tactic more often than any other. It is only the third most often used in nonprofit organizations. Government and higher educational institution leaders ranked this tactic as their second most often-used tactic with subordinates. People working in small work units and in organizations of fewer than one-hundred people use training and orienting others very frequently. It is less frequently resorted to by members of organizations with opposite characteristics. It is a favorite tactic for service-oriented organization members, but less so for professional–technical–clerical workers.

This tactic is the single most effective power tactic used by superiors and toward subordinates. It ranks first in use with this target group and third overall. Women find training and orienting others to be a little more effective than their male counterparts. Persons of all ages find this tactic to be effective. Training and orienting others and developing others are the two most often-used and the most effective tactics in working with subordinates. Similar findings come from analysis of supervisors–nonsupervisors and bored–excited workers. These findings are also present when we analyze the respondent pool for characteristics of the organizational environment of the power users.

Again, training and orienting others and developing others are the most ethical of all the power tactics used toward subordinates. No one responding found training and orienting others to be unethical and only a few saw it as ethically neutral. Indeed, all kinds of power users examined and those working in all organizational situations find this tactic to be ethically okay.

Subordinates use this tactic as an initial behavioral approach to alter subordinate actions. This is a uniform finding for this tactic. Persons using this tactic do so primarily as an initial, not a fall-back, method of impacting subordinate behavior to achievement of their desired results.

Summary

Training and orienting others is a positive, effective, and often-used power tactic in subordinate relationships. It is uniformly effective in gaining compliance from subordinates. While a commonly used approach in organizations, we have not recognized its power dimension. Recognition of the power implications of this organizational activity can aid us to better use this tactic. This recognition can help one to decide when to use it rather than an alternative cluster of behaviors.

DEVELOPING OTHERS

This tactic involves efforts to increase the individual capacities of others, thereby increasing the overall capacity of the group and our ultimate power. Developing others is one of the two most frequently used power tactics with subordinates. It is the single most effective tactic used with this classification of power-use targets. It defines a positive cluster of power behaviors that try to build up the total power in the individual and in the total group.

The developing others tactic assumes the premise that follower capacity, skill, and ability can increase. As subordinates increase capacity and direct it toward mutually accepted goals, overall power is enhanced as well. Having better-prepared and -qualified people working with us increases our power. There is a risk inherent in the use of this tactic. We risk that the better-qualified follower might wrest control from us. Nevertheless, developing others is the most effective power tactic available. Increasing follower capacity multiplies available organizational power and innovation in ways that are not possible under systems that rely solely on the leader's capacity or potential (Fairholm, 1991).

Nyberg (1981) discusses this tactic, which he calls fealty, in his excellent work on power. Fealty, or faithfulness or loyalty based on trust and mutuality, he says, is the highest form of power use. It is the most stable form since it rebounds to the mutual benefit of the parties involved. This research confirms his position that most of us sometimes behave in developmental ways in our downward relationships with group members.

American culture does not encourage us to think of power and caring together. The Judeo-Christian tradition separates these two concepts. As noted, many often relate power to authoritarianism and exploitation—both the antithesis of love. Also noted in the discussion of the history of power is the idea that power has two dimensions: domination and development. This second dimension of power seeks to build others rather than to make them weak. The developing others tactic follows this theoretical line of thought.

The development of others includes efforts we make to enhance the capacities and self-confidence of our associates. We can find examples when leaders delegate formal authority widely, share information, and encourage participation in policy and decision making. As leaders share power in these ways, they increase the power in that group. Fellow workers also grow. They see in conformity an opportunity to develop their individual talents and skills.

As we use the developing others tactic our followers feel protected and comfortable. In this assurance, they can apply their capacities and energy to the plan of action leaders promulgate. They need not reserve some energy and talent to protect themselves from possible negative actions. This is power use in its most effective, most socially positive dimension.

Analysis

Many people report using this tactic in their relations with subordinates. More than 73 percent of all respondents use this tactic in downward relations. Developing others is part of a cluster of three tactics (with training and orienting others and dispensing rewards) that dominate downward power use. Almost 75 percent of all leaders report frequent use of each of these three clusters of power behavior.

This situation adds support to the current orientation toward participative management and leadership styles. Apparently, many people engage in behavior that is at least partially aimed at increasing the overall (general) capacity of subordinates. This is quite apart (or, at least, in addition to) efforts to get them to perform the required organizational tasks. They report frequent and effective use of this kind of power behavior. Data suggest that people use the developing others power tactic also in some peer–peer relations, but rarely in subordinate-to-superior relations.

Men engage in developing others activities most frequently. Women use this tactic also, but use both dispensing rewards and training and orienting others more often. Those more than 40 years old use this tactic most frequently in subordinate relations. Those under 40 follow the women in using training and orienting others and dispensing rewards more often. Supervisors use this tactic frequently, as do those workers who are either bored or excited about their work.

Government, business, and higher educational institution workers all use developing others as a favorite power tactic. In each case, however, they report using several other tactics more often. Not-for-profit organization members do not use this tactic in statistically frequent amounts. They report use of only three power tactics toward subordinate targets: those of controlling decision criteria, training and orienting others, and legitimizing control. Members of larger organizations and those with longer tenure in their work groups report frequent use of this tactic. Perhaps it takes time and the accumulation of trust-building associations in order for people to use this tactic with comfort and assurance.

Developing others, as noted, is the most effective tactic identified in those tactics used toward subordinates. Men find this to be the case, but women report developing others as only the fifth most effective tactic they use. Both older and younger organization members find the developing others tactic to be very effective. So, too, do both supervisors and nonsupervisors and those with bored as well as excited attitudes about their work.

The characteristics of the organization in which we work does not have a significant bearing on the feeling that this is a very effective tactic. Members of all types and kinds of organizations analyzed find this tactic to be effective.

Uniformly, both superiors and subordinates find this tactic to be ethical. No one found this tactic to be unethical. This ethical rating is uniform through all classifications and types of people and all organizational situations in which we find ourselves. We find more consensus on the ethics of the developing others tactic than for any other single power tactic studied.

Looked at in the aggregate, the developing others tactic is seen as an initial approach mechanism to secure subordinate compliance. All classifications of people and organizational situations reflect this position. No significant variations from this norm can be seen.

Summary

The developing others tactic is an effective and ethical cluster of power behaviors frequently used by organization members toward those subordinate to them in the hierarchy. It is appealing to people in all organizational situations and with varying personal characteristics. It is enhancing of the subordinate and of the power user's positions and goals. This sharing of power tactic differs in at least one critical dimension from other power tactics. Development defines a set of behaviors that aim at sharing available power and of multiplying its impact. Most other tactics treat power itself as a limited resource that we should husband and control. This is a positive, popular, and effective cluster of power behaviors favored almost universally by those participating in organizational life.

DISPENSING REWARDS

This tactic is similar to allocating resources. Individuals can use a variety of rewards, some resources-based, some psychological, and either positive or negative, to gain influence over and support from others. Dispensing rewards is a very frequently used and effective power tactic. It, with developing others and training and orienting others, enjoys wide popularity among superiors in working with their subordinates to sway them to desired behavior. There is some ambiguity, however, in its use. Many people report that dispensing rewards is unethical. And, people often use it as a response to failed earlier tries to influence subordinate behavior.

Giving something that we value to others in return for allegiance to our decision choices constitutes the use of the reward tactic (Hartsock, 1983). Use of proxemics and other size and distance factors of the physical situation (such as size of office) is an application of this tactic. Also included here is the allocation by the power holder of accoutrements such as windows, furniture, cars, and other facilities and symbols of status. It also includes the more obvious raise in salary or promotion.

Space and time/space factors can add to or detract from our perceived power potential. When leaders reward a follower in this way, they enhance their perceived power and the perceived power of the individual who controls these rewards. This tactic, then, can be developmental to the individuals involved as well as to their organization.

The use of rewards to induce compliance or the threat (or imposition) of punishment for noncompliance is as old a management behavior pattern as any. It is at the heart of management compensation systems, productivity improvement programs, and most other management systems, methods, and techniques. Because leaders use this tactic frequently does not lessen its importance as a power tactic. Rather, the utility of this tactic in society is testimony of the ubiquity of power in organizational life. Power is indeed a universal concept in social science.

Analysis

Dispensing rewards is the third of the cluster of three subordinate power tactics employed most often by leaders who want subordinates to conform their behavior to desired results. Women find this the most often-used tactic toward subordinates, while men rank it fourth in these kinds of relationships. Supervisors also rank their use of this tactic in fourth place, but nonsupervisors use it most frequently. Maybe nonsupervisors find they can dispense psychic and other rewards in situations where they cannot undertake training, developing others, or others of the nine power behavior clusters that are more often within the control of supervisors.

Government, higher education, and business organization members also rank dispensing rewards very highly. Their nonprofit colleagues, however, do not use this tactic often in their relationships with subordinates. Surprisingly, they do not report using this tactic in these relationships. This is an interesting finding in the face of conventional wisdom that suggests that psychic rewards would be a part of the compensation system in human service, religious, and eleemosynary institutions, from which agencies these data come. The use of this tactic in other organizational situations does not reveal significant deviations from the overall ranking of this tactic. It is an often-used power tactic.

While often used by most organization members, dispensing rewards is not seen as an effective method of using power. Men find it effective, but women do not. Younger workers rate it as effective; older ones do not. Supervisors see it as effective. Nonsupervisors do not rate it as effective. Neither those excited about their work nor bored with it find this tactic effective in a statistically significant sense. Education, government, and nonprofit organization leaders report it to be effective in their work, but businesspeople do not. Nor do leaders working in product-oriented organizations, professional–technical–clerical workers, those with five or more years seniority in their work, or those in small work teams. Others rate it as effective.

Dispensing rewards is not seen as an ethical pattern of behavior, either. Overall respondents see this tactic as unethical. Both men and women so rate it. Older and younger people, both supervisors and nonsupervisors, and those with attitudes of excitement or boredom about their work also see it as unethical. Members of organizations of all classifications and kinds are unanimous in rating this tactic as unethical.

People bring dispensing rewards into play most often as a response to failure in earlier tries to influence subordinate behavior. No classification of individual nor organizational situation worked in showed variation from this overall style of use position.

Summary

Dispensing rewards is a frequently used tactic, but one that is seen by most people as ineffective and unethical. People use it most as a response to subordinates who evidence resistance to other power-use efforts. Those with control over resources needed by subordinates use this tactic to induce desired behavior. Most often these efforts do not prove successful in attainment of the desired behavior results. It is seen to be unethical, an inappropriate use of available resources. This may be because of the implication of unequal distribution of these resources among the subordinate core. These findings of ineffectiveness and unethicality provide another perspective on this cluster of behaviors, one that questions some long-standing assumptions about management and human dynamics.

CONTROLLING DECISION CRITERIA

This tactic concerns the selection of decision criteria in the decision process and application of those criteria in ways that favor our position. This tactic is an unobtrusive tactic of power use. It deals with our actions in instituting problem-solving or problem-evaluation criteria that organizational participants will use in analyzing and deciding group issues. The idea is that if the parameters of problem analysis are set in specific ways, the resultant decisions (or recommendations) will conform to our desires.

People exercise power in situations of competing choice. This tactic is an indirect expression of power. It is one in which we introduce criteria others will use to judge the utility of the decision system or process. Setting decision criteria removes the need that the leader intervene directly in the decision-making process. Often, determining the criteria others will use is less threatening to others than is engaging in a conflict over specific decisions or solutions. Selecting this tactic assures control over the decision result without the risk of confrontation or the appearance of domination.

An application of this can be seen when a lower-level manager wants to buy a particular item of equipment or service. If he develops specifications (goals) that only one supplier can meet, it is not possible for higher management to choose any but the desired item. The leader has exercised power in this decision process without direct involvement in the decision event and without the risk of confrontation.

The dominant coalition frequently tries to design structures that reduce the discretion of lower-level participants. Bachrach and Baratz (1970) suggest that one of the significant advantages powerful people have is the power of nondecision. That is, the ability to suppress or thwart challenges by preventing consideration of an issue is effective. And Pfeffer (1981) concludes that we determine decisions largely by the premises used in making them. Control over the basis for decision making can affect results as surely as direct tactic in the decision process itself. Controlling decision criteria is an effective, yet unobtrusive means of gaining follower compliance.

Analysis

This tactic is the fourth most frequently used power tactic toward subordinates. Peers use it only infrequently in their relationships and only rarely toward superiors. Both men and women use this tactic often, as do supervisors and nonsupervisors. Those bored with their work find this the most often-used tactic engaged in. Those excited about their work find frequent occasion to use this tactic also, but find three other tactics more useful. Setting decision criteria is uniformly seen as a frequently used power tactic by all classifications of people and types of organization members.

Respondents uniformly confirm the effectiveness of this cluster of power behaviors. Men and women, older and younger workers, supervisors and nonsupervisors, and workers in all kinds of organizations surveyed report that efforts to control decision criteria work well in subordinate relationships.

Controlling the criteria subordinates use to decide is seen by most respondents to be entirely ethical. Only a few classifications of workers disagree. Understandably, nonsupervisors did not find this cluster of behaviors ethical, nor did those workers less than 40 years old. Interestingly, only government employees found this tactic ethical; the remainder rate it as neutral.

This tactic falls fully in the initial power-use group of power tactics. Only nonprofit workers find this tactic more useful as a response to resistance. All kinds of people surveyed report infrequent use of this tactic in that situation.

Summary

Controlling the criteria, and not the decision itself, is a commonly used tactic in securing subordinate compliance. Most classifications of organization members find this to be an often-used, effective, and ethical initial approach to subordinates. It is an unobtrusive, effective method of securing desired results from subordinates. It apparently conforms to current norms of superior–subordinate behavior. It produces expected results enough of the time to make it an often-used cluster of power behaviors toward subordinate targets.

LEGITIMIZING CONTROL

This tactic includes our efforts to formalize our right to decide through appeals to hierarchy or to the legal right associated with either our position or that of another in the hierarchy. The legitimizing control tactic defines a set of power behaviors intended to energize the formal authority system present in the situation. This is an effective kind of power action. It is also common in subordinate relationships (as many would expect). It is interesting that this classic form of organizational power in downward relations is only the fifth most frequently used power tactic in these situations. And, importantly, most of the more often-used tactics rely on sharing power behavior rather than system-based kinds.

Legitimizing control is the most commonly used power behavior by superiors toward subordinates. It relies on organizational authority. The basis of the legitimizing control tactic is legal, organizational, procedural, moral, ethical, or customary values, proscriptions, and mores (Molm, 1990). It adds the "force of law" or custom to our decisions or behavior choices.

Reducing organizational relationships to official organization charts is a common example. Promulgation of standard operating procedures, requiring prior (or post) approval of subordinate decisions or actions, and an overadherence to organizational traditions exemplify ways to apply this tactic.

Weber (1968) emphasized legitimacy as a base of power. As a tactic, legitimizing control uses this base of power in a wide variety of ways. All applications of legitimizing control aim to ensure compliance of others because they come to see the leader as acting appropriately, legally, in "the right manner." Examples of legitimizing control include any of the following list of specific behaviors. They serve to illustrate this power tactic and are by no means presented as an inclusive list of this very commonly used tactic. In using the legitimizing control tactic we:

command others to obey our directives;

use rules to ensure compliance;

install decision or procedural processes that ensure maintenance of our power position;

check other's work regularly;

require people follow specified channels;

appeal to higher organizational authority;

justify our orders on the basis of regulation, tradition, or law;

relate our orders directly to organizational purpose;

use rules as a way to surveil subordinates;

require sign-offs, prior to or after performance of assigned tasks;

require justification in writing.

Legitimizing control ascribes our orders to someone or something else. In using this tactic we present ourselves as acting for some higher authority that all members of the organization respect and obey. People often use legitimizing control in situations where our targets perceive themselves and us as part of some encompassing organization. We do not use legitimizing control often when we act independently (McKinney and Howard, 1979). Obviously, the legitimizing control tactic is common in delegation situations. It is most in evidence in delegations since much of the assignment of work and energy to activity is through delegation.

Analysis

Legitimizing control defines a set of power behaviors that find their basis in the formal authority and traditions of the organization. For many, this tactic represents the sum total of power use in organizational life. Its ranking as the fifth most frequently used tactic is, therefore, instructive. There are at least four other tactics more often used. Indeed, legitimizing control is just one of nine tactics that this research discovered to be significant in getting subordinates to alter their behavior in desired ways.

When not used toward subordinates, legitimizing control is used in peer relations and to a limited extent in relations with superiors. Both men and women find this tactic useful, as do participants of all ages and supervisors. Understandably, nonsupervisors do not find significant opportunities to use this tactic. When looked at for compatible organizational environment, we see people use legitimizing control in all kinds of situations except among workers in product-oriented organizations. In this case, while the use is frequent, it did not meet statistical tests of significance.

This tactic is effective. However, most users rate it as about average in effectiveness. About as many tactics are seen as more effective as there are less effective than legitimizing control. There is no major difference in this finding among the several classifications of people or kinds of organizational environments studied.

Surprisingly, most respondents do not feel the legitimizing control tactic to be fully ethical. By the same token, none see it as unethical. The neutral rating on the ethical scale is surprising given its extensive use and the theoretical and experiential support this kind of behavior enjoys.

Men do not find this tactic ethical, but women demur. For them it is a neutral behavior. Both supervisors and nonsupervisors see legitimizing control as ethically neutral, although supervisors rank it closer to being ethical than their counterparts. Neither age nor attitude about our work affects the overall ethically neutral ranking of this tactic. Of the four kinds of organizations considered, only nonprofit organization members, those working in organizations with more than 1,000 people, and those working in professional–technical–clerical organizations see this tactic as ethical. Others confirm that it is a neutral behavior set.

Legitimizing control is a power tactic most people use to counter resistance in subordinates. Only for people working in nonprofit organizations is this a tactic of choice for initial power action toward subordinates.

Summary

The legitimizing control tactic is a fully useful tactic in subordinate relations. It is seen as effective, ethically neutral, and a way to respond to resistance in subordinates. The legitimizing control tactic is referred to often in the literature as a typical supervisory approach to subordinates. This research suggests that it is only one of several available options to influence a subordinate's behavior and direct it in desired ways. Its base is legitimate authority. It uses force and authority forms of power more than any of the others.

ORGANIZATIONAL PLACEMENT

This tactic involves the conscious manipulation of the hierarchical structure of the organization to place our delegates in strategic positions. By this means we can place people we control in critical positions. Another version is to restructure the organization system to isolate our potential opponents. When accomplished, persons who owe us allegiance can provide us with needed resources, information, or control over other important resources. Organization members use this tactic often and view it as effective, if unethical.

The attempt to place in key positions people who will support and defend our decisions is a common practice. Also common is an effort to restructure major work systems to isolate opponents or potential opponents (Grimes, 1978). As far back in organization and management history as the early Hawthorne experiments, people have seen that social location can influence performance. And, too, dislocation can affect many in threatening ways. We use control over the placement of others to aid us in getting them to do what we want them to do.

One example of this occurred when the chief engineer of a large state highway organization was effectively isolated from key decisions. When efforts to reorient the decision-making processes of the chief engineer about highway construction priorities failed, the administrative officer took other steps. She initiated a low-key and unpretentious project to automate the mechanics of the project decision work-flow system. This system monitored the flow of a project through the department from initial plans to final construction.

On initiation, it effectively removed the chief engineer from decisions of consequence on all new projects. These decisions were automated and controlled by underlings employed and guided by the administration officer. The ostensible reason for this was the minor changes in procedures would "improve productivity." It resulted in removing the chief engineer from effective control over project initiation, progress, design changes, and timing.

While isolation of an opponent is a common version of this tactic, another is placing allies in strategic positions throughout the organization. Persons with like philosophies, similar skills, or who are under obligation to us can be helpful in securing compliance from other individuals or groups. Research supports the idea that allies strategically located throughout the organization can ease communication, provide critical information, and otherwise increase our power potential (Yukl, 1981).

Placing ourself in specific positions in the organization is also a power behavior falling under this tactic. As we analyze organizations, we can identify strategic, critical, and central positions in the hierarchy and occupy those positions to increase our power. In competition for power, physical settings often represent a critical resource because of its placement in a communication network, its physical proximity to powerful people or critical resources, or its symbolic impact potential. Centrality, in this sense, is seen in competition for office location, selection of prestigious neighborhoods, the popularity of tall building locations, and similar facts of contemporary organization life.

An interesting version of this tactic is the conscious reordering of the environment of the target of power. Kotter's (1977) research confirms that changing the job surroundings, redefining jobs, and similar structural adaptations also can affect our influence over those affected by the changes. Other research (Siu, 1962) is explicit in suggesting that restructuring of the environment is an important element of leader–follower systems. Several examples of loss of power because of work design action are clear. Location affects our ability to govern when employees move from our direct control. It can entail loss of power through dispersal of employees geographically or spatially, or when changes take the tasks we ask employees to do beyond the understanding of the leader. These examples illustrate the range of behaviors from which we can draw in structuring the environment to increase or maintain our power position vis-à-vis colleagues or competitors.

Analysis

Placing self or others in central or critical positions within the organization structure is a commonly used tactic many find effective. Most see this power behavior as unethical. When used, it is most effective as an initial, not a fallback, action. Having our person on the spot in a critical part of the organization enhances our capacity to know about and to do what is necessary to organizational success. The literature often references this behavior set and has conventional wisdom support.

The sixth most often-used tactic toward subordinates, organizational placement is often used in peer, as well as occasionally in superior, relations. Men find this tactic useful and resort to its use often. Women do not find this tactic a proper one and so use it less often. Women do not use this tactic significantly. Understandably, supervisors use this tactic. Nonsupervisors find little opportunity for its frequent use.

Leaders of governmental organizations use this tactic. Neither business, higher education, nor nonprofit workers use it often. Workers in their immediate work team more than five years use this tactic frequently. Those with shorter tenure do not. Nor is it used often by professional–technical–clerical workers.

Placing self or organizational colleagues in central positions in the organization is an effective power tactic. Only nonsupervisors and people working in product-oriented organizations found this tactic to be ineffective. Other organizational situations did not affect the overall ranking of organizational placement as an effective tactic in power use with subordinates.

Most people use this tactic but find it to be unethical. This is the case with men, nonsupervisors, those under 40, and those excited by their work. Women, supervisors, older workers, and those people bored by their work find it ethically neutral. These findings are reasonable, given the different orientations about their work and the general work environment of the kinds of people reporting. Placing self or others in critical positions requires some command of organizational resources and systems. Those without that authority or those resources, risk subjugation to those who do. A reluctance to view this power behavior pattern as ethical is logical for this group of people. Those with such resources at their command can take a more positive position. Only persons working in business see this tactic as unethical; the others see it as neutral. Most other people see this tactic as neutral.

When used, people apply organizational placement most often in initial contacts to influence subordinate reactions. Workers in nonprofit organizations use it to counter resistance from subordinates.

Summary

Organizational placement is an effective power tactic often used by supervisors and others with control over critical resources. It is an initial tactic, one used frequently by many organization members.

USING SYMBOLS

This tactic employs physical or psychological objects, ideas, or actions to authenticate our power position or to expand it. A cross section of organizational workers see this power tactic as unethical. They use it as an initial contact approach to influence subordinate behavior, and find it effective and frequently used. Some of the ambiguity of these findings may stem from the ambiguity of this concept. Symbols rarely have precise and universal meanings for all participants in a given situation. That many resort to using symbols to help them in swaying subordinates is not unusual. Nor, given the complexity and multiple meanings potential in using symbols of power, is it unusual that many find its use unethical.

Symbols can be used to indicate or amplify power. For instance, commitment to organizational or personal goals is sometimes facilitated when managers "involve'' followers in discussion or decision events whether or not the decision outcome is changed as a result of the process. The symbolic value of participating (even without real impact) can enhance cooperation and commitment to decision outcomes.

This tactic is used in a variety of contexts. For example, a new executive developed the appearance of power though the simple mechanism of a signature. By signing his name on all kinds of correspondence in large, bold letters with a black felt tip pen he made his signature recognizable and ubiquitous. People throughout the organization recognized the signature on papers crossing their desks and that of others. They perceived him to be involved and influential in all aspects of the organization. He added to his formal power in this way simply by making his signature a perceived symbol of power.

Symbols play an important part in communication, personal interaction, and organizational relationships. Sharing a language is the most powerful of all symbol systems. Berlo (1960) makes a strong case that all language communications is affective, intended to influence the actions or thoughts of the communication targets, and that symbols play a significant part in these communications. Indeed, words themselves are symbolic of the reality they are coined to depict. Language is perhaps the most effective symbolic medium that we employ routinely to secure compliance from our coworkers.

Symbolism in organizations takes many forms in addition to language. Window offices, carpet, special deference, automobiles, stock options, retirement packages, and other perquisites of rank play a role in the power hierarchy in all organizations—both formal and informal. These can represent status symbols, identify the playing field, and the pieces of the power game. They represent also the rewards of effort. These symbols can be counted to determine relative status vis-à-vis competitors. Careful observers of the organizational scene can interpret these kinds of symbols and determine where group members stand in the power ranking system at work.

Manipulation of symbols as a power tactic operates primarily in the realm of the intellect. Symbols impact on attitudes, emotions, sentiments, beliefs, mores, and values more than they do on realities of position or control over tangible resources. While there is a link between substantive reality and symbols used in social intercourse, the connection is often tenuous and subject to individual interpretation. Power users adept in the use of this tactic find that to succeed they must be sensitive to the perceptions of power targets as much as to any other factor.

Analysis

The symbol tactic is the seventh most frequently used power tactic with subordinates. People also use this tactic occasionally with peers and in relationships with their superiors. Men use this tactic; women seldom do. It is not a particularly significant behavior pattern for women. Older workers also use it more than younger ones. Interestingly, both supervisors and nonsupervisors use this tactic often, as do workers whether or not they find their work exciting. Only business organization members do not make statistically significant use of this tactic.

Using symbols to get our desires realized is effective when used, however. Women rank it more effective than do males. This is the second most effective tactic women reported using. Men ranked it seventh most effective. Other breakdowns of the respondent pool point to a generally felt feeling of effectiveness, except for workers in governmental institutions.

While often and effectively used, the use of symbol power tactic is seen by most people to be unethical. Perhaps the element of manipulation power present in perceptions of this tactic accounts for this fact. When it is used, it is seen in initial contacts with power targets. There is no significant deviation from this pattern of use seen in the survey data.

Summary

Symbols appeal to the intellect and the emotions. The use of this power tactic is seen in a complex array of power-tinged behaviors. It is relatively often used, is effective when used (mostly in initial contacts with our power targets), and is seen as unethical by most users.

RITUALISM

Ritualism is the name coined here for any attempt to induce institutionalized patterns of behavior in people or in organizational units and practice that enhance one's individual power. It is the eighth most often-used tactic by superiors toward subordinates. It is, nevertheless, seen as the third most effective tool in these kinds of relationships.

Any collective experience can fall victim to rigidities. As organizations evolve, formal practices, relationships, procedures, and work processes develop and become institutionalized. When these customary modes of behavior are consciously developed and pressed on the organization's workers to institutionalize action patterns that consolidate our power, the ritualism tactic is in use. The rituals developed also can have the effect of diminishing available energy that might otherwise be used to counter our power use. Or, it can be used to counter competing behavior of other powerful organizational actors.

Examples of the use of the ritualism tactic can be seen in the operation of most organizations. For instance, in one agency the chief executive officer consistently refused to consider any issue for discussion in staff meetings until she initiated the topic in some way. Once this ritual was completed, anyone was free to comment on the issue, support it, disagree, or suggest alternatives. But, if the CEO had not introduced the subject, it would not be recognized if raised by another person.

It is also common in many organizations to subject every suggestion for change to a complex system of sign-offs and clearances. This ritual ensures that customarily powerful people continue to exercise power. It also has the effect of dissipating the available energies of organization members not a part of the power structure. Part of the red tape of government is due to the ritual of clearances that intends that initiation of and approval of change stay in designated hands.

Most organizations have several ceremonies that serve to mobilize support for the powerful or to quiet opposition. These rituals serve to retain power in the hands of the already powerful. Several forms of this tactic are evident.

Intimidation of Opponents

O'Day (1974) describes four intimidation rituals he observes in organizations. He suggests that power users progress through these four ritual behavior sets in their efforts to silence opposition: (a) nullification of the target's initiatives, (b) isolation of the target from the action scene, (c) defamation of the target on a personal and/or professional level to denigrate him and his action alternatives, and (d) expulsion from the group as a last-step ritual. Both the individual steps in this escalating process and the process itself constitute an organizational ritual.

Standing Rules

The design and promulgation of standing operating procedures that maintain our relative position of power is another iteration of this tactic. Making decision and policy approval mechanisms routine solidifies our power and makes alternative power relationships more difficult to develop and institutionalize. It should be noted that Crozier (1964) describes a situation where a unit not routinized in its task accomplishment systems gained power over those who were. In this situation, Crozier appears to be describing the proactive tactic in the same environment as the ritualism tactic. Of course, one power tactic might be used to counter another power tactic.

Information Control

Specifying the flow of information generally and the specific dissemination patterns for selected items of information often is ritualized in organizations. Setting up of committees to investigate deviations from the norm, reporting to specified individuals in the power structure, routing information through prescribed channels serially, all represent possible ritual behavior aimed in part at maintaining extant power relationships—sometimes beyond their useful, productive lives.

Organizational Structuring

Organizational structure also is often used in (power) ritual ways. Designing and maintaining an organization structured in a certain way perpetuates certain patterns of power over other possible forms or patterns. Any form of structure favors one power system over competing possibilities, and in this way constitutes a ritual pattern of behavior, work flow, and action relationships.

Custom and tradition also can have a powerful impact on performance. Conscious attempts to formalize practices or relationships that favor our power potential over that of competitors represent use of this tactic (Molm, 1990). John Gardner (1964) says that vested interests exist and are among the most potent factors producing rigidity in our organizations. This is the essence of the ritualism power tactic.

Analysis

Ritualism is used frequently by superiors toward subordinates, but less frequently than the seven other tactics discussed above. It is only occasionally used toward our peers or superiors. Men and people in all kinds of organizations use this tactic more than women, who do not find it relevant to their work. Neither do nonsupervisors use this tactic, perhaps because of their lack of formal authority and control over work systems. In all other cases the use of this tactic is relatively frequent.

People find this tactic effective in getting their way regardless of their organizational situation. They also see it as generally ethical, except for workers in higher education and nonprofit organizations. These people rank this tactic as neutral. The ritualism tactic is most commonly used in initial, not resistance, power situations. Ritualism describes a common cluster of behaviors people use toward subordinates to sway them to desired actions. While common in all organizations, it is nonetheless an effective power intervention, commonly used by most organization members.

Summary

Available data suggest that this is a ubiquitous power tactic employed by most of us in our relationships with subordinates. People generally see this intervention as effective, ethical, and an initial power ploy in these relationships. Many kinds of organizational behavior fall into this cluster of power activity. It represents a known, understood mode of behavior in organizations. Institutionalized patterns of behavior are power-tinged. They are also commonly used to enhance our power positions vis-à-vis subordinates.

INCURRING OBLIGATION

The tactic, incurring obligation, relies on the development of obligations in others as the basis of our power. This power tactic is frequently a part of superior-to-subordinate (and peer) relationships. Obligation is created out of an unequal exchange between two or more people or groups. Powerful people may provide information, money, material things, psychological support, friendship, or other needs to others and then use the sense of obligation—debt—incurred later to ensure that the other person(s) complies with our demands in another context.

Several versions of obligation as a power tactic can be identified:

1. Obligation is incurred when a person promises another specific action or reward for current cooperation. Obligation is a kind of conditioned compliance founded upon the specific or implied promise or expectation of reward.

2. Friendship can be a form of obligation. Most people prefer to deal with friends. Friendship helps reduce tension and encourages trust, facilitates communication, and eases discomfort in social situations. As the power user develops office friendships with others, they tend to want to comply with his or her wishes in order to retain friendly relations (Siu, 1979). Of course, friendships may be present without overt power implications. It is nevertheless a common form of power use.

3. Exchange of favors is also an example of the obligation tactic. Many peer relationships are, in fact, based on this kind of exchange of energy, information, and skill. It is also common in superior-to-subordinate relationships.

4. Self-sacrifice may seem altruistic and moral, but it can also become a power behavior. The superior moral position of having sacrificed self in some way can be used to dominate the other person in direct ways.

5. Finally, obligation can be incurred through praise. Most people want the good wishes and respect of others and will comply with the orders or requests of the person who continues to find value in their behavior and is willing to express that value in praise and compliment.

Analysis

A complete discussion of the incurring obligation tactic is part of Chapter 6. It is sufficient here to remind the reader that this tactic is operationalized with subordinates in about the same way it is with peers. The essence of this tactic is not on the formal elements, or resources, or structure. It is, rather, on the nature of the personal relationship extant. It is a personal power tactic that ensures target compliance though reliance on personal favors or debts and the resultant need to pay back past favors.

Summary

Incurring obligation is used least often of the significant subordinate-oriented power tactics. When analyzed in terms of specific characteristics of users, we find the context of use similar to that employed with peers. It is used frequently but is not considered fully ethical. There is a manipulation element in this tactic, one that puts people off. And, too, many organizational actors do not see it as an effective tactic when compared to the other power-use options open to them in their dealing with subordinates.

Part IV

Comparisons of Use
of Tactics

Comparing the individual tactics according to their use by men and women, supervisors and nonsupervisors, and leaders in various kinds of organizations is instructive. While the information contained in Chapters 9, 10, and 11 is preliminary, at best, it does point in interesting strategic directions. The "cross-grain" findings presented in Part IV are valuable for their intimation of other possibly significant findings as more research attention is directed toward organizational politics. The findings of the next three chapters discuss power use in operational contexts. They provide a new perspective—a political one—about what goes on in the organizations in which we spend so much of our time and personal energy. As more of us engage in a dialogue about work system uses of power, we can forecast significant enlargement of our understanding of the specifics of organizational politics—a process of energy exchange in return for needs satisfaction.

Chapter 9 illustrates the range of uses of the various tactics according to organizational type. While people in all kinds of organizations make routine use of the power tactics in their political maneuvering, they differ a little in their perception of effectiveness, ethics, and style of use. These findings point up that developing others, proactivity, training and orienting others, allocating resources, and displaying charisma are often-used modes of power action regardless of organizational environment. While definite differences are found in the specific application of the twenty-two power tactics, there appears to be little fundamental difference in power use among workers in the four kinds of organizations studied. Business and nonprofit organization members differ most; business and higher education workers are the most similar in their uses of power.

Chapter 10 describes how both supervisors and nonsupervisors engage in political power use. The general frequency of power use and the range of power tactics used attest to the fact that both are prepared and active power participants in organized relationships. This chapter compares power tactic uses by supervisors and nonsupervisory professionals in a variety of organizations. The conclusions reached in this chapter suggest that supervisors use power tactics in expected ways—based on control over resources. Supervisory uses of power do not call forth much personal involvement or use of personal aspects of self. Nor do they employ expensive tactics like allocation of rewards, using outside experts, or incurring obligation in their subordinates. They rely mostly on power tactics based on traditional ideas of authority and official ceremonies and rituals.

Understandably, nonsupervisors make more use of power behaviors that rely on personal power factors. They also employ trade-off tactics, ritual-building tactics, and risk tactics a little more than their supervisors. Thus, they use indirect tactics like coalition formation, building favorable images, quid pro quo, controlling decision criteria, and use of surrogates and symbols more than do supervisors.

Finally, Chapter 11 provides interesting, if preliminary, findings that may point to differences in organizational politics demonstrated by men and women leaders in their institutional uses of power. Both men and women use all of the identified tactics and find them useful and effective in about the same ways. Where there is difference, it is mostly in degree of use, or in their perception of the correct context in which to use a specific tactic. These differences may be important. They define demonstrably different power-use orientations. Men appear to use consent-based tactics like developing others and training and orienting others more frequently than do women. Women, while involved in sharing, collaborative power behavior, do not commit to these behaviors quite as much as some have thought.

Most difference between women and men is in feelings about the effectiveness and ethicality of specific power tactics. While they agree on many tactics, women rate system-based tactics like using symbols and surrogates, quid pro quo trade-offs, displaying charisma, and using outside experts more effective than do men. While the full meaning of these differences is unclear, it does suggest the possibility of a discrete female pattern of perception and use of power.

Men make full use of tactics based on personal power. They value tactics like developing others, building a favorable image, and ritualism as more effective than women do. These findings run counter to conventional wisdom ideas that women are more personal and men more system-based.

The three comparative chapters in Part IV may form the nucleus of a future research agenda about organizational politics and power use. They begin to identify an agenda for more definitive and comprehensive studies of specific similarities and differences between organization members—leaders and followers—as they function in today's complex environments and relationships. Power remains an essential element in all interrelationships. These findings may be helpful in taking more effective control over our intraorganizational lives.

9

How Business, Higher Education, Government, and Not-for-Profit Organizations Use Power

The people making up our organizations frequently involve themselves in using power. This is true whether the formal organization has a profit, an educational, a governmental, or community service orientation. In this chapter we discuss findings that shed new light on the specific power orientations workers routinely display in each of these classes of organizations. We will use four specific organizational classifications: business organizations, higher education organizations, government organizations (including personnel from local, state, and federal agencies), and nonprofit organizations. Data were collected from workers in each organization class. Table 9.1 shows this breakdown and data about the size of each cohort.

Persons who work in these organizations sometimes differ in the power tactics they use as well as in the kinds of power behavior they see as effective or ethical. Also, some similar power uses can be seen in our analysis of the power behavior of people in each classification of organization. This chapter summarizes pertinent data about frequency of use, effectiveness, ethics, and timing of use of each tactic by persons in each classification of organization studied. This analysis elaborates the major similarities and differences found. These data deal with

Table 9.1
Survey Demographics: Power-Tactic Use by Class of Organization

Class of Organization	Number	Percent
Business	30	27.8%
Higher Education	13	12.0%
Government	55	50.9%
Nonprofit Organization	10	9.3%
TOTAL	**108**	**100.00%**

overall findings and differences between one kind of organization and other classes.

FREQUENCY COMPARISONS

Members of organizations, regardless of classification, find occasion to use each of the twenty-two identified tactics. Some coalescing around frequency of use are seen in the tactics of developing others, proactivity, ritualism, training and orienting others, displaying charisma, and use of resources. These tactics are the most often used by workers regardless of class of organization. Similarly, all classes of organization members use brinkmanship infrequently, if at all. Nor do they use the tactics of using outside experts, incurring obligation, use of rewards, controlling the agenda, or organizational placement very frequently in their relationship with colleagues. The Appendix (see Appendix Table A.6) lists tactics by overall frequency of use and for each individual classification of organization.

Table 9.2 repeats some data found in the Appendix and highlights the most frequently used power tactics. This table shows the highest rankings of power tactics for each classification of organization. There is overall similarity in the tactics most used by people in each kind of organization studied. Each makes frequent use of developing others, proactivity, training and orienting others, and displaying charisma. The differences in rankings may be instructive for the individual working in each kind of organization. For example, government workers may do well to recognize their colleagues have an orientation toward independent (unapproved) action, but it is generally directed toward helping the coworker grow. Businesspeople should be able to see some tendency on the part of their colleagues toward development of others, but it is done in a context of system (ritual and legitimizing control).

Similarly, data amassed suggest that workers in higher education tend a little more to use ambiguity as a way to get their way. They also tend to rely a little more than others do on the use of resources. The members of not-for-profit

Table 9.2
Frequency Rankings of Tactics by Organization Type

Business	Government
1 Developing Others	1 Proactivity
2 Ritualism	2 Developing Others
3 Displaying Charisma	3 Training and Orienting Others
4 Legitimizing Control	

Higher Education	Not-for-Profit
1 Developing Others	1 Proactivity
2 Using Ambiguity	1 Ritualism
2 Proactivity	2 Displaying Charisma
2 Allocating Resources	2 Developing Others
3 Displaying Charisma	2 Legitimizing Control
3 Rationalization	2 Building a Favorable Image
3 Teaching and Orienting Others	3 Using Ambiguity
	3 Allocating Resources
	3 Co-opting Opposition Members
	3 Quid Pro Quo

Note: Some tactics are used with equal frequency by workers in a class of organization. The ranking numbers indicate this.

organizations differ most from their colleagues in other organizations. They use many of the same power tactics as those in other kinds of organizations, but rely also on proactivity, building a favorable image, ambiguity, and co-opting opposition members tactics. These tactics are appropriate in a less hierarchical organization. They also use the trade-off tactic, quid pro quo, frequently.

In summary, frequency ranking of each class points up some interesting findings. It appears that brinkmanship is the least frequently used power tactic by workers in all organization types. And, they all find developing others or proactivity as the two most frequently used power tactics. Business, government, higher education, and nonprofit organization members agree that training and orienting others is another frequently used tactic.

There is a general similarity in the frequency of use of several power tactics among members of each of the four classes of organizations studied. Workers in most organizations make about the same use of:

controlling agenda preparation
forming coalitions
developing others
legitimizing control
proactivity
allocating resources
ritualism
using symbols

brinkmanship
controlling decision criteria
building a favorable image
organizational placement
rationalization
dispensing rewards
using a surrogate
training and orienting others

Nonprofit organization members differ more from the remaining three classes of organization members than does any other organizational group. Business-people and those in higher education show more similarity in power behavior than any other organizational class. Government and nonprofit organization members also show a general similarity in rankings of frequency of use of these tactics. Members of both business and government organizations also display some general similarity in their frequency choices of these power tactics.

EFFECTIVENESS COMPARISONS

Members of all four organization types rate all tactics as effective. Some minor aberrations are, however, apparent. For example, research summarized in the Appendix (see Table A.7) suggests that businesspeople think dispensing rewards is not effective for them. Other classes of organization members find this tactic to be effective. Government workers find brinkmanship and incurring obligation to be ineffective. Nonprofit organization members agree only in finding brink-manship to be ineffective.

Several differences in effectiveness rankings are also clear from Table 9.3 data. First, higher education workers find ambiguity more effective than those in other classes of organization. They also rate co-opting opposition members as highly effective. Higher education workers think building a favorable image is one of their most effective power tactics. Other classes of worker rate it near the bottom on this measure. Higher education workers also see legitimizing control, organizational placement, and rationalization as more effective than the average of the other worker groups. And, finally, workers in higher education think use of surrogates is an especially effective tactic. It is one of the four most effective clusters of power behavior they identified. Workers in all other classes of organizations found this tactic to be only one of several effective power tactics.

Second, some interesting facts about business organization members are clear. Business workers use coalitions frequently. They find this tactic effective when used. They, with those in nonprofit organizations, find this tactic to be more effective than do government or higher education workers. Businesspeople do not rate developing others as very effective. This is in sharp contrast with workers in the other classes or organizations. It is only the fourth most effective for businesspeople. It is the first or second most effective power tactic for the others.

Table 9.3
Effectiveness Rankings by Class of Organization

Business	Higher Education	Rank	Government	Not-for-Profit
Allocating Resources	Developing Others	1st	Dispensing Rewards	Developing Others
Forming Coalitions	Building Favorable Image	2nd	Developing Others	Training/Orienting Others
Ritualism	Using Surrogates	3rd	Training/Orienting Others	Displaying Charisma
Displaying Charisma	Training/Orienting Others	4th	Proactivity	Dispensing Rewards
Developing Others	Dispensing Rewards	5th	Displaying Charisma	Forming Coalitions

Business workers do not find using outside experts as effective as do those in other classes of organizations. They rate this power tactic as fourteenth most effective for them compared to general average of sixth most effective for other workers. Neither do they find training and orienting others particularly effective compared to their counterparts. They do, however, see proactivity as a highly effective power tactic.

Third, nonprofit organization workers rank quid pro quo as more effective than do the members of other kinds of organizations—especially business workers. They rank it ten levels higher than do businesspeople. Both business and nonprofit workers rank forming coalitions as very effective.

Government workers appear to value the effectiveness of most tactics in ways that are similar to the average of the other classes of workers. They rank use of rewards, developing others, and training and orienting others about the same as the average of all workers. They are alone in ranking proactivity as more effective than other tactics, although businesspeople also value this tactic highly as an effective way to achieve their goals. Government workers are also unique in their ranking of incurring obligation as ineffective. This finding does not jibe with the conventional wisdom ascribing a political orientation to government service, an orientation typically involving workers in multiple trade-off situations. The five most effective tactics identified by workers in each class of organization are shown in Table 9.3.

ETHICAL COMPARISONS

[Members of all classes or organizations find developing others to be an ethical tactic.] People in all four classes of organizations also find that training and orienting others, proactivity, displaying charisma, forming coalitions, and building a favorable image are ethical tactics. They also uniformly find brinkmanship and dispensing rewards to be unethical power behaviors. Study findings show these and other comparisons on this measure. The Appendix (see Appendix Table A.8) highlights the classification of organization studied that ranks each tactic most (or least) ethical or whose ethicality rankings were similar. The most

Table 9.4
Ethical Rankings of Power Tactics by Class of Organization

Business	Higher Education	Rank	Government	Not-for-Profit
Developing Others	Developing Others	1st	Developing Others	Developing Others
Training/Orienting Others	Training/Orienting Others	2nd	Co-opting Opposition Members	Proactivity
Ritualism	Using Ambiguity	3rd	Proactivity	Forming Coalitions

ethically appropriate tactics for each class of organization worker are shown in Table 9.4.

Most differences in ethical findings are seen in the following:

1. Only government workers find ambiguity unethical power behavior. Higher education workers see ambiguity as very ethical, while other classes of organization workers rate it above average on this measure.

2. Higher education and business workers rank control over agenda preparation as ethical, but government and nonprofit workers see it as ethically neutral.

3. Higher education workers find dispensing rewards to be neutral. Others find it unethical.

4. Higher education people also find incurring obligation ethically neutral while others see it as unethical.

5. Controlling decision criteria is seen to be ethical in government and higher education worker's relationships and unethical for those in business and nonprofit organizations.

6. Controlling the agenda is unethical to business and nonprofit workers and ethically neutral for the other two.

7. No one in higher education ranked brinkmanship as ethically positive.

8. Similarly, no one in higher education organizations ranked ritualism, using ambiguity, training and orienting others, developing others, using a surrogate, or quid pro quo as unethical.

9. No class of organization workers found brinkmanship ethically positive.

STYLE COMPARISONS

All four classes of organization workers find using ambiguity, displaying charisma, developing others, building a favorable image, proactivity, allocating resources, ritualism, and training and orienting others to be initial-use power behaviors. Some difference is seen (see Appendix Tables A.9 and A.10) in other tactics, but the preponderance of use is initially also for controlling decision criteria, organizational placement, and quid pro quo.

Power tactics used to counter resistance for all four classes of worker based on organization include: controlling the agenda, brinkmanship, co-opting opposition members, rationalization, dispensing rewards, and using a surrogate.

Most people in most classes also see forming coalitions, using outside experts, and legitimizing control as resistance-coping behaviors.

Not-for-profit organization workers use forming coalitions as an initial behavior tactic. The other three classes of workers use it mostly to help overcome resistance to their initial power-use tries. Similarly, nonprofit workers also are unique in selecting to use legitimizing control and rationalization as initial power-use options. Their counterparts in other kinds of organizations use these tactics as fall-back approaches to get others to comply with their desires. In the same vein, business workers use quid pro quo as a fall-back approach. The others use it most often as an initial cluster of power behaviors.

Comparing the tactics used initially with those most often used to counter resistance reveals some interesting findings. It appears that initial-use tactics rely most upon resources controlled directly and overtly by the power user. They fall within the range of normal, accepted organizational behavior for most people. That is, these power tactics rely for their success on the image others have of the power user, the general perception of resources controlled, the in-place operating systems used, and in-use interpersonal relationships patterns. They also make use of personal dynamism. Importantly, two power tactics used initially focus on the personal needs of the power target. Developing others and training and orienting others focus on getting the other person to do what we want because of what we do for them as well as environmental resources or situational context we may control.

Resistance-coping tactics rely more on secondary resources and subterfuge. The resistance-coping tactics are riskier and generally less effective, although use of rewards and co-opting opposition members are two exceptions to this statement. The resistance tactics also appear generally to be seen as a little less ethical and are only ordinarily effective. Nevertheless, they are well within the range of normal power behavior of those people surveyed.

SUMMARY

As a summary statement, we can say that the way people use power in carrying out organizational political action in the four different classes of organizations is similar. Members of each class use all the power tactics. They vary somewhat in frequency of use, but find developing others, proactivity, training and orienting others, allocating resources, and displaying charisma often-used modes of power action. They agree also in that brinkmanship is only very infrequently used. They agree that it is not effective in swaying others to our point of view of power use and on timing of use of specific tactics. Business and nonprofit organization members are the most divergent from the norms. Business and higher education workers are the most similar in their uses of power.

The few differences present tend to be scattered. That is, each class of workers seems to differ in the specific uses of individual tactics. For example, several findings are counter to the "conventional wisdom." Thus:

1. Businesspeople find dispensing rewards ineffective.
2. Government workers use incurring obligation only infrequently and find it when used.
3. Controlling the agenda, a low-key activity on the surface, is seen as unethical.
4. Higher education and government workers find coalition building a less effective power tactic than do those people in business organizations.

How Supervisors and Nonsupervisors Use Power

Much of our thinking about power is in formal organizational authority terms—that is, power based on superior hierarchical position. There is a large body of information to guide supervisors in their use of authority (power). There is much less information available, especially in applied terms, about how nonsupervisors exercise power. This research confirms that nonsupervisors as well as supervisors routinely drain energy in power-use behavior. They typically rely on several power forms including, but certainly not limited to, authority power.

Experience confirms that nearly all organization members—supervisors and all others—use authority, as well as the other forms of power. These other forms (e.g., force, manipulation, persuasion, threat–promise, and influence) can be useful ways of controlling coworkers where formal authority alone will not suffice. Targets of power use do not always recognize or understand the formal authority held by the supervisor. And, while they may recognize it in one situation, they may not in another. Also, the formal and informal sanctions the superior can impose in a situation may not be important to the subordinate. In this situation it dilutes any real impact formal authority may have. One conditioning factor in power relations between supervisors and nonsupervisors may lie in these kinds of perceptions by nonsupervisors. Another important factor is the impact of nonsupervisor power resources on the relationship.

While often at a disadvantage in relative formal authority held when compared with supervisors, nonsupervisors hold considerable advantage in the more personal forms of power. Mechanic's (1962) work suggests that nonsupervisors rely on persuasion, manipulation, threat–promise, and personal influence forms more than force or authority power forms. Nonsupervisors engage in power-use behaviors both for personal goal accomplishment and to achieve organizational goals.

The work of Allen, Madison, Porter, Renwick, and Mayes (1979) suggests that much of what we call organizational politics describes the power activities of nonsupervisors. It encompasses most effort spent in trying to get others to alter their behavior to enhance the nonsupervisor's personal or organizational aims. Research by the author confirms the fact of routine involvement by non-supervisors in power activity. It suggests that nonsupervisors use the same power tactics supervisors use, but with some unique variations.

This research (summarized in the Appendix) confirms that nonsupervisors are frequent users of the twenty-two power tactics. It helps validate a growing literature suggesting that persons not in high-level positions in the hierarchy have and use power to get their way. Data amassed suggest that nonsupervisors engage in power use about as much as supervisors do. It also suggests that supervisors and nonsupervisors, while using all the tactics, do not always do so in similar ways. There are some interesting and instructive differences, as well as some important similarities, in use of specific tactics by each group of organizational participants. Some elaboration of this data is presented in the sections that follow to show both similarities and differences in their uses of power behavior by supervisors and their nonsupervisory colleagues.

FREQUENCY COMPARISONS

Both groups use all the power tactics identified. Supervisors use proactivity most frequently; nonsupervisors use developing others most often. The five most frequently used power tactics for both groups are displayed in Table 10.1.

Both kinds of organizational workers use many of the tactics in very similar ways. Supervisors use only two tactics most frequently; nonsupervisors use fifteen more often than any others. The rest of the power tactics are employed in about the same level of frequency by both groups of workers. Analysis of these data reveals some interesting findings in this connection. For example, both groups rank similarly the frequency of use of the tactics of co-opting opposition members, legitimizing control, proactivity, ritualism, and training and orienting others.

Significant differences in frequency of use are seen in the rankings of a few tactics (see Appendix for details). A major difference in frequency of use is seen in the use of the symbols tactic. Nonsupervisors use this tactic much more often than do their supervisors. This finding is counter to the generally held feeling that supervisors possess more symbols useful in power relations than those people they supervise. A similar wide variation in use of a few other tactics can be noted in the tactics using outside experts, incurring obligation, organizational placement, quid pro quo, allocation of rewards, and use of surrogates. Super-

Table 10.1
Most Frequently Used Power Tactics by Supervisors and Nonsupervisors

Supervisors	Rank	Nonsupervisors
Proactivity	1st	Developing Others
Allocating Resources	2nd	Proactivity
Training/Orienting Others	3rd	Training/Orienting Others
Developing Others	4th	Ritualism
Building a Favorable Image	5th	Legitimizing Control

visors use these tactics much more than do nonsupervisors. Each of these tactics shows at least a five-place difference in rankings between supervisors and nonsupervisors.

It appears that nonsupervisors use trade-off tactics significantly more, for example, incurring obligation, organizational placement, quid pro quo, and allocating resources. They also employ a variety of tactics that have the general result of involving others in direct and indirect ways in impacting their supervisors. These tactics include those of forming coalitions, rationalization, and controlling decision criteria. And they make significantly more use of personal displaying charisma than superiors do in getting their way in the organization.

In terms of frequency of use, it is evident that nonsupervisors make as much use of the tactics as their supervisors do. Nonsupervisory workers in our organizations are fully engaged in power activity. It is a part of their organizational life, one in which they gain considerable practice. This finding casts the nonsupervisory worker in a new, more proactive role in our organizations. It represents a major change in our thinking about organizational direction and control. The organizational reality is that nonsupervisors engage fully in power behavior intended to attain their (as opposed to the organization's) goals. Leadership to integrate this independent behavior becomes a more critical element in the dynamics of organizational life. Our traditional management and leadership theory must accommodate this new reality (Fairholm, 1991).

EFFECTIVENESS COMPARISONS

Supervisors feel developing others is their most effective tactic. Nonsupervisors rated allocating resources as their most effective tactic. The listing in Table 10.2 compares the five most effective tactics for each group. Both groups see developing others, allocating resources, training and developing others, and displaying charisma as among their most effective power tactic options. Supervisors rate proactivity as another very effective tactic, while nonsupervisors see ritualism as a very effective tool in attaining their individual agendas.

Both supervisors and nonsupervisors demonstrate some uniqueness and some

Table 10.2
Rank Order of Most Effective Power Tactics by Supervisors and Nonsupervisors

Supervisors	Rank	Nonsupervisors
Developing Others	1st	Allocating Resources
Allocating Resources	2nd	Ritualism
Training/Orienting Others	3rd	Training/Orienting Others
Displaying Charisma	4th	Developing Others
Proactivity	5th	Displaying Charisma

similarity in their perception of individual tactic effectiveness. These findings are displayed in Table 10.3. Overall, Table 10.3 data confirm a general uniformity in a few other tactics also; that is, tactic of brinkmanship, co-opting opposition members, decision criteria, legitimizing control, incurring obligation, organizational placement, and use of surrogates. The data in Table 10.3 compare supervisors' and nonsupervisors' feelings about the effectiveness of individual tactics. Most differences in effectiveness rankings come on the using ambiguity tactic. Nonsupervisors find it three times more effective than do supervisors. Using symbols is also a highly effective tactic used by nonsupervisors in their group relations. Other tactics found to be more effective by nonsupervisors than for supervisors are those of controlling the agenda (four ranking difference) and building a favorable image (three rankings). Nonsupervisors find those kinds of tactics that involve nonsystematic sources of power and those involving manipulation and persuasion power forms to be most effective.

Their supervisor counterparts, however, rated the effectiveness of some other tactics more highly. Tactics found more effective by supervisors include those of forming coalitions, developing others, using outside experts, quid pro quo, and rationalization. These are also indirect forms of power use. They depend much more on control over available organizational resources for their success. This difference pattern is reasonable and expected, given the relative control over institutional resources available to each kind of worker surveyed.

Significant difference is also found in perceptions by supervisors and nonsupervisors about which tactics are not effective at all. Supervisors found that the brinkmanship tactic alone was not effective at all in their power-use experience. Nonsupervisors agreed. They added several other power tactics that they felt to be noneffective. These other tactics not seen as effective by nonsupervisors include incurring obligation, organizational placement, rationalization, and dispensing rewards. One expects that nonsupervisors would find these tactics ineffective given their generally nonresources-controlling status in most groups.

Supervisors rate five tactics most effective; nonsupervisors list six power tactics as their most effective, as shown in Table 10.2. Both groups of organizational

Table 10.3
Most Ethical Power Tactics by Supervisors and Nonsupervisors

Supervisors	Rank	Nonsupervisors
Developing Others	1st	Developing Others
Proactivity	2nd	Building a Favorable Image
Training/Orienting Others	3rd	Proactivity
Ritualism	4th	Training/Orienting Others
Building a Favorable Image	5th	Co-opting Opposition Members

workers see the balance of the tactics in about the same light as far as effectiveness in getting their way is concerned. (See Appendix Table A.11 for more detail.)

ETHICAL COMPARISONS

The fact that a given power tactic may be used and considered effective does not determine its moral or ethical vitality. Study findings suggest that even given effective use, some tactics are considered unethical. Both supervisors and non-supervisors find nine power-use tactics ethically negative:

controlling agenda preparation
using outside experts
organizational placement
rationalization
using symbols

brinkmanship
incurring obligation
quid pro quo
allocating rewards

Supervisors add to this list of unethical tactics the using ambiguity tactic. Nonsupervisors also see both decision criteria and legitimizing control as ethically negative. Perhaps this is because of the element of manipulation they see in the use of these tactics by supervisors in interrelationships with them. When compared to the data displayed above (in the sections on frequency and effectiveness of use of the power tactics), we can say that these perceived negative tactics are nevertheless used on occasion by both supervisors and nonsupervisors.

Supervisors and nonsupervisors alike find the tactics of rationalization and quid pro quo both unethical but relatively effective in getting their way with others. They also find using outside experts an effective and often-used power tool in this connection. The other unethical tactics noted are used relatively infrequently and found to be only marginally effective.

Nonsupervisors find a few tactics significantly more ethical than supervisors (see Appendix for details). For example, nonsupervisors see using symbols as ethical, while supervisors specifically rate this tactic as unethical. Nonsupervisors find this tactic more ethical by three rankings. Supervisors, on the other hand, find ritualism a little more ethical than do their subordinates. They also find using a surrogate to be ethical in differentiation from nonsupervisors, who find it ethically neutral.

Supervisors find five power tactics more ethical than nonsupervisors: forming coalitions, controlling decision criteria, legitimizing control, ritualism, and use of surrogates. These are power tactics closely associated with the supervisor's hierarchical position and prerogatives. It is logical that they would use these tactic more than their colleagues and find them ethically okay. Nonsupervisors, on the other hand, find seven power tactics more ethical than their bosses. These include displaying charisma, co-opting opposition members, using outside experts, building a favorable image, incurring obligation, rationalization and using symbols. The pattern here is also logical. Nonsupervisors lack the formal authority and control over organizational resources of their counterparts. It is natural that they typically use these tactics more and find them morally supportable.

Both groups agree generally on the most ethical power tactic in use today. They both find the developing others tactic to be the most ethical of all of the power tactics identified. There is general agreement also about the ethicality of the proactivity and training and orienting others tactics. Only ten tactics are identified by both supervisors and nonsupervisors as ethically acceptable. They include, in addition to the three already noted, (developing others, proactivity and training/orienting others) displaying charisma, forming coalitions, co-opting opposition members, building a favorable image, allocating resources, ritualism, and using a surrogate. With only ten of twenty-two possible power tactics seen as ethically correct, it is easy to understand the moral and ethical dilemma some see, even today, in the routine uses of power in our organizational relationships.

Table 10.3 displays the tactics either supervisors or nonsupervisors found to be most ethical. Other tactics are ranked about the same by both groups.

STYLE COMPARISONS

Supervisors and nonsupervisors are unanimous in their choice of the timing of specific tactic use. Both groups selected the same list as initial approach behaviors and as resistance-countering tactics. (See Table 10.4.) There is some variation in the specific rankings of frequency of use in each of these style factors. Both groups see each tactic in about the same way. Both groups find system-based power tactics (those requiring organizational support for success) to be most effective on initial contacts. They are similar also in their use of some of the unethical and ineffective tactics when countering resistance. Apparently some power behaviors are used though felt to be ineffective or, even, unethical, because of the need to "do something." Both supervisors and nonsupervisors used the tactics shown in the Appendix as initial and resistance clusters of behavior in impacting targets.

Table 10.4
Initial and Resistance-Countering Tactics' Combined Ranking: Supervisors and Nonsupervisors

Initial Power-Use Tactics	Resistance-Countering Tactics
Using Ambiguity	Controlling the Agenda
Displaying Charisma	Brinkmanship
Controlling Decision Criteria	Co-opting Opposition Members
Developing Others	Using Outside Experts
Building a Favorable Image	Legitimizing Control
Organizational Placement	Incurring Obligation
Proactivity	Rationalization
Quid Pro Quo	Dispensing Rewards
Allocating Resources	Using Surrogates
Ritualism	
Using Symbols	
Training/Orienting Others	

SUMMARY

The sum of the findings discussed in this chapter is to the effect that political behavior in organizational relationships between supervisors and nonsupervisors normally conforms to expectations formed from one's experience and readings. Supervisors use power tactics based on control over resources. They do not use tactics that require indirection, much personal involvement, or use of personal aspects of self (like displaying charisma, rationalization, or using symbols) as much. Nor do they find the need to get others to do what they want them to do by employing expensive tactics like allocating rewards, using outside experts, or incurring obligation in their subordinates. The simplest and most economical power tactics for them are those based on traditional ideas of authority and official ceremonies and rituals.

Nonsupervisors understandably use more power behavior that does not rely on formal authority or institutional mechanisms. They, nevertheless, fully involve themselves in power use. Nonsupervisors use developing others more than their counterparts. They also employ trade-off tactics, ritual-building tactics, and risk tactics a little more than do supervisors. We can characterize nonsupervisors' uses of power as more indirect than are those of supervisors. Thus, they use tactics like forming coalitions, building favorable images, quid pro quo, controlling decision criteria, and using surrogates and symbols more than do supervisors. This is logical, given the general paucity of control nonsupervisors exercise over formal institutional systems and resources.

Nonsupervisors' ethical determinations conform to expectations, given their place in the hierarchy. That is, nonsupervisors find a few tactics such as using symbols to be more ethical than supervisors do. They also disagree with supervisors who find ritualism and use of surrogates as ethical power behavior. Solidifying one's power through manipulation of organizational resources is commonly seen as ethical by supervisors. These tactics are not viewed quite as ethically okay by nonsupervisors.

Nonsupervisors engage fully in power use in a variety of ways, using a variety of tactics toward a variety of targets. They reflect special aspects of power use founded on their general lack of control over positional bases of power. The general frequency of power use and the range of power tactics used attest to the fact that both supervisors and nonsupervisors are prepared and active power participants in organizational relationships.

11

Comparing Power Use: How Men and Women Use Power

Power may be the most important issue of the 1990s. It is coming into focus in more and more contexts: in leadership, in management, in families, in friendship relations, and in most other interpersonal contacts. Research evidence provides some interesting insights when we compare how men and women use power. Sex-based perspectives of power as a political aspect of relationships may offer guidance to both men and women as they use power in their interpersonal relations. How each uses power, what tactics each emphasizes, and when and in what contexts they use it are critical to full understanding of power use (Abrahams, 1989). How men and women differ in how they value its use may help us clarify some of the knotty problems now facing participants in the workplace as women assume more prominent positions.

More women are taking their place in significant positions in organizations. We can expect that their special ways of using power will result in significant differences in power use in informal or formal institutions. Of course, this assumes that the signs of differences alluded to in earlier chapters are sustained over time. Key among these emerging changes are those dealing with alteration of the male-dominant culture typical in many organizations (White, 1990). We may see dramatic changes in the sociology of organizational life.

Some writers have tried to distinguish methods, results, or situational constraints on power based on sex. McClelland's work (1975) in power motivation concluded there is little evidence to support the idea that women have different power needs than men. He does conclude, however, that women express their needs for power in different ways. Winter (1973) verifies this overall finding. He confirms that, contrary to myth, women also want and seek power. And once obtained, they use power differently than men do. White's (1990) work suggests that women need to spend more time in culture-coping activity than do men. They need to overcome a male-dominated culture in order to perform their work. This need may entail significant extra energy expenditure. The sum of this research provides empirical evidence supporting some differences in tactic use.

Wagner and Swanson (1979) also conclude from their study of this question that there is no difference in need for power, but tactics differ. They find that women express power in internal ways. They use power to build inner strength more than to seek external power bases. They also found that women are less intense than men in their use of power. This orientation to power is a generalist's one. Women exercise power in different ways, depending on the situation. Their uses of power are eclectic, focused, and situational. Women do not see using power as an aspect of career-developing others, which, Wagner and Swanson conclude, is the primary way men use power. Women vary power use according to the context within which they find themselves. Women's use of power, they found, is more relationship-oriented, while that of men more task-oriented.

It is clear from this research that women behave differently from men in their application of power. The following summary may be helpful as an introduction to this discussion of the differences in the way men and women use power. Several tables in the Appendix summarize pertinent information developed from survey data about the twenty-two power tactics as actually used by men and women. Analysis of these data points up several factors. First, both men and women workers make routine use of all tactics. Second, men and women use many tactics in similar ways. Third, both use more than half of the tactics about equally. Fourth, both sexes are similar in finding most of the same tactics to be effective or ineffective. Fifth, they converge also on many ethical evaluations. And, sixth, they agree on the characteristics of an appropriate situation in which to use a specific tactic. That is, both use the tactics in about the same way in either initial contact or as a method to counter target resistance.

Close analysis of these findings also points up some important differences in power tactic use, effectiveness, ethics, and timing patterns. We must assess these differences also. For it is in the differences that the most insight about current power-use behaviors can be garnered. The remaining sections of this chapter offer more detailed comparisons and analyses on the basis of frequency of use, effectiveness, ethics, and timing of use patterns. Both similarities and significant differences are noted. As women take their place in our organizations in more numbers and at all levels, their special (if indeed, it is special) perspectives on organizational politics will be important new information all managers must acquire.

FREQUENCY OF USE COMPARISON

As a general statement, both men and women report frequent use of all twenty-two power tactics. Specific approaches to use of the individual power tactics

Table 11.1
Comparison of Frequency of Tactic Use by Gender

Men	Rank	Women
Developing Others	1st	Proactivity
Training/Orienting Others	2nd	Ritualism
Proactivity	3rd	Using Resources
Ritualism	4th	Developing Others
Legitimizing Control	5th	Displaying Charisma

vary somewhat. For example, men use (in rank order of frequency) developing others, training and orienting others, proactivity, ritualism, and legitimizing control most frequently. Women use (also in rank order) proactivity, ritualism, allocating resources, developing others, and displaying charisma most often. Both use brinkmanship least, along with incurring obligation, dispensing rewards, and controlling the agenda.

Tables in the Appendix compare frequency of use decisions of both men and women. They highlight the tactics most frequently used by men and those most often employed by women along with those used about equally frequently. Men and women differ significantly in how often they use the developing others tactic. Men use this cluster of power behaviors most frequently. Women use three other tactics more frequently. Women favor using outside experts, on the other hand, by three rankings. Men use building a favorable image more frequently. They rank their frequency of use of this tactic eighth to the women's ranking of fourteenth—a difference of six rankings. Women use quid pro quo more frequently than do men (by four rankings). Women also opt for allocating resources by four rankings. Men favor training and orienting others much more than women—a difference of five rankings.

Table 11.1 compares the five most frequently used tactics for men and women. Men appear to favor power tactics associated with enhancing followers along with traditional tactics associated with authority and system. Women, contrary to some popular wisdom, find reason for more frequent use of proactivity, system, and allocation of organizational resources. They also employ power in personal (personality) terms more frequently than do their male counterparts.

EFFECTIVENESS COMPARISONS

Women rate all tactics except brinkmanship and dispensing rewards as effective. Men follow suit; they rate only two tactics as ineffective: brinkmanship and incurring obligation. Women and men find the tactics listed in (Table 11.2) most effective.

The Table 11.2 comparison shows that, while both men and women use displaying charisma, women use it more often. Women also find it somewhat

Table 11.2
Comparison of Effectiveness of Tactic Use by Gender

Women	Rank	Men
Displaying Charisma	1st	Developing Others
Training/Orienting Others	2nd	Allocating Resources
Using Symbols	3rd	Training/Orienting Others
Allocating Resources	4th	Ritualism
Developing Others	5th	Displaying Charisma

more effective. (See Table 11.2.) We also find significant difference in effectiveness rankings between men and women in their use of displaying charisma. Study findings (see Appendix for detail of ranking differences) suggest that women find this the most effective tactic they use, favoring this by four rankings over men. Men, on the other hand, use developing others more often than do women and find it more effective than their female counterparts. They also value ritualism (ten ranks' difference), rationalization (difference of seven ranks), and building a favorable image (three ranks) as significantly more effective than do women. In addition to displaying charisma, women ranked using symbols (difference of sixteen ranks), quid pro quo (seven ranks), using outside experts (three ranks), and incurring obligation (also three ranks' difference) significantly more effective than men. These may be interesting shades of difference between men and women in their use of these power tactics.

Both sexes rank the effectiveness of the tactics using ambiguity, forming coalitions, proactivity, and dispensing rewards similarly. Comparisons of tactics by perceived effectiveness point up similarities and differences in effectiveness perceptions by sex of the power user. From the data in Table 11.5 we see that women rely a little more on institutional bases of power and authority forms than men do. Aside from the developing others power tactic, men seem to focus most on tradition, logic, and image as the basis for power success. Women gravitate more toward tactics that involve others, the organizational structure, personality, and symbolic references. Both find power use based on legitimacy and personal competence effective at about the same level of intensity.

COMPARISON OF ETHICALITY

When looked at in ethical terms we see that men ranked eleven tactics as ethical in normal usage; women listed twelve. Both sexes included the following tactics in their lists of ethical clusters of power behavior:

developing others
training and orienting others
building a favorable image
displaying charisma
co-opting opposition members

proactivity
ritualism
allocating resources
forming resources
controlling decision criteria

Women added two more that men did not list as ethically positive tactics: using ambiguity and using a surrogate. Men also found legitimizing control an ethical tactic. Women did not.

Determinations of the differences in ethicality of tactics by men and women are also shown in this research. Both sexes agreed on four unethical power tactics:

brinkmanship

dispensing rewards

incurring obligation

controlling agenda preparation

Men added organizational placement as another unethical tactic, while women think the rationalization tactic is unethical.

Major differences in ethical rankings between men and women are seen in several tactics, for example, using ambiguity. Women find this tactic more ethical than men do by eight rankings. Women also differ with men in their ranking of the ethics of using outside experts. Men find the following a little more ethical than do women.

building a favorable image (seven ranks' difference)

legitimizing control (five ranks' difference)

rationalization (five ranks' difference)

allocating resources (three ranks' difference)

STYLE COMPARISONS

Both women and men see some tactics as being most effectively used in an initial power approach in impacting others. They also agree on which tactics to use to counter resistance to their power ploys. Table 11.3 shows details of these common choices.

Additionally, women also see incurring obligation and using outside experts as initial power-use behaviors. Men listed using outside experts and incurring obligation as resistance-countering clusters of power behavior.

SUMMARY

Both men and women use all the tactics. Both sexes find them effective (with a few exceptions, notably brinkmanship). Both use about the same tactics as

Table 11.3
Comparison of When Tactics Are Used by Both Men and Women

Initial Use	Used Upon Resistance
Using Ambiguity	Controlling the Agenda
Displaying Charisma	Brinkmanship
Controlling Decision Criteria	Forming Coalitions
Developing Others	Co-opting Opposition Members
Building a Favorable Image	Legitimizing Control
Organizational Placement	Rationalization
Proactivity	Dispensing Rewards
Quid Pro Quo	Using Surrogates
Allocating Resources	
Ritualism	
Using Symbols	
Training and Orienting Others	

initial approaches to influencing target behavior and both use about the same tactics in countering resistance from targets. Power use, and application of the specific power tactics, is similar regardless of the sex of the power user.

Where there is difference, it is mostly difference in degree of use. Or the difference is one of perception of the correct time and place in which to use a specific tactic. However, these differences are significant and define demonstrably different orientations to power use. For instance, men appear to use developing others and training and orienting others more frequently than do women. These are tactics based much more on consent than coercion. They represent a variance from many stereotypical orientations about men and women now current in our literature and thinking.

For example, White (1990) concluded that women and men differ in overall management approach. She concludes that women are more indirect than men, and more participative and people-oriented. Wagner and Swanson (1979) found that women were more internal, preferring to share, rather than to aggregate personal power. Their work, like White's, has its base primarily on attitudes, not examination of actual power behavior. It may be that role stereotypes have left us with a conventional wisdom at some variance with actual power-use experience.   Women, while involved in sharing collaborative power behavior, do not commit to these behaviors quite as much as previously thought. And they do so a little less than male counterparts in overall power use. Women are also a little less like men in their behavior in seeking to develop others through sharing to enhance colleagues, the organization, and themselves.

Most differences in power-tactic use between women and men are in feelings

Table 11.4
Differences in Male–Female Uses of Power

Factor	Women	Men
Motive Base	*No real difference in power need based on gender*	
Cultural Pressure	To be submissive toward power use	To be aggressive toward power use
Bases of Power	Internal: self	External: situational
Autonomy	To control own life	To control environment and others (and through that, to control own life)
Proactivity	Internal: building self, find strength as a resource	Aggressive: find strength in action
Sociability	More involved in clubs. Associate with others for the intrinsic benefits	More involved in formal organizations. Associate with others because it is the "thing to do."
Values	People	Things
Decision Style	Contextual, integrative	Factual, analytical
Power Style	*Both have a generally similar overall style*	
Power Forms Used	Authority, and then manipulation—persuasion	Persuasion, and then manipulation and influence
Power Tactics Used	System-based	Personal

about their effectiveness and ethicality. Both find about the same cluster of power behavior to be effective. Nevertheless women do rate system-based tactics like using symbols and surrogates, quid pro quo trade-offs, and use of outside experts help more effective than do men. They also rely on displaying charisma more than men do. Whether this shows a sex-based tendency or is merely a function of their relative newness in organizational environments is not clear. It does represent a definable pattern of perception and use of power by women.

Men find the most effective power-use tactics to be those we can classify as based on personality. They rate tactics like developing others, building a favorable image, and ritualism as more effective than women do. They also find displaying charisma, forming coalitions, proactivity, and training and orienting others as very effective. These findings imply a reversal of current stereotypes that have women being more personal and men more system- (structure-) based.

On balance, both men and women agree on ethical questions of power-tactic use. Men and women also agree on questions of timing of tactic use. They report similarities in style of use while exhibiting some variation in specific uses of individual power tactics.

Available research is beginning to clarify the nature of differences in male and female uses of power. The summary in Table 11.4 may be helpful in analyzing these differences.

Part V

Power Use in Our
Lives: Theory and
Application

Thus far this book has been about how people use power to achieve individual and group aims—whether or not those aims correspond to organizational goals. It has been about the technology of organizational politics. Part V chapters provide a theoretical, operational, and moral basis for our analysis of the tactics of power use identified in earlier parts of this book. It is less about the process and practice of organizational politics and more about the theory and dimensions of power, the key tool of organizational politics.

The chapters in this part will be generally known to the expert in power. It may provide another perspective for the practitioner by placing operational power use on a foundation of theory, process, and ethics. The Part V overview of past and more recent research on the use of power is focused to underscore the new view of power developed in this book: an applied perspective. It sets the intellectual and conceptual foundation for the analysis of current power behavior, which is the centerpiece of this book.

Part V chapters develop the historical and ethical foundations for modern-day application of power in our large-scale organizations. These chapters focus primarily on tracing the idea of power through history and organizational and management thought. Chapter 12 delves briefly into the theoretical dimensions of power use. It traces the idea of power to our central activities as human beings and relates power to social, political, and ethical ideas. The sense of Chapter 12 is that power is a tool we all frequently use. Organizational politics, that is, political behavior in the administrative aspect of our interactions, is an example both of power use and the results of that use.

We see power in use in any of a variety of forms. Chapter 13 identifies six archetypical forms in which we see persons use power. These forms are force, authority, manipulation, persuasion, threat (or promise), and influence. Sections of Chapter 13 define the parameters and interrelationships of each form. This exposition relates each power form to the others on a coercion–consent continuum.

Chapter 14 examines the sources of power available to us in normal social relations. It reassesses French and Raven's work, criticizes it, and elaborates on this historically popular model. Chapter 14 identifies alternative bases of power that help the reader understand how to acquire and use power in work contexts.

Chapter 15 examines the ethical dimension of power use in organizational life. It is appropriate to end this analysis of organizational politics on an ethical note. While we all use power to negotiate the attainment of our desired outcomes in the groups to which we belong, some people sometimes see this behavior as being somehow wrong. Chapter 15 guides the reader through the ethics of power. It makes the point that power per se is not ethically negative. It is morally wrong only because we use it in some ways and for some purposes. It is "right" because we use power for other purposes and in other ways. This chapter concludes that power is essentially neutral ethically. The ethics are "added" by individuals in a given situation.

Together, the intent of Part V chapters is to acquaint the reader with definitional, historical, and ethical dimensions of this critical and common interrelationship.

12

The History and Theory
of Power

Power is a part of all life. Viewing our relationships with others from the perspective of power can assist us to understand our success or lack of success in attaining our aims (Pfeffer, 1992). A power perspective can add insight about human interrelationships that no other perspective can. We can, of course, gain insight about our group behavior when we view our actions from the standpoint of communications. Other insight is possible as we analyze our relationships on the basis of conflict, or change, or motivation, or a number of other technologies. These perspectives are well known and well documented. Techniques and models abound to help the individual understand group behavior in these terms.

An organizational (political) power perspective in leadership is new. Little has been written that develops a holistic model of human relationships in work organizations based on power usage. A careful review of the literature reveals significant insights about power in use. It is only recently that writers have begun to abstract working models and strategies applicable to leadership (Pfeffer, 1981; and Allen and Porter, 1983). The ideas contained in the following discussion relate sometimes disparate power ideas into a synthesis hopefully useful to practitioner and academic alike.

BACKGROUND

Society is a condition of inequality. Whether in the animal or human realm, there are the ordinary and the extraordinary, the leaders and the led, the powerful and the relatively powerless. The patterns of dominance and subservience found in nature are mirror images of systems present in our social systems all over the globe. Consider this listing:

1. The leader displays the trappings, posturing, and gestures of dominance—sleek, calm, relaxed, and purposive.
2. When challenged he scares his foe with aggressive charges.
3. If needed he can—and does—overpower his opponent.
4. He is not only physically strong, but is cunning, quick, and intelligent also.
5. He reinforces his dominance on the group by maintaining harmony, thereby ensuring his position.
6. He develops a cadre of assistants who help him maintain the safety of the group. He rewards them with relative freedom of action and closer association with him.
7. He protects his subordinates, thus ensuring the continuance of the group.
8. He determines the movement of the group. They go where he goes, work when he works, and rest when he rests.
9. He is continually reassuring the group members of his affection and love for them.
10. He assumes command in times of danger and is in the forefront of battle.

This account could be a description of the modern business executive. In fact, it is an outline of the ten commandments of dominance in baboon leaders described by Desmond Morris in *The Human Zoo* (1969). Human society follows this natural pattern. Granted, the immense difference in power between the powerful and the relatively powerless are no longer as striking as they perhaps once were. The relative power of the slave and the holder of 10,000 slaves is not the same as the CEO with 10,000 subordinates over whose livelihood he has suzerainty. Nor are the depredations of the Spanish inquisition similar to the egalitarianism of today's governments or modern religious ecumenicalism.

Whether or not the individual need for dominance has atrophied over the centuries is debatable. Its gross manifestations appear to have at least moderated. The plain fact remains, however, that those individuals with power act in ways uncommonly similar to the ways those in power in ancient times acted. And both are similar to the actions of the dominant ape.

Anyone with even a little energy, concern for others, or a drive to accomplish anything wants to and does exercise power. We all exercise power. Parents use power, as do ministers, teachers, policemen, athletes, and leaders of any social group. Within reason, we consider the exercise of power by any of these people as normal and routine. In these cases, power use is not a matter of concern for anyone—not for the object of power, nor the power holder, nor for the social scientist who may study the episode.

When we exercise power within normal limits, those exercising it are useful, valuable, and acceptable functionaries in our social system. It is only when the person of power exceeds group norms that power becomes a threat and the object of derision, scorn, and elimination. Within acceptable norms, power is a natural part of life. Beyond those norms, it is a threat many fear and try to eliminate—or ignore. In these cases, many people see this type of power as evil, unethical, and hurtful, and oppose its use.

THE PROGRESS OF POWER IN HISTORY

Krieger and Stern (1968) have aptly synthesized the evolution of power in theory. Their survey of power evolution (restated here) is instructive. For Plato, power was a necessary aspect of the good and the principal ingredient of power was knowledge. We should, therefore, respect power and those who use it. Aristotle concentrated on means and ends distinctions. For him there was a reciprocity between the powerful person and the target of power. Power is a function of change we can use to achieve good ends. The good ruler is a good and wise man.

The Romans, on the other hand, saw political power as independent from ethics. They saw power in terms of origins, not ends. Power for them was position-based; it came with the decision to involve oneself in the political life and institutions of the society. We grant the public leader power, but also constrain him by the prerogatives claimed as part of the role of public controller. Greek thought placed power in ethical terms around ends sought. They distinguished ethical ends from the forms of power defined by Roman tradition.

These ideas were separate through the Middle Ages, but gradually merged into one theoretical system. Thomas Aquinas argued that God, being the author of all nature, must also be the final source of political power. Kings must accede to the rule of theology while attending to the business of caring for social systems.

Machiavelli demurred from this ecclesiastical construct, preferring to argue that power must be served. His ethics were those of the realist. State power existed to serve the protection and security of the state. Nonetheless theological primacy over temporal rulership continues into our times. English political traditions implied a divine right to rule theory until the seventeenth century. Then consent of the governed in the form of social contracts replaced the divine right to rule. The Social Contract philosophers saw power as residing not only in kings but in commoners. The assertion of this power took the form of rights granted to citizens in cultural and economic matters. The king's role became one of concern with the protection of these rights and for the general welfare of his subjects.

While historically much of the view of power is in political terms, there is a much more encompassing arena for the study of power today. The modern organization and its ruler, the leader-executive, are a prime locus for the study of power today. The large-scale organizational executive exercises a power no less encompassing than that of the political executive. His power is pervasive and strong; his impact on the quality of life is broad.

Power is a major theoretical thread in U.S. business and government as well as political and social theory. Much of the theory coming to us from past research forms three distinct tracks: Political Power Theory, Psychological Power Theory, and Organization Power Theory. Following is a brief recapitalization of some of the salient ideas of some of the thinkers in power theory. This treatment of the key themes in power theory is intentionally brief and intended only to place this current work on the use of power in a theoretical context. It then lets the reader know where to go for more in-depth treatment of this complex and interesting topic.

Power in Political Theory

From a political perspective the distribution of power in the United States is continuously and comprehensively considered. Perhaps one of the most helpful treatments has been the work of C. Wright Mills. His book *The Power Elite*, published in 1957, establishes the thesis that political power in America is in the hands of a few people whom he called the power elite. The power elite is made up mostly of political, military, economic, and community leaders. These people occupy strategic positions in the social system of the community at every level in America: national, state, regional, and community. Their positions at the top of organizational institutions making up the social infrastructure make it possible for them to command in significant community decisions (Dahl, 1961).

Mills's research concentrated on the military, political, and economic leaders of the community. Familial, religious, or educational leaders, he found, were not particularly effective in using power to run community institutions or processes. They are subject to the more powerful community leaders. These people often are relegated second-level roles in community decision making.

The power elite Mills defined formed a kind of interlocking directorate at the top of the community leadership system. They are, of course, conscious of their power and their relationship to each other. While not a monolithic, formal body, they were, he said, conscious of each other and of their relative position in the power oligarchy. The membership is typically shifting. Over time members are moved out and replaced with others on a continuing basis. These changes are based on the particular issue on the public decision agenda. The elites are, nevertheless, present at any given moment and are a known, and knowable, body of community power notables. They cooperate and conspire to exercise decision-making power over significant community action issues.

Another significant contributor to elites theory of power is Floyd Hunter. In two works, *Top Leadership, USA* (1959) and *Community Power Structure* (1963), Hunter elaborated Mills's work. Studying community leaders in Atlanta and nationally, Hunter found that top leaders came from more than the military, economic, and political cadres. They include labor, recreation, professional, and financial leaders also. Hunter saw the power elite as being more homogeneous than Mills, suggesting that the elite is often highly centralized and structured. Their hierarchy includes at least policy councils as well as general membership.

This monolithic orientation to power structure is a unique contribution of Hunter to our thinking.

Perhaps it was this highly definitive structure of power that challenged others to move into the power discussion. At any rate others quickly took the field to offer counterarguments. Most notable was Robert A. Dahl in *Who Governs?* (1961). He took issue with the monolithic model of power use in community life. His research led him to the conclusion that power was apparent in the community in a pluralism model, rather than a monolithic one. For Dahl, power is exercised in the community by a series of shifting coalitions, differing in membership with the issue under study. Community public works concerns will bring to the fore a markedly different power cadre than, say, one concerned with education. Dahl has had a significant impact on power theory since 1961. Others support his work. For example, Arnold Rose's book *The Power Structure* (1967) develops a multi-influence thesis to explain the working of the body politic in community issues resolution.

The theoretical debate on these two issues—elitist versus pluralistic—continues today. Both sides amass data to support their contention. The issue is not a settled one by any means, but the rhetoric may be abating somewhat. Each side appears to have taken a more moderate position as evidence mounts that both sides have empirical research support. There is indication that some communities have a more or less stable power hierarchy while that of others shifts with the issues.

Current research attention focuses on the basis for the monolithic or pluralistic decision-making pattern in a given community. While the controversy is very much in evidence, the dogmatic posturing has given way to a more empirical accumulation of the evidence. This posture may provide a future resolution of this critical issue in political power theory.

Power in Social Theory

Since at least the time of Plato, men have written about power in society. Plato's ideal state was one where passions were in check, the philosopher-king was in charge, and the despot banished. Later Hobbes, Machiavelli, Nietzsche, and Adler concluded separately that we can explain man's nature and origins in society in power terms. Today we are using power ideas to described many different social events: war, social movements, race turmoil, political activism, the counterrevolution. In the process of widespread use the word has acquired many meanings, so many as to make the term misleading and its use confusing.

As an element in social theory, power is more often a negative idea than a positive one. Plato saw power as essentially good. He cautioned that its misuse can be destructive. It can be the basis for man's propensity for acquisition. He viewed it as a corrupting influence destructive of man's higher propensities, even of life itself. This view has, as noted elsewhere, persisted. Lord Acton's dictum that power corrupts has been a hallmark of social theory. However, we can discern an alternative perception in social thought. That is that power, while basically appealing to the lower instincts, is second to social altruism. Adherents to this perspective see power as a way to social advancement. Ideas such as duty, responsibility, legitimacy, and love have been at the center of this branch of social thought. Power, they, say has a role in defining and applying these higher ideals.

In this century, the power literature is more complete and the approach more realistic. Writers now are dealing directly with concepts like authority, force, control, and conflict as significant elements of social relations and as mechanisms to both describe and predict situational alternatives (Wrong, 1973). The terminological taboo under which the idea of power has suffered for decades has lifted in this latter part of the twentieth century. Instead of one coherent concept, there are many. While we can relate them all to the underlying idea of power, they have not coalesced into a power theory. Among the ideas that are beginning to shape a power theory are those of motivation, self-esteem, competence, and control. Others include causation, helplessness (powerlessness), stimulus response, and locus of control.

These ideas all relate directly to power use and have done much to clarify individual aspects of power theory in social science. None has achieved the pervasiveness it would need to dominate in either power theory or the broader field of social science. Each has added significantly toward this goal. In sum, over thirty years after Cartright's seminal review of power theory, it is still a subject in search of a discipline.

Social science boasts many distinguished and helpful minds. Some of the best have devoted their time and talents to the study of power. In this review, we will refer to only a few; specifically, we will review the work of Machiavelli, Hobbes, Russell, Nietzsche, and Weber.

Machiavelli, of course, has achieved a degree of fame (even infamy) as a result of his work to apply power in public life. His advice to rulers on how to gain, maintain, and accrue power is commonplace by today's standards. It finds its uniqueness in that it blatantly advocates a separation of statecraft from the ethical and moral dimensions of public life. In a backhanded way, Machiavelli focused public attention on the ethical dimension of power use. Before his work, and for generations after, others have kept these ideas hidden. Ethics is still a central theme in social theory and in organizational practice.

Hobbes, a generation or longer later, provided a more systematic analysis of power. His task was to build a comprehensive system of human behavior based on principles of motion and egoism. He based his definition of power on hedonistic ideas. For him power was the present means to secure some future good. Since people seek pleasure, power becomes the means by which they can gain that goal in the face of competition (even conflict) from others. Carried to its logical conclusion, this drive in people for hedonistic pleasures leads to conflict and war.

The solution for Hobbes was in some form of social order. For him, the logical option was a formal covenant among the people. The social contract is the basis of much of our political and social theory as well as the theory of human interactions. The contract creates a superior governing entity—the Hobbesian *"Leviathan"*—a self-perpetuating, autonomous social order, one, like Machiavelli's, separate from moral or religious constraint. While less important today to social scientists, his ideas have significantly influenced our thinking and our theory of social systems.

Others proffer other solutions to the challenge of power use among the members of social systems. The utopians' and the rationalists' views were much more in vogue in the past than today. Both grappled with the central issues of power use and distribution among the members of the society. Bertrand Russell follows these theorists. His task was to deal with the corporate version of man in society. Power in modern industrial society becomes a different order of involvement. Power exercised by the organizations of society become more impersonal, and anonymous and relate more to abstract roles than previous, more individualistic constructions. For Russell, the key to understanding power in industrial societies lies in understanding the structure of society and its major institutions. Power in this context relates to institutional values. His definition of power as the production of intended effects is, then, entirely compatible with an organizational focus.

Nietzsche's work still has currency among social scientists in elaborating power at the psychological level. His *Will to Power* (written during 1883–1888) uses power as an elastic term as well as a specific one. He incorporates a widely diverse list of concepts in defining power as well as the concrete idea that power is the essential and irreducible prime motive for action. For Nietzsche, man's internal, prime desire is for power. Other desires are incidental to this central drive. He specifically defines power to mean self-overcoming, an idea not dissimilar to Maslow's self-actualization ideas. The antisocial uses of power come as people experience powerlessness, the antithesis of self-overcoming power. Hence, power use to dominate others is an expression not of self-overcoming power, but of the absence of this central drive in man.

Max Weber's work has had a significant impact on power theory. His power studies are classic and simultaneously completely up-to-date. His social conflict perspective is as contemporary and appropriate to our present postindustrial society as it was to industrial societies. He deals with power in a structured context as did Russell. His three types of legitimacy (traditional, legal, and charismatic) are especially useful in describing organizational life and in analyzing change in the organization. His discussion of charismatic power also provides a useful paradigm for analysis of individual power relationships.

Recent analyses have tried to place power in a behavioral context or see it as a process of interactions within the confines of the group. Both of these perspectives have added insight into the social theory of power. A process orientation lets us see power in dynamic interaction. It becomes a transactional process. The behavioral focus brings power into the immediate. It allows us to deal empirically with what is, and has been, an abstract and complex issue. Both of these perspectives hold promise of further elucidation of this central element of social theory.

POWER USE IN ORGANIZATIONAL THEORY

Power is both an enigma and a central theme in organization theory. It is an aspect of formal and informal relationships. While it is common in organizations, it is but little discussed or analyzed. Bennis (1966) called it the last dirty word in management. By that, he meant that power is the last (latest) implicit component of organizational life to be exposed to systematic review and analysis.

Power has both psychological and social dimensions. It partakes somewhat of the stimulus-response model of education theory. That is, specific power use often can evoke predictable responses in our targets. The research support for this idea is limited, but the idea makes intuitive sense (Nyberg, 1981). In social situations its use also has distinct value dimensions that bring us into confrontation with ethics and morality. Using power has ideological, methodological, procedural dimensions. Its use is systematically connected to the world of ideas. It presents at once a special aspect of organization theory and the essence of that theoretical discipline (Daft, 1989).

There is a visceral connection between power and organization. We feel the relationship as much as we see it in day-to-day operation. Power, authority, dependence, and independence are related terms that describe aspects of the modern large-scale organization. They are critical to the functioning of the organization and to the fulfillment of the democratic traditions of our cultural life (Bacherach and Lawler, 1986). The organization is a social grouping of at least two people involved in some common enterprise with accepted goals, methods, and structure. The organizational construct is in every respect one of power. We cannot consider organization apart from the idea of power.

Power in organization and management theory spans Marks and Machiavelli, Hobbes and Russell, and Maslow and McClelland. To review so universal and complex an idea in the theory of organizations is to attempt the impossible. Yet power has had a direct impact on organizational theory building and we must consider it a central issue. Some reference to the theoretical underpinnings is necessary to proper understanding of the framework within which we place the data on power use.

Early organization thought centered around rational models of human interaction. It tended to concentrate on authority issues and structure and ignore the knottier problems of power in use (Backerach and Lawler, 1986). Power was an implicit, but unidentified, part of the background of the organization within which we discuss specific functions (such as communications, decision making, planning). Initially we viewed organization theory mechanically and dealt with power (largely in its authority form) only as it added to the logic and predictability of the organizational system (Daft, 1989). Understanding authority helped us to rationalize the system of people in relationship. We noted deviations in practice, but these were seen as human flaws in performance, not in the underlying rational theory of organization.

Rational theory flowed out of an autocratic past that gave place to structured methods of ruling and controlling subordinates. Rational theory was a way to focus on the government of tangibles (parts of the "organizational machine") rather than on the government of people with their unpredictable impacts on the governors. While power was not a part of this theory (except for authority), it is plain to see its shadow cast on doctrinaire systems of rationality.

Twentieth-century problems and an awakening concern for the impacts of social relationships on people in organization brought the issue of power again into focus. Operationally, power entered organizational theory through the firm. Theorists see ownership as theoretically similar to political monarchism and the owner's treatment of employees equivalent to the ruler's treatment of subjects. The human relations approach to management, popular in the mid-century, was a direct effort to democratize the firm (Drucker, 1973). The approach was similar to the way that political scientists were trying to democratize political society in that same period (Waldo, 1947).

Because the human relations school of organization theory did not deal with power squarely does not gainsay its members' concern for recognition of the role of power in organizational life. They challenged the mechanistic school of the classical theorists and brought the people factor of organization life into public focus. While they mostly ignored power per se, they opened the way for later theorists to place this concept in proper perspective. They defined a mode of organizational life built on both rational decision making and emotion.

The kind of accommodation people make in the organizational system is a function of both mind and heart. The allocation of power and the system of power arrangements in place in the organization have a significant impact on the kind of adjustment people make or can make within the organization to achieve their desires—needs for achievement, affiliation, or power (McClelland, 1975).

We can credit the group dynamics theorists with the contemporary awakening to power dimensions of human interaction in organizations. This movement was simultaneous with the development of human relations and was, indeed, a part of this movement. Their concern with interactive, participative elements of organizational effectiveness led them into consideration of alignments of people's goals with those of the organization. They also focused on exchange transactions present in the organization where trade-offs take place to assuage both organizational and personal needs and with the determinants of leadership. One impact of the Michigan and Ohio State studies is that today we see active expansion of discussion, research, and theory building in the power areas of organizational and management theory. Three theoretical constructs among several deserve some attention here: exchange theory, alignment theory, and contingency theory. These ideas have encompassed much of the essence of current theoretical thinking on power use.

Exchange Theory

Power is a natural result of the drive to subdivide organizational functions and people into homogenous elements. The basic tenant of organization (i.e., division of labor) has created an environment where people must depend on others for resources of information, energy, and instructions necessary to accomplish individual or group purposes. The logical mechanism of division of labor is exchange (Backerach and Lawler, 1986). One individual or one group must necessarily get help from other individuals or groups in the organization. The exchange transactions that result from efforts to ameliorate these needs provide a fruitful field for the analysis of power. The reality that desired results is beyond the capacity of any one individual or group leads naturally to power use. The controllers of desired commodities must negotiate for advantage in trade-off situations. Power must be used under these circumstances to attain desired results (Molm, 1990).

We can describe organizations as marketplaces for the exchange of goods and services, information, labor, and intellect to achieve both organizational and individual goals. This marketplace is a political (i.e., power) arena within which participants engage in power use to make real their own result desires. The organization is an environment where people negotiate for advantage and then act out the terms of their exchange negotiations.

The participants may occupy various places in the hierarchy. The negotiation between individuals depends on whether the relationship is superior-to-subordinate, subordinate-to-superior, or peer-to-peer. The relationship is, therefore, one of equals against equals (powerful against powerful) or equals against unequals (the powerful against the relatively powerless). It can be both a balanced or an imbalanced situation with power concentrated in one party. Dennis Wrong identifies these relationships as intercursive and integral, respectively (1979). Regardless of which we employ, the results expected are the same. One party tries to affect the balance of rewards and costs in the relationship. The more one party gets, the less the other enjoys.

Exchange theory flows out of the work of many people. Key in its development and elaboration is the work of Simon (1957), Cartright (1965), Bierstadt (1950), Homans (1958), Thibaut and Kelley 1959), and Gouldner (1960). They saw power in the terms of symmetry–asymmetry, as systems of control over information and affection, as a function of prestige. They also saw it as a balance of values prominent among competing participants in the exchange relationship.

Alignment Theory

The work of Culbert and McDonough (1980), while not a full-blown theory, suggests a dimension of the power-use problem that is worthy of consideration. They propose that each time we enter an organizational situation, we need to align our personal goals and values with those of the organization. We must seek a compatible, congruent relationship between our skills, interests, and personal values and the aims, methods, needs, and values of the host organization. The alignment that is successful is that which optimizes both our personal pursuits and organizational expectations. The alignment once achieved is a convenient lens through which to view organizational events and their impact on the organization and the individual.

Not all alignments are effective for the individual, however. Some people's orientation toward the organization is remote from either (or both) organizational demand or personal need satisfaction. The alignment in this case is ineffective. Effective alignment must orient our actions, values, and views of reality in ways that allow us to achieve important self-interests while meeting organizational needs. Power use is the instrument through which leaders can help followers make such alignments and the force that allows the individual to maintain a fruitful alignment.

The idea of alignment is keyed to organizational culture. The organizational culture, customs, and traditions must match (or be made to match) those of the members in real ways if a useful relationship is to evolve. Cultures that focus on a central power figure emphasize the power dynamic more than do cultures focusing on position, role, or task (Franks, 1989).

Contingency Theory

Much has been written about the impact and force of contingencies in the environment on organizational success and individual capacity to achieve personal goals. We need not summarize this literature here. We need only consider the element of this theory that impacts directly on power use. Simply stated, when we use power by controlling scarce resources, then control over these "critical contingencies" becomes a prime source of power in the organization. People who control critical contingencies are better positioned to use power to achieve their aims than others who do not control critical contingencies.

Contingency theory also flows out of the organizational practice of division of labor. As one compartmentalizes work functions, we defer to those people or units who come to control critical work elements (critical contingencies) essential to organizational success. They become more powerful in relation to others in the organizational system (Crozier, 1964).

Contingency theory is a dynamic concept. As the organization and its host environment change, so, too, do those factors that we consider critical. And as criticality changes, those who control these evolving critical factors supplant the former powerful organization members (Kipnis, 1976). We can summarize contingency theory with a cogent comment attributed to Nord (1978). His epigram, a variation on the Golden Rule, is simply: "Them that has the gold make the rules."

13

Forms of Power

As we have seen, power use is a central activity of life. Its use in the many contexts we find it takes many forms. In a real sense, it becomes *the* central activity of life. And, precisely because power use is so ubiquitous in life, the terms we have to describe the various forms of use have become confused. At the risk of perpetuating this confusion, in this chapter I will try to redefine common language and some popular power terms. The intent is to relate these terms more precisely to the forms that power takes in organizations.

Securing our desired results in the face of opposition characterizes much of our interpersonal life activity. Depending upon the individual persuasions, writers define power as harmonious with influence or opposed to it. They use the ideas of power and force synonymously. Others define it as disparate ends of a continuum of control. That is, some see power as authority or as antithetical to it. Others see coercion as power made manifest, or as merely one form of power. Confusion in the literature is rampant. The result is that the lexicon of power terms is almost useless in distinguishing power-use mechanisms. We need a new language to reconceptualize power terms in ways that admit precise meaning and unambiguous application. To do this, however, is to introduce further ambiguity into the language and discussion of power.

Defining power as a personal capacity that allows the individual to get his desired results in the face of opposition encompasses much of current research. It removes, also, the need to construe too narrowly much of the important work now being done to extend and operationalize power usage. Power defined in this way allows us to see it manifest in a wide variety of settings and in increasingly multiple forms. It is thus a potential for organizational and individual imposition of sanctions and any preliminary steps that induce the target to comply or incur the threatened sanction.

Power is explicit in any of these forms (that is, as threat or actual imposition of sanction). It is also present in situations where someone substitutes logical argument for threat of or actual imposition of sanction. This is a much more comprehensive construction of power than Robert Bierstadt's (1950). His definition more accurately follows the argument of Bachrach and Baratz (1970). Their important critique of power use in making decisions and nondecisions equates power with a capacity to compel obedience even over resistance. However, they reject the idea that power is present in persuasion situations where little resistance is present—a construction of power that others support. A more inclusive analysis would support a definition of power that includes instances of compliance due to persuasion, intrinsic logic, or even like-mindedness (Goldhammer and Shils, 1972).

Undoubtedly power use takes a variety of forms to produce intended and effective results. It is a process based on a desire to induce change in others in conformance with a predetermined plan. The forms it takes range from coercive application of force to benign and sympathetic persuasion to joint action based on common values and ideals. Figure 13.1 identifies six forms of power within the overall umbrella of a coercion–consent behavior impact process. These archetypical power forms serve to distinguish the various forms of power available to the individual. Some forms tend to flow out of coercive means the individual holds and some tend to flow from consensus. Figure 13.1 also depicts this general relationship. It recognizes the general tendency of individuals to favor one basic approach but to use the others also in some circumstances. Briefly, the basic power impact process described in Figure 13.1 suggests that people exercising power behave in ways and for goals that result in impacting another's behavior, values, ideals, or attitudes. The process by which this change takes place we call a power or an impact process. We derive power from our capacity to coerce others' compliance and from our capacity to attain voluntary consent from them. The process of power is one of change; the sources are self and role in the group hierarchy.

The actual use of power takes any of several forms. The specific form adopted depends upon the individual, the situation, and the needed, scarce resources controlled. These forms of power (force, authority, manipulation, threat (or promise), persuasion, and influence) encompass a continuum of control ranging from coercion to consent.

The various forms of power use are, then, linearly related to each other on this coercion–consent continuum. At one end of the continuum, the forms rely heavily on coercion to secure compliance. At the other end, power use relies on informed, cooperative consent as the basis for compliance. The forms are archetypes of power. Descriptions of each follow. In this section we also elaborate on other elements of the basic power model to try to integrate the power use into an overall process.

**Figure 13.1
A Basic Impact Power Model**

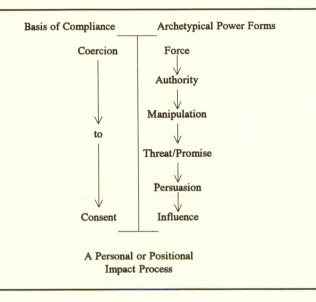

Basis of Compliance   Archetypical Power Forms

Coercion   Force

Authority

Manipulation

to   Threat/Promise

Persuasion

Consent   Influence

A Personal or Positional
Impact Process

THE IMPACT PROCESS

Power is an impact process. Any time we impact others in ways that change their behavior, values, ideals, or perceptions, we can say that power is in use. Power in this construction is a process of affecting another (Handy, 1976), regardless of the method, approach, or foundation upon which we achieve that effect. It matters only that we impact another to behave in a way that the person would not otherwise have behaved.

The impact process is pervasive and tied to interpersonal relationships. It is not merely a function of hierarchy. The impact process is the mechanism for the exercise of power. It is the process by which we direct power and focus it. Madison (1980) uses a financial simile to distinguish impact from its activating source—power. Wealth, he says, is finite (countable). And, cash flow is the process by which one puts wealth into use in ways that the holder of wealth desires. Madison equates impact with wealth and power with cash flow. The impact process, then, is the mechanism by which power is activated and made useful in affecting the power holder's world.

We apply power in any of its six forms in given situations via this impact process. It is a central social process. It is the mechanism upon which, Moscovici contends, all other processes (in social psychology) depend (1974). The sources of power are personality or position held. Falbo (1977), in analyzing ways people get their way in social situations, identified sixteen different approaches. Fundamentally, however, we can order these approaches based on position held in the group or personal characteristics held.

Position

Position as the basis for power use is a part of the analysis of even the earliest works on power. Anciently, Epictus (first century A.D.), in describing freedom and coercive power, made this penetrating point, "no one is afraid of Caesar himself, but he is afraid of death, loss of property, prison, disenfranchisement. Nor does anyone love Caesar himself . . . but we love wealth, a tribuneship, a praetorship . . . when we love and hate and fear these things, it must needs be that those who control them are masters over us" (quoted in Krieger and Stern, 1968). Position *per se* grants to the incumbent resources useful in exercising power to get our way, such as rewards and punishments.

Position makes available specific reward or punishment potentials. Position may be instrumental in achieving control over reward or punishment potentials held by others higher up the group hierarchy. Hollander (1978) suggests that superior position in the group carries with it control over specific rewards but also control over opportunity for experience that subordinates value. It also conveys control over information, values that are acceptable in the group, and over uncertainty, hope, and optimism.

Position in the hierarchy also allows the incumbent to control setting of norms, values, and other socialization processes. Gouldner (1960) identifies this social binding capacity as a significant source of power supervisors control in their groups. People in superior status positions often have the right to prescribe behavior patterns for others in the group.

Personality

Notwithstanding the above, it is also true that we may love Caesar. People of merit or with outstanding personal qualities or characteristics attract us. We allow people who can provide us with affection, recognition, and time and attention to exercise power over us. People whose qualities or appearance we value can satisfy needs for affiliation, recognition, association, sympathy. These people can also punish us through rejection, disengagement, attitudes of detachment, or even by formally excluding us from their company. Rosen, Levinger, and Lippitt (1961) and Bass, Wurster, and Alcock (1963) say that we want to be valued and esteemed by others that we value and esteem. We endow such people with power based on aspects of their character or personality.

Personal power as a basis for activation of the impact process in social situations is also important. It is an aspect of power use that has only recently received major attention in the research literature. Its impact on organizational life, however, is, and has always been, significant. Weber (1968) identified charisma as one of three primary sources of power (along with traditional and legalistic foundations). Charisma, a transcendental idea of supernatural power, also incorporates ideas of strong emotional bonding between charismatic leaders and followers. This bonding may be strong enough to incite intense commitment, fanatical loyalty, and even mass suicide, as the example of the Reverend Jim Jones attests.

COMPLIANCE: COERCION OR CONSENT

Power is effective only as the target of power follows the wishes of the powerful person. We use the impact process to induce others to obey our orders, instructions, requests, or implied wishes. Compliance is the power-use result intended. And compliance can be voluntary (consented to) or coerced. The form of power use taken will rely more or less heavily on either coercion or voluntary consent or a combination of these two kinds of compliance. The goals will be the same: compliance by the target of power.

Consent

All of our instructions or commands depend on acceptance or compliance of the commanded. Achieving compliance is, therefore, the aim of power use. Compliance takes many forms. Nyberg (1981) relates it to consent, a sensed willingness on the part of the target of power. At times we acquiesce under threat of coercive sanction. This is coercion. Sometimes we consent to another's wishes because we have thought about it and concluded that the suggested course of action is logical for us. This is voluntary consent (the highest form of compliance). Between these two polls we obey based on varying degrees of coercion or of voluntary consent based on understanding. That is, we gain compliance in others according to the validity and scope of our information, interest, and available alternatives.

Consent implies respect for the idea or the personality of the individual asking us to comply. Consent is a voluntary reaction to another's requests. It is evoked out of our willingness to be guided by the actions or words of another person because we admire, respect, and are attracted to that person or his/her ideas.

The problem of ensuring compliance, through voluntary consent, to our orders or wishes is universal in social units (Etzioni, 1961). It is a basic element of all social relationships. We relate in one-to-one and one-to-group relationships to get others to behave according to our wishes. We want others to relate to us in specific ways (i.e., in ways that we feel appropriate, given our power resources). We attain this objective through power use.

Coercion

Coercion implies required compliance—the ability to force another to behave in desired ways. It is, therefore, important in power use. In its extreme form, coercion is naked force or violence. Coercion is also a part of many orders we receive from those in authority over us. Threats of violence or force are less dramatic manifestations, but also are examples of coercion. Supporting this concept must be the plausibility of enforcement. That is, unless we have the means to exact the violence threatened, no power is exercised. Coercion, therefore, is one foundation, one basis, for power use. This is the connotation given it by French and Raven (1959). For them, coercion is one base upon which the individual can rely in exercising power. Assuming we have the ability to exact sanctions for noncompliance, and we know the situation, in most cases there is little need for direct coercion.

Coercion implies the absence of alternative actions. If we and our target have antithetical values or needs, one must sacrifice his or her values to the other (Kipnis, Schmidt, and Wilkinson, 1980). Coercion, as a basis of power, can be legitimate or illegitimate; for example, a robber's coercion of a victim. This foundation of sway, nevertheless, has impact regardless of the legitimacy of the underlying ethical values.

A key idea here has to do with information. The cliché is that information is power. The relative availability of information in the power relationship is critical in defining coercion and consent. The presence or absence of information to targets of power helps clarify whether or not the relationship is a consensual or a coercive one.

Compliance, then, is the goal of power use. The form taken roughly conforms to the range of the forms of consent eluded to above. Some examples of power use rely more heavily on coercion. Other forms rely more on voluntary consent for compliance to our wishes. Both of these extremes are examples of power use, as are all of the intervening options that are open to us. Achieving target compliance shows effective power use. This is true regardless of the form employed.

THE FORMS OF POWER

The Basic Power Model defines six forms of power; forms that range the continuum from coercive to consensual. The six forms represent archetypes; that is, they depict major types of power use, each identifiable from the others in some specific dimensions. Actual power use may take any of these archetypical forms. It is, perhaps, more common that a power try may also overlap one or more forms. Indeed, power use typically will partake of characteristics of two or more forms of power.

Force

Force power refers most often to physical or biological force. Force is the ability to impose obstacles restricting the another's freedom or inflict pain or discomfort (physical or psychological), including the taking of life itself (Yukl,

1981). This capacity to cause pain, restrain freedom, or take life underlies power use on two levels. First, French and Raven (1959) identify force (coercion) as one base for the use of power. We have force power if we can control another's behavior to exact compliance. Bierstadt (1950) defines all power in force terms. For him, the power (impact) process involves three kinds of power: power, or latent force; force, or manifest power; and authority, or institutionalized force. Force is one form of power. It is the most effective form in the sense that people respond more directly to its application than to any other power form. Dennis Wrong (1979) conceptualizes power as having four forms: force, manipulation, persuasion, and authority. His analysis supports Lanski's (and this discussion) in defining force as one form of ''power in use.''

Second, force has relevance to a study of power not only as a basis for power use, but also as a form of power use. Force power is at one end of a continuum that includes authority, manipulation, and persuasion as well as threat. Manipulation is an aspect of force, for once the target is in the forcer's grip, he has no option as to his course of action. Both force and manipulation have nonrational implications. Persuasion and authority are more rational manifestations of power.

The most direct form of force is violence—direct assault on the body. However, nonviolence is also a form of force. The recent experience with nonviolent movements (for example, Ghandi in India, the nuclear nonproliferation activists, and the U.S. civil rights activists) shows clearly the impact nonviolence can have on other people. Sit-ins and freedom marches as much as any other tactic were instrumental in forcing official attitudes and many private ones to change about civil rights. Depriving certain customary conditions is also an example of nonviolent force. Denying sleep or subjecting prisoners to intense, continuing light or making them stand for hours all have been used and can be effective in forcing compliance of others to our wishes.

We see force in situations where someone threatens violence: ''Your money or your life,'' a fist shaken violently in our nose, and so on. The difference between these and a shot fired or a punch thrown is significant, but in power terms both are examples of force. They describe situations where the power user gets compliance based on coercive control over the available options. In one case the situation is direct; the other is a situation where force is abstract or symbolic.

Some (Arendt, 1951) contend that force is the behavior of choice in the face of a breakdown of power (for example, authority or threat power forms), not an example of power itself. Rather than seeing these two ideas an antithetical, a more logical approach is to view them as separate examples on the power continuum. This is the option taken here. We may, in fact, adopt force to ensure compliance when other applications of power—say, threat (or promise) or persuasion—fail. Even so, it is not inconsistent with logic to say that in these cases, we adopt another form of power. We do not move from power to something else.

Force is effective both in achieving desired behaviors and in forestalling undesired ones. But it is perhaps in the realm of prevention of undesired behavior that we employ force most often. Force limits our ability to behave in desired ways. It limits freedom and independence. And it is expensive. For example, to kill a person will indeed prevent undesired actions, but it limits future relationships drastically. And, too, in work contexts, we can seldom achieve compliance by forcefully manipulating someone's fingers, hands, or head in desired ways.

Force can forestall, but has only limited effect in getting positive action. In its psychological dimension, we apply force to forestall others' acting in undesired ways or to withhold psychic rewards. It also has psychological limitations in that while it can inhibit undesired behaviors, it has little effect on encouraging desired ones.

Authority

Authority is power sanctioned by the group (Simon, 1950). It is legitimate in that we base authority on externally sanctioned law, custom, or common practice. Authority comes from position held and on the expectations of the follower corps that assumes obedience to the authority figure. It is therefore coercive in nature. As a form of power use, we base authority on sources external to the individual. We get compliance as targets obey because it is implicit in their relationship with the group to behave in such ways.

Authority power is commonly exhibited through orders we issue to someone subordinate to us. Barnard (1948) defines this power-use form as part of the character of a communication in a formal organization by virtue of which it is accepted as governing or determining what a member does or is not to do in so for as the organization is concerned. The authority form of power is a coercive resource we get by virtue of power (authority) grants from those above and below us in the social structure. It is often logical, reasoned, legitimate, and systematic in its application and use. It, nevertheless, is a coercive form.

Weber defined three ideal types of authority: rational–legal, traditional, and charismatic authority (1968). Each type implies a separate foundation upon which authority functions. One's authority may come from role (position) legally granted by superior hierarchy. It can be a delegation in the traditional sense. Habitual modes of behavior and interaction also can provide the basis for structured authority relationships. An example is where we defer to one person consistently because it is expected. We take authority relationships for granted because we feel that this is how relationships work in this organization at this point. And, finally, we also can base our authority upon our special traits and capacities, personality, charisma, or specialization.

Authority power appears to have a relationship to acceptance (perceived or real) by the subordinate to the authority figure. Delegation can bestow an amount (domain) of authority on us. Until others perceive that grant as legitimate, reasonable, and acceptable, given the situation, no real capacity to achieve intended results is possible. Some group consensus (Grimes, 1978) must be present. Sanction-meting-out ability (coercion) is present in any authority-based power-use relationship. We activate our authority only as followers grasp an underlying logic, rationality, or sense in the order. They must see the order as sensible to the organization, the current situation, or the relationships then extant between the authority figure and them. Barnard (1948) suggests that if the subordinate cannot see this relationship as logical and consistent with his perceptions of the organization and its operation and his personal interests, he will not accede to the order even though sanctions can and will follow—that is, force will be used.

Authority represents, perhaps, the most ubiquitous form of power use in organizations. It is, of course, the basis for division of labor in large-scale organizations (Bell, 1975). It ensures coordinated action, responsibility, and accomplishment. Authority power is direct, whereas some other forms, such as influence (at the other end of the continuum), are subtle. Authority can be ''seen'' and its coercive format attacked more openly and more consistently.

Actions based on authority are, to some, more anxiety-laden than some other forms of power. McKeachie (1969) suggests that fear of aggression and retaliation is often present in authority figures. Some of the ''loneliness at the top'' may derive from the adverse psychological impacts of the exercise of authority. People maintain their authority by using the group resources that gave it rise. We maintain it also by a wide range of social and interpersonal pressures and norms that sanction the relationship and define what is acceptable. The maxim ''love flees authority'' adds conventional wisdom to this idea. Authority power induces remoteness, psychological distance between followers and leaders. Gaining and using authority increases our vulnerability to group members. Krupp (1961) contends that as use of authority increases vulnerability, power use increases. Following Krupp's thesis, then, power use is evidence of stressed authority relationships that need attention.

Manipulation

Force is overt; manipulation is covert. In a force situation, the target of power is aware of the application of force. In some respect he or she is aware of the use of other forms of power. There are circumstances where we conceal forms of power. In these situations, the power user is employing manipulation. Wrong (1979) asserts that sometimes people use manipulation alone as a single power form. Often, we use it in combination with another form, say, persuasion or influence. The key to manipulation is masking intent to affect the other person's behavior directly.

Manipulation does not evoke counterreaction from the target, since the target does not know our hidden agenda. Manipulation may even evoke feelings of freedom and choice (see Dahl, 1961). Manipulation is widespread, although counter to American norms. It connotes calculation, premeditation, and detachment, not openness, sharing, or candor.

People exercise manipulation in several ways. In one scenario, we use the technique of concealing our intent through control over the information sources available to the target. Advertising and public relations technicians sometimes fall into this class of user. These methods employ symbolic communications to limit or selectively determine the information supply, or to inculcate desired values or attitudes. In another scenario the technique is for us to manipulate the environmental surroundings of the target person and in this way evoke the desired response. Price setting in the marketplace is an example of this technique of manipulation. Manipulation also is a part of our efforts to create conducive physical surroundings. Thus, we see manipulation in the case of the man who provides his date with candlelight, flowers, music, and a good meal to influence her to his point of view about his desirability as a mate. And, finally, there is the Machiavellian manipulator who cunningly, devilishly sets out to undermine another's position, reputation, or honor.

It is hard to oppose manipulation openly, since the target is unaware of the use of this form of power. There is no action to oppose, no order to disobey, no adversary to face. Manipulation is, therefore, the most dehumanizing form of power. It is more dehumanizing than physical force where the adversary is at least known and confrontable. Much of the negative reputation that power enjoys today may have come from negative experiences we all have had with manipulation.

We can, of course, use manipulation to aid individual and group development. Its covert character places it in a precarious position in terms of acceptance by adherents. This form of power use, however, is a fact of organized group life. Group members must deal with manipulation both theoretically and operationally as they function in the real world. Advertising, propaganda, control of information flows, and plain deception are a part of life. Other forms of power use are available besides manipulation. We can manipulate others on only a limited basis in an age of increasing awareness, enhanced information availability, and multiple information sources. Authority, threat, persuasion, and influence are other forms of power that we can adopt and use to counter manipulation.

Threat/Promise

Threat is a distinct form of power use. Threat power is exercised when others obey because of their desire to avoid a future state of being that we predict will result from their disobedience. We sometimes get other people to change as a direct result of the threat of deprivation of something they desire. The statement, "Do this or else," is a power paradigm.

For this form of power to be effective, there must be recognition by our targets that we have, in fact, the capacity to deprive. Unless the power target knows this and the possible deprivation is important enough to the target of power, threat is not operative (Bachrach and Baratz, 1970).

This power form is not like force where we take the options of the target from him. When we use threat, the target retains the option of noncompliance. The decisive factor is the degree of desire he has not to be deprived of the threatened sanction. Our past uses of force, however, can act to strengthen later use of threat power. In fact, theorists justify the occasional use of force on the grounds that it lets us use the less coercive threat power more. Newstadt (1960) illustrates this idea clearly in his description of the events surrounding President Truman's firing of Gen. Douglas MacArthur. The firing of MacArthur (an instance of use of force) represented a failure of threat power. When threat failed, the alternative of force become the only viable option left to a beleaguered president. Once accomplished, however, the firing provided the basis for an increase in the perceived power of President Truman. Truman's power increase extended not only in military realms but throughout the scope of his presidency. Others in the administration perceived him to be aggressive and contacts with him carried the implicit threat that he could and might also fire them.

Bell (1975) agrees, although he calls this form of power influence. He imputes to influence (read threat) an aspect of prediction of future happenings. He suggests that we use influence (threat) when someone warns another of dire results given a specific source of action. Threat is also explicit when we use influence in forecasts that positive results will follow desired behavior on the part of the target of power. Bell follows Bierstadt in saying threat is more persuasive (and therefore, more consensual) than coercion.

As Bell implies, promise is like threat in theory and application. A promise also predicts a future state of being, one desirable to us. It is equal to threat power as a means of ensuring compliance. In this version, we secure compliance from others through the technique of painting a picture of a desirable future that someone can attain upon compliance with our wishes. Both threat and promise induce compliance in others by predicting the future—one dire, the other desirable.

Persuasion

Persuasion is argument—successful argument. It is a relationship in which one person independently weighs and accepts the ideas, instructions, and values of another who elaborates his position to the first. In this form of power use, the decision of the first person to accept our argument is essentially unconstrained by considerations of penalty or reward (except via the logical results of this "desired" behavior). When we use argument, we suspend use of force or authority. Persuasion is a form of give-and-take in which both parties interact in relative equality. Persuasion is egalitarian power use.

Persuasion is a power form characterized by sharing. The individuals in the situation begin with different views, information, ideas, values, biases, and so on. The resulting dialogue convinces one of the other's point of view and, therefore, to action that that person would not otherwise have taken. Individuals in relationships almost always differ in their talents, information, intelligence, and logical capacities. As they interact, they engage in relationships that employ these talents of persuasion, negotiation, and selling others on their ideas.

Persuasion depends on resources held or controlled by the individual that give him an advantage in rhetoric. Persuasion depends on known capacities held that are in advantage over others in the relationship. In this characteristic, persuasion is like other forms of power. As one must have force in superior quantity to exercise force successfully, so must one be more persuasive than others to use it in power situations. Properly directed, persuasion is an effective form of power use. It is one of the most effective and reliable forms in existence precisely because it is so common in social interaction. We often see one person trying to persuade another to laugh, to cry, to like him, or in any other way to get another to do what he wants.

Influence

For Bachrach and Baratz (1970), influence is a function of power without the use of actual or threatened sanctions. If we use sanctions, force power is in play. If we only threaten, threat/promise is the form of choice. Influence power is affecting another's behavior without resorting to either tacit or overt threat or imposition of severe deprivations. Influence differs from manipulation also in that there is no masking of intent. In using influence, we do not disguise our power use; in manipulation we do.

Influence relates to respect. We comply with other's wishes when we respect them, honor them, admire them. Influence is confused by some with persuasion. Persuasion power is power based on argument in the present situation. Influence is respect for the other person arising from past or other relationship experiences.

Influence flows out of common values, ideals, and goals also. It is noncoercive power used in a nonthreatening way. Persuasion and influence are distinguishable, but the line is narrow. Influence is operative where a young man submits to the orders of an older gentleman because of admiration for the older man's capacities and accomplishments and agreement with his values and ideals. If obedience is because of another reason, it is not an example of influence. For example, if that older man is also his rich uncle, then the situation might involve threat of loss of inheritance. In this case the power situation is an instance of threat power use.

Similarly a legislator may vote as he does because he comes to value the president's political philosophy and the policies of the administration (influence). Or, she may vote because she is convinced by rhetoric or debate (persuasion). Finally, the legislator may vote as she does because of fear of retaliation if she goes against the administration's recommendation (an instance of threat power use).

These kinds of situations multiply thousands of times in our experience. They complicate life. The observer cannot easily unravel them for analysis. Furthermore, in many situations persuasion and influence are self-reinforcing. While the differentiation of the various power-use forms may be difficult in a strictly objective definition, the distinctions are clear in our experience.

Bases of Power

The basis of power is control over needed and scarce resources. We may define resources as anything physical or psychological we own and make available to others and valuable to them in meeting their perceived needs. To be useful for power purposes, the target must see the resources as available only (or most economically) from us. In effect, power comes to us when others perceive us as having resources in some kind of monopoly (Kipnis, Schmidt, and Wilkinson, 1980). The scarcer the commodity, the more useful it is to us to achieve our desires from those who want that commodity. The more of these scarce resources we control, the more powerful we are in the eyes of those persons in need.

Any discussion of power bases must include the seminal work of French and Raven (1959). They distinguished five types of power: reward power, coercive power, expert power, referent power, and legitimate power. Briefly, they define these very commonly referenced bases of power as follows:

1. Reward power—based on our ability to provide benefits to the target.
2. Coercive power—based on our ability to provide punishing effects to the target for noncompliance.
3. Expert power—based on the special ability and knowledge that we have that the target would like to have or use.
4. Referent power—based on desires others have to identify favorably with us or with what we symbolize to them.
5. Legitimate power—based on the feeling others have that we have the right and authority to exert influence over their activities. This feeling results from acceptance of our grant of power by the formal organization or through historical precedence.

This typology has dominated thinking about power sources since its presentation in 1959. These five bases of power have been useful as a foundation for understanding of the sources of power. Unfortunately, they also have served to limit additional thinking about and research into other, alternative foundations of operationally used power.

In fact, the French and Raven typology is inconsistent and limiting. Patchen (1974) correctly challenged the French and Raven typology as being inconsistent to identify the range of power resources. He says that the five bases of power distinguished by French and Raven are not described in a conceptually parallel way. Instead, different types of power are defined in terms of different aspects of the process underlying successful influence. Reward and coercion power are described in terms of resources. Referent power is couched in terms of motivation of target (influence subject) and expert power is in terms of characteristics of influencer. Finally, legitimate power is described in terms of the target.

Patchen concludes that French and Raven are not discussing types of power but instead different aspects of power itself. These nonparallel aspects make it difficult to make comparisons between power types and to treat power in a systematic fashion. The result has been that many theories and empirical studies of power ignore sources of power other than the five provided by French and Raven, augmented by a few simplistic elaborations of their basic model. Simple observation shows that many other sources of power are available to the active power user. These other sources help round out and complete the nature of any working power system.

Following is a discussion of power bases using parts of the French and Raven analysis. This discussion expands their work to include other sources not typically presented as power bases. They are equally valuable as possibilities for us to consider in using power in our interrelationships. This inventory of power bases may be useful in expanding our insight into effective power-use options.

POWER FLOWS FROM CONTROL OVER REWARDS

Power flows to the individual who can provide desired rewards to others. Our ability to provide benefits allows us to control others' behavior and achieve desired results to the extent of others' need for that reward. Rewards can take the form of physical emolument or psychological "strokes." Rewarding someone with a promotion in return for desired performance is an example of this power base. Giving praise, a smile, our attention, or association to another in return for compliance are psychological rewards. In either case, we base our capacity to reward on our control of rewards desired by others.

Use of this base of power is more common in people in the higher reaches of the hierarchy. They typically have more access to materials, information, or psychological emoluments than do subordinates in the hierarchy. Subordinates are less able to gain control over rewards useful in organizational task-accomplishment contests. They typically must rely on nonmaterial or non-institution-based resources. Perhaps their most useful power base is their own energy and skill. Superiors are dependent on subordinate energy, time, expertise, information, and experience to get the organization's work done. Subordinates can reward superiors by applying these resources in appropriate ways in exchange for results they desire from superiors. Besides energy and skill to do the work, employees can marshal recognition, esteem, and friendship rewards to induce coworkers to behave in desired ways.

POWER FLOWS FROM COERCIVE FORCE

French and Raven suggest that this base of power lies in our ability to command compliance physically. Like rewards, in some respects, this base of power allows us to effect others' behavior because of our ability to impose undesirable results. Noncompliance with our desires can result in the imposition of punishments in the form of sanctions or the withholding of desired rewards. This situation is a coercive power situation.

Schermerhorn relates coercion power to a military model. In military and militaristic organizations (for example, police and criminal organizations) members marshal power through control over violence and the capacity to inflict violence. Violence provides much of the basis for directive action by those in control. Coercion is also evident in some respects in economic organizations. Managers sometimes control resources to deprive others of essential materials or impose punishing consequences on those who fail to obey. Of course, economic resources are a potential reward system that people use to secure compliance. This is obvious as a base of power for those higher in the hierarchy. We also can see this base of power in lower-level group members.

POWER FLOWS FROM THE LEGITIMATE RIGHT TO COMMAND

Power may come to those whom the organization appoints to command. Authority legitimizes our right to impose obedience on those who profess allegiance to the source of our legitimacy. The perception of legitimacy in the power target's mind is critical. Unless the target sees us as having a legitimate right to command, there is no basis of power use possible in a situation. Legitimacy unaccepted is not legitimacy at all, regardless of the official nature of the delegation or right.

While legitimacy comes from delegation by the organization and the acceptance of the delegation by those affected by it, it also can flow out of traditional relationships. Usual and customary modes of interaction and cultural expectations are also sources of power in the group. A ubiquitous example of this kind of routinized behavior is that occasioned by standard operation procedures. Standardized procedures allow us to legitimize power relationships without fanfare. They proscribe behaviors in direct and specific and legitimate ways. Legitimacy bestows capacity to control information, material resources, and esteem symbols held by the legitimizing institution. Group members can hold these bases of power independent of the formal legitimizing structure. Or they can be a part of the legitimate positional foundation certain numbers of the organization occupy vis-à-vis other members of the organization.

Legitimacy is, therefore, a position-based source of power. Relationships and roles set within the organization and the community define and delimit the allocation of legitimate power. It is a combination of people in an organization with material and other resources held in common. Our legitimate right to command flows through the formal mechanisms of the organization. Its impact, obviously, extends largely to organizational members. Only marginally does legitimate right in one social group provide a basis for power in another social group. Examples of this, of course, are clear. A ready example is available in the politician who is dominant in his governmental role as well as in social and economic spheres. This is a kind of halo effect.

POWER FLOWS FROM IDENTIFICATION WITH POWERFUL OTHERS

Association and affiliation with powerful people augment our power. Thus, power derived by reference to "a powerful other." Identification power defines our capacity to achieve our desired results by positive identification with others known to be powerful. This kind of power can come from a personal relationship such as that of a secretary with an executive. In this example, the secretary can achieve desired results because of the closeness perceived by organizational members between the secretary and the CEO. Targets of the secretary's power behavior cannot easily differentiate the secretary's personal agenda from that of the CEO. In some instances, the secretary couches her instructions in terms that are similar to those used by the executive. Or the actions requested conform to the overall pattern of action the CEO has issued in the past. In either situation, the target obeys because of the identification of the secretary with the CEO, not because of intrinsic power resources she controls.

Identification can be personal, as with the secretary, or symbolic. We can attain or increase our power by adhering to the ideals, norms, or goals others value. Identification with ideas, values, methods, or goals of powerful people can add to our perceived power in the same way that direct association does.

POWER FLOWS FROM EXPERTISE

For French and Raven (1959), a prime source of power is expertise. Power flows to those people who have skills, knowledge, and abilities needed and respected by other people. If a person sees his potential for goal accomplishment enhanced by the skills or ability we have, then we enjoy power. People respond to competence. Pettigrew (1972) identified competence as a prime base of power in staff groups. And competence comes from expert ability to perform regardless of role in the hierarchy. This is an important power base in that anyone can exercise power over others depending on the special skills possessed.

The increasing complexity in the modern organization and organizational growth both suggest that this power base will be increasingly important in the future. David Mechanic (1962) concludes that expertise is important as a base of power because targets come to depend on the expert for performance needed in the organization.

This is an especially useful power base for lower-level organizational members. Their special and needed expertise can impact high-level group members in ways that make them conform to the lower-level expert's wishes. Subordinates can, therefore, exert power beyond their role in the organization.

POWER FLOWS FROM CRITICALITY

We are powerful to the degree that our contributions are important to the group or to individuals in the group. Whether the other person(s) desires our energy, our resources, or our expertise, or any kind of contribution, to that degree we have power over them.

Criticality is equivalent in many respects to importance. And importance applies to either party in the power relationship. We exert power to the extent of the importance (criticality) we attach to the resources the other person controls (Rubinoff, 1968). Similarly, Mechanic's (1962) research points out the direct relationship between effort expended by a powerful person and his interest in the result. We expend energy in power behavior to the degree of our interest and if we feel the outcome to be critical, important, or interesting. In this, as in many other aspects of interpersonal relationships, perception of the fact is as important as the fact itself.

Motivation is also a helpful factor in understanding this base of power. When we feel a certain behavior is critical to our success, we are motivated to achieve that behavior. To that degree we will expend energy in power behavior.

Burns links motive (see Howard, 1982) to control over resources. Unless both sufficient motive (importance) is present and necessary resources are available to apply to the proposed activity (power behavior), we will not resort to power behavior. Without resources, motive, no matter how strong, cannot be applied to a particular result. Both must be present before movement to achieve our desires can take place.

Johns (1983) found that before we expend energy in power behavior, we must feel we control strategic contingencies. That is, people exercise power when they or the group perceives that they can control events or resources critical to others. Falbo (1987) applies this idea to clergymen. He suggests a direct link between the congregant's perception of the clergyman's role and the acceptance of his power by followers.

Individuals who can get critical information or expertise needed by the organization will be more powerful than those who control only marginal or non-critical resources. Whatever is critical at the time of need is a source of power in our relationships.

Implicit in this discussion is the idea that power comes to those who control needed expertise. A more accurate and useful idea is that power flows to those who control needed, scarce resources—material, psychological, or other. Dennis Wrong (1979) lists a wide array of resources useful in this sense. He includes money, personnel, presence, popularity, legitimacy, legality, and solidarity.

The ability to allocate resources needed by others is a base of power use. (The actual allocation is an example of power in use.) Rosebeth Kanter (1979) classifies these resource into three sources. Lines of supply refers to control over resources available from the larger environment. Lines of information describes control over information necessary for organization movement. Finally, lines of support refers to control over information or manpower necessary to deal with nonroutine job situations—that is, situations where routine skills, knowledge, and ability or materials cannot cope successfully. Kanter's typology also implies a power base dependent upon control over scarce resources in both routine and nonroutine situations.

POWER FLOWS FROM SOCIAL ORGANIZATION

Bierstadt (1950) adds another power base, social organization. Power, he says, also derives from structured relationships in which people combine individual strength to meet group goals. James MacGregor Burns (see Howard, 1982) says the same thing in another way. He sees the power of leaders as deriving from the power of followers. In the final analysis, goal accomplishment comes as powerful individuals mobilize and transform followers who, in turn, transform leaders. For him, social interaction is a base of power. It is a multiplying of individual power.

Power is a function of group cooperative interaction and jointly applied individual power. Power can come from coalitions of independently powerful people who join together to multiply strengths to attain a sufficient critical mass to achieve desired results. Power can flow from group solidarity as much as from individually special people.

Power is potential also in organizational work systems. Coenen (1988) reports that information systems are becoming instruments for the exercise of organizational power. Leaders of information systems may design and implement them for various reasons. When the reason is to effect change in the organization or among its members, the information system becomes a source of power for that leader. System power, like traditional positional and personal power, can let the information system leader gain his or her desired results.

Power also can accrue in mere numbers of people. Persons who are part of a dominant coalition in the organization are powerful. They control group behavior. Perhaps the main sources of power in emergent unions is in the mere fact of numbers—a germane coalition. On at least one dimension, the amount of power held is in direct proportion to the size of the group represented (Szilagyl and Wallace, 1983). Rule by the majority is a common form of political government and it extends to most social and economic institutions as well. It is a part of our cultural value system and it is operationalized in everyday behavior. Those who proceed with their goal-directed behavior without a solid foundation of support from at least a (power) majority of the members of the applicable organization must risk failure without some countervailing power base.

Examples of solidarity as a base for goal-directed activity are common. Politicians assure themselves of a solid core of constituent loyalty before they introduce major policy initiatives or, even, run for office. The civil rights movement achieved a measure of success only as it drew support from many citizens. The war in Southeast Asia ended only by the efforts of many individuals coalesced around this goal. Nations, groups, religions, military forces, and political activist organizations all seek to grow on the theory that might makes right.

POWER FLOWS FROM USE OF POWER

Failure to exercise power can result in its loss. Conversely, the use of power tends to increase power (Wagner and Swanson, 1979). And, perceptions by others of our failure to use power (whether true or not) can result in a deterioration of support. Failure to act or acting imprudently can erode power and the support of others necessary to its continuance. Power itself, then, is another base of power. Used judiciously, it increases, or at least maintains, our power level. Using power inappropriately, or not at all, decreases or dilutes that power already held.

POWER FLOWS FROM CHARISMA

Personality attracts and attractive people command the obedience of others. This is true especially when this personal capacity is scarce. Attractive people are more likely to be in the inner circle of influential cliques and have access to influential people in the hierarchy. They are also likely to have bonds between people who are attractive and those with whom they interact. Whether the interaction is between the attractive individual and those in key positions or between the individual and the masses, the bond is the same. One depends on the other. Followers depend on the attractive person to present their needs to those in power or to satisfy needs that the attractive person can supply. These needs may be anything wanted, including, for example, affiliation and affection.

Charisma as described by Weber (1968) and referent power identified by French and Raven (1959) fit somewhat into this base of power. People with attractive personalities are likelier to enjoy access to others and to exercise control over them than those who are not sought after.

POWER FLOWS FROM CENTRALITY

Strategic placement of the individual in the organization is also a basis of power use. Physical location in the center of activity or in relationship to powerful people adds to the development and effective use of our power. Centrality is a significant in power terms in both physical and social dimensions. Propinquity affects opportunities for interaction with others and control of information and materials (Mechanic, 1962). Mechanic amasses many logical examples to make the point that lower-level subordinates in the organization can add to their power position by association with needed material and social/psychological resources. Mechanic believes the best way for subordinates to gain power is to control expertise, energy, information, or space, and to form coalitions to multiply individual power. For him, the more central a person is in an organization, the greater is his access to persons, information, and instrumentalities of power.

SUMMARY

We gain, maintain, and expand power when we have control of any of several bases of power. The bases listed are those group members use most often. They are available in large-scale organizations today. Analysis of these bases of power reaffirm much of the literature on power foundations:

1. Power is resource-based. Control over needed or desired resources of any nature or description adds power to the individual who controls them.

2. Scarcity is critical to acquisition of power. Any resource may be a potential source of power. Only those resources that are scarce are actually helpful in gaining, maintaining, and increasing power. Scarce and needed resources are critical to enlarging power. No one will alter their behavior when someone offers something they already have or can get easily from multiple sources.

3. Control is enough to impute power. We need not own the scarce resources to have power. We need only be able to control their distribution or use, or appear to have this capacity, to be powerful.

The Ethics of Power

For many, using power to secure personal goals is somehow ethically wrong. For them, power is the capacity to force others to do something they would rather not do. Power lets one person dominate or subjugate another. They say one employs power when other forms of influence fail. This negative face of power translates ethically into a view of power that sees it as constraining on the target of power and, somehow, demeaning to the user. Much of the negative image of organizational politics stems from these kinds of feelings.

An alternative construction sees power as a value-neutral tool in conducting human intercourse. This power tool is neither intrinsically good nor bad. It is only in the ethics of the user that power use contributes to or detracts from the accepted values, mores, and standards of the society.

In this chapter we lay out for review some of the ethical considerations of power use as a foundation for detailed discussion of discrete power-use tactics presented elsewhere in this book. The tactics described in previous chapters constitute a series of systems of behaviors one may adopt to impact the actions, thoughts, or beliefs of others—superiors, peers, and subordinates.

Understanding something of the intellectual basis of power ethics will help us make more informed power decisions. We can make better decisions about when to use power, specific tactics to employ, and the ethical implications of its use. Because, whether we like the idea or not, power use is a part of all life. We engage routinely in relationships that can be better understood from the perspective of power relations. It is central to understanding how we relate to others. It is critical to success in these relationships.

The capacity to influence others has always been a part of the history of people and ideas. Kings, priests, and philosophers from our earliest history share a fascination with the idea of influencing others to procure desired results. Who influences whom? Who is more dominant in a given situation? What resources can I control with this individual or group? These are the stuff of leadership and power and are traceable in the history of mankind.

Religiously, this theme has a rich and varied history. Cain's problem with Abel had a power basis. Moses pitted his power against Pharaoh to "let [his] people go." Later he represented the epitome of organizational power as he sat in judgment over the people of Israel during part of their forty-year pilgrimage. The current pressures in the Catholic Church stemming from the power-tension between Rome and local bishops is a modern iteration of power in religion (Laeyendecker, 1989).

For Jews and Christians, God is the center and source of all power. Power is the center of Hindu theology. The *Bhagavad Gita's* central episode deals with exercising power in warring against chaos. The Chinese *I Chang* focuses on taming power in both the prominent and modest, and of the power of light and darkness. To McClelland (1975) it seems that religions represent changes on the eternal theme of how to deal with man's power relationship.

From a philosophical perspective, power has occupied the interest and writings of every significant theorist. Beginning with the works of Thucydides, Socrates, and Plato, the ideas of power both attract and repel us. And, since Machiavelli, this issue has attracted social scientists as well (Desmond, 1969). Philosophical and ethical writers have dealt with power themes in at least the following ways:

As an element of domination–independence relationships.

As a factor in self-discipline systems.

As the central element of justice.

As a factor in sacrifice and service to others (altruism).

As an element of equality (as a corollary to, or opposite of, freedom).

As an element of personality (instinct, self).

However, the literature does not highlight a truly sustained and comprehensive analysis and synthesis of power—either scientific, religious, fictional, or pragmatic. The theory of power is vague and incomplete. Definitions of the ethics and morality vary and are inconclusive. The theory is ideological, not operational. In fact, the discussion of power is ambiguous and its relationships to major themes implicit rather than explicit. Its association with the knowledge of mankind, as captured in the history of ideas, is shadowy, spotty, and inconclusive. Nevertheless it persists! While largely ignored as a central issue, power is implicit in the dynamics of history. To ignore it—as many have—is to become prey to those who do not.

Indeed, power use is an accepted part of life. Both leadership and management theory imply power use to control others. All social control, the control of one person or group by another, of one society by another, is critical to our life and our history, and control implies power use. In a word, power is ubiquitous in social systems. Without power there would, in fact, be no society, no cooperative effort of any kind (Smith and Tannenbaum, 1963).

Power is the basis of social organization and action; it is the opposite of chaos. Power exercised produces the noble and modest acts of both hate and love. Nyberg (1981) makes the connection between power and two major human traits: the tendency to relate to others and the need to accomplish. The first he calls love, the second power. Power is an essential aspect of human life. In many ways it defines and describes human activity in more helpful terms than any other analytical concept.

We cannot choose whether or not power will be a part of our relationships. It is. We can only choose how we will use it in those relations and how we will react to its use by others. Only as we understand more about power can we become powerful in relationship to others—a situation some suggest is the essence of freedom. Power liberates the powerful and can be the mechanism for expanding the horizons of those in relationship with the powerful person.

The determining factor in the results we achieve is in the purposes and methods of the power users. Theodore Roosevelt summed up this idea in his contention that power undirected by high purpose spells calamity, and high purpose by itself is utterly useless if the power to put it into effect is lacking. Power use is, in this sense, ethically oriented. But, it is not power, but the underlying motivating purpose of the power user that directs its use to morally useful or harmful effects. The ethics of power is in the user, leader, manager, or follower.

AMBIVALENCE TOWARD POWER USE

American ambivalence toward power use is a result of our failure to deal frontally with power. On the one hand our teachers teach us to expect that we can become what we set our minds to become. On the other hand, they also teach us to reject—even fear and oppose—domination by others. Some of our religious leaders say that power is the polar opposite of virtue. We connect power and evil symbolically. And power, because of its negative overtones, is largely absent from education theory. Our acculturation places the two ideas of freedom and power as opposites. We want power for what it can do *for* us and to oppose the powerful for what they can do *to* us. We see it as part of our capacity to achieve and as a threat of external control.

Perhaps the most famous quote about power, one that has set its ethical dimension, is that of Lord Acton. In a letter to Mandell Creighton criticizing his "History of the Papacy during the Reformation," Acton wrote, "Power tends to corrupt and absolute power corrupts absolutely." While widely quoted, this statement is only partially valid. Surely power corrupts some people in their capacity to control others. But surely powerlessness is no less corrupting of the soul and of individual capacity. As Hannah Arendt (1951) has said, violence (a power idea) is the expression of impotence. Powerlessness transformed into violence accounts for at least as much of the depredation history records as does power exceeding moral constraints.

The moral definition of power use must rest in the results desired and achieved. Admittedly, power use in some ways corrupts both the user and the victim of power. Equally obvious, experience teaches us that power enriches us, ennobles us. It lets us achieve our highest potential as individuals and as groups. The will to power, as Nietzsche said, is one of self-realization and self-actualization. In this sense, the moral obligation is toward power, not away from it. The pull toward power is strong. The counterforce against its use is also strong.

While results attained are determined by power use, this is not always a simple cause–effect relationship. We all can think of situations in which power users have deceived themselves as to the moral utility of an outcome attained through power. It is, of course, possible to rationalize power use to attain an end that, when attained, turns out to be destructive. And often an outcome obtained through power use may have more than one ethical result. That is, a power result may be good for some, but destructive to others. Ethical complexities abound in both the literature and actual power-use situations. Its ubiquity in our relationships demand that we understand power and become expert in its use. Far from treating power as a negative term, we can view power as a fundamental process of life, growth, and development (Madison, 1980). Power may corrupt, but so does powerlessness.

Our cultural attraction–rejection attitudes toward power must surely account for some of the lack of concerted analysis of it found in sociopolitical theory. It accounts for some of the confusion many feel when dealing with power in their interpersonal relationships. The ambiguous terms used to discuss power are really euphemisms reflecting the confusion we feel about its use both by us and on us. Influence, leadership, charisma, and control are substitutes for power. We often delude ourselves into thinking that we exercise "leadership" when we try to influence others for their own good. When we are successful, someone will likely accuse us of manipulating others.

NEGLECT IN DISCUSSING POWER USE

Ambivalence and largely negative constructions of power have led to a situation where, until recently, little discussion of applied power use in nonpejorative terms has taken place. Even casual review of the many books and articles with the word "power" in the title reveals that most are not, in fact, about power. Indeed many books in the social, political, and organizational disciplines do not even list entries for power in their appendices. As Bennis (1966) suggests, power is the last dirty word in organizational thought. Because many hold this perception, power is only just beginning to receive the analytical and applied treatment it deserves. Power is one of the central motivating forces in individuals and in organizational life.

Power is constantly in action. Management–labor negotiations are overlaid on a base of power relationships. Political maneuvering between nations balances on a power fulcrum. Religious strife and persecutions involve on at least one level a struggle of leaders for the fealty of their followers. The basis of development of cultures, their dissolution, economic enslavement, political conquest, and organizational health and growth is power, regardless of other explanations promulgated.

Men and women, nations, and institutions have used power constantly throughout history. They have developed arguments to justify its use in any context. The power users base their use of power on the intrinsic logic of the situation. That is, on the wisdom of the message, on the ideology, on the philosophy espoused by the powerful. The political doctrinaire, the religious zealot, and the economic revolutionary all have advanced their dogma from the foundation of the internal justice, validity, or the utility of the idea of the moment.

We also justify power use on the basis of personal values. Much of the growth of this nation and the influence of our economic institutions is traceable to the general acceptance of the profit motive. The profit motive is a central reason for the use of power in organizations. We justify our actions on what we, as individuals, value. Our personal motives are laudable; those of the opposition are not nearly so justifiable. Hence we justify our use of power sometimes on the basis of our *good* motives against the *bad* motives of the opponents. One example may suffice to clarify this justification: American missiles are defensive; enemy buildup of arms is offensive.

We also commonly justify our use of power on the rationale that it only counters the negative, aggressive acts of others. Hence we justify both the use of power by opponents and our uses on the basis of aggressive tendencies found in society—indeed, in all individuals. Fighting fire with fire is an old and often-used rationale.

Power-use-produces-change-and-change-is-progress-and-progress-is-growth. Much of justification for applying power in society is through this chain of logic. We base power use on a commitment to the growth and development of whatever organizational or institutional system to which we belong. And, too, we justify our use of power on the basis of a need to do good. As we (who are good) and our good institutions prosper, so does mankind, and, in order to prosper, we must use power on occasion to ensure necessary progress. Its use permeates our individual and institutional acts on all levels and in all activities. We justify our use of power because its use adheres to us benefits we want. Refraining from using power does not.

BEHIND THE TWO FACES OF POWER

Recent treatments of this theme have noted that power is not a uniformly evil tendency in people, not a wholly negative aspect of their interrelationships. While based in conflict, we can and do use power to attain both positive and negative values. McClelland's (1975) much-quoted treatise defines "two faces of power." One is a positive, outward-oriented, social dimension, the other a negative, inner-directed, selfish dimension. The negative face seeks to dominate others. The positive face directs us toward helping others develop their full potential.

THE IMPORTANCE AND UTILITY OF POWER USE

Rather than being a dirty word in the business of the social sciences, power is one of the key concepts in defining and testing reality. Understanding the nature and uses of power can help both the analyst and the participant in understanding and successfully dealing with the exigencies of organizational life. Donald W. Howard (1982) suggests that in its ontological meaning, power is good. That is, power is the capacity to act, to be an effective force in the society and among our associates. Power makes it possible for the individual to "be." Power lets the individual have impact in life and in society, and to this extent all power is good, since "being" is good. Plato in *The Sophist* says that anything that has power has real existence; it is. The more power we have, the more capacity for affecting others and the environment we have and the more "good" that capacity becomes. This idea explains part of the attraction of power. It grows with fulfillment, and that growth is in both the power wielder and the target of power.

If we learn not to dominate, not to treat others as pawns, but use power to enlarge others' capacities we make them feel powerful. Then power can become one of the most helpful resources we can use in enlarging our world (Backarach and Lawler, 1986). It can make it a better place in which to live. In this sense power is empowering of other.

The evil in power, then, consists not in its being, but in the way we use it. Negative power is merely power applied to constrain and dominate others. It limits rather than expands the human talent. This limiting of another's chances is what has turned many away from even the discussion of power. Used this way, it hobbles the human being. Bertrand Russell said that the benefits to the powerful are so potentially massive as to corrupt the individual. Power for Russell (1938) is evil largely because of the corrupting influence power has due to the potential (benefits or harm) it can bring.

A better construction of history and of power ideas is that power itself is ethically neutral. It is a personal capacity held that allows us to get our desired results, whether or not those actions are ethically positive. The ethical quality perceived in its use flows out of the motives of the user, not out of the essential "stuff" of power. It is the misuse of power that may be evil. That is, power can harm others. In just the same way, the proper use of power can be ennobling to the group members. We need not place power into one discrete ethical classification. Power is neither nourishment in the sense Nietzsche meant it, nor is it poison as Henry Adams said. Power is like fire: It can be useful (even lifesaving); it can be pleasurable. But it needs to be watched, or it can destroy us. The proper intellectual and practical attitude should be respect.

The thread of power ethics moving through history is a clear if only a minor thread in the fabric of human interrelationships. Indeed, the historical treatment of power is an important, if minor, counterpoint to more explicit social systems and activities. We often can see power in use in the great events and actions of history. Unfortunately, historically we have only meager explanatory or theoretical models with which to analyze or evaluate this tool. Nevertheless, the theory of power use is available to the careful observer.

The principle threads in the evolution of power as a tool in social intercourse formed the basis of Chapter 12. In this chapter we saw how the idea of power as a tool of social intercourse is continually evolving toward a specific technology of power in use. This power technology is beginning to be codified into discrete sets of power behavior. These behavior sets are coalescing into definable tactics we can use to secure our desires.

We get things done in our organizations through the effective use of power in interpersonal social situations. The way leaders and others in the organization use power determines their success in personal and organizational goal attainment. It is also the way to insure organizational survival. We all use power to accomplish our ends. It is part of the process of human interaction. The tactics described in this book describe leader and group member behavior in the process of leadership. Familiarity with this technology of power facilitates attainment of our objectives, our individual development, and that of our social system of organizations and institutions.

Appendix: Survey of Power Use by Executives

INTRODUCTION

Organizational politics is a routine fact of our organizational and group life. Based on power, it is ubiquitous in our social relationships. There is some theory to guide us in using power in sociological and political arenas. But little is available to guide us in terms of using power in organizational politics. Unfortunately, research and theory building in this kind of operational usage of power is in its infancy. A few attractive concepts have evolved that have been described and in a few rare cases tried out in practice. In the last decade, especially, a spate of studies has been written on power use in organizational situations and in leadership (Fairholm, 1985, 1991).

This book pulls together some of this research about power and the specific tactics we use, or can use, in office (organizational) politics. Primarily, however, the data upon which the power tactics described in this book are derived come from practitioners. The research methodology employed was analysis of descriptive statistics from more than one hundred detailed questionnaires completed by members of a variety of complex organizations. These data were coupled with in-depth analysis of case studies of specific instances of power use. Analysis of power-tactic use by individuals, the coworker targets of this usage, and the results reported form the basis for conclusions drawn in the various parts of this book.

METHODOLOGY

Using commonly accepted survey techniques coupled with interview and observational data, the author surveyed a variety of individuals in several types of

Table A.1
Demographic Data: Power Study Respondents

<u>Personal Characteristics of Respondents</u>

Total Respondents	109*	
Sex	71	Male
	36	Female
Age	72	Less than 40 years old
	37	More than 40 years old
Work Experience	11	Less than 1 year of work experience
	46	1 to 5 years of work experience
	51	More than 5 years of work experience
Supervisory Experience	86	Some
	23	None
Attitude about Job	17	The job is boring and/or routine
	90	The job is exciting and/or varied

<u>Organizational Environment of Respondents</u>

Kinds of Organization	30	Business
	11	Educational
	55	Governmental
	10	Not-for-Profit
Type of Organization	21	Product-Oriented
	70	Service-Oriented
	15	Professional/Clerical/Technical
Size of Organization	33	Fewer than 101 workers
	37	101 to 1000 workers
	36	More than 1000 workers
Size of Work Unit	46	Fewer than 11 people
	50	11 to 50 people
	14	More than 50 people

* Not all data in this table totals 109. Some respondents did not complete all questions. Some questions call for more than one answer.

organization. The focus was to explore the kinds of operational (tactical) power behavior they engaged in routinely on the job. Table A.1 identifies the kinds of people surveyed and pertinent demographic data. The executive pool described in Table A.1 constitutes a small, but statistically significant coterie of people from a variety of organizations. Together they provide a useful foundation for the major conclusions drawn here and in the foregoing chapters about power usage in the workplace. A summary of some specific findings about the tactical use of power by these respondents is found in the tables in this appendix.

The research focus was on specific behaviors engaged in by organizational members to ensure achievement of their desired results. Analysis produced the twenty-two separate power-use tactical interventions analyzed in the body of this book. They define specific behavior patterns individuals employ in organizational politics to secure their desired results. Respondents specified (a) which tactics they have used in organizational political action and (b) which ones were the most effective in achieving their desires. They also provided data about (c) their perceptions of the ethics of use of tactics and (d) the kind of relationships in which specific tactics were employed.

These power tactics have been validated by a formal study of over 100 organization members and have been tested informally with over 350 people— clerical, technical, professional, and managerial—who have passed through the author's graduate-level classes. The tactics have proven to be statistically discreet behavior patterns, patterns of behavior that are commonly engaged in by people at all levels in the organizational hierarchy.

SURVEY FINDINGS

Identification of Twenty-Two Power Tactics

Study subjects illustrate sufficiently broad-based characteristics to form a sound platform from which to describe power use in organizational politics in work situations. Data collected were subjected to several statistical procedures. The results show that specific power behavior interventions are discreet. That is, the twenty-two power tactics produced do not duplicate each other. Neither are any tactics related to each other in statistically significant ways. The Kendall Tau B statistic was used and confirmed that there is no evidence that respondents treated any question in a statistically similar way to any other question used. Each power behavior tactic appears to be unique and was perceived as such by those responding to the survey. The correlation was at least to the .5 level in all cases. The twenty-two organizational politics power tactics are defined as follows (see Table 4.1 in Chapter 4):

Twenty-Two Power Tactics

Controlling the Agenda: Determining beforehand the issues, subjects, or concerns for group action or decision.

Using Ambiguity: Keeping communications unclear and subject to multiple meanings.

Brinkmanship: Disturbing the equilibrium of the organization to control choice options.

Displaying Charisma: Using the respect that others have for our character traits, presence, or method of operation to effect another's behavior in desired ways.

Forming Coalitions: Securing allies, both employees and other stakeholders in the organization or associated with it.

Co-opting Opposition Members: Placing a representative of the opposition group on our decision-making body to induce the representative to favor, rather than oppose, our interests.

Controlling Decision Criteria: Selecting of the criteria by which decisions are made so that desired decisions result regardless of who decides.

Developing Others: Increasing the capacities of others, thereby increasing their overall power.

Using Outside Experts: Involving congenial experts in organizational decisions, thus allowing us to effect results without personally deciding.

Building a Favorable Image: Creating a persona of skills, capacities, values, or attitudes to which others defer.

Legitimizing Control: Formalizing our right to decide through appeals to hierarchy or legal precedent.

Incurring Obligation: Placing others under obligation to us so they do what we desire.

Organizational Placement: Placing allies in strategic positions or isolating potential opponents.

Proactivity: Unilateral action to secure desired results.

Quid Pro Quo: Negotiating trade-offs with others to secure our desired results.

Rationalization: Consciously engineering of reality to secure desired decision results.

Allocating Resources: Distributing resources under our control in ways that will increase our power in relationships to others.

Dispensing Rewards: Rewarding or punishing others to win their support.

Ritualism: Inducing institutionalized patterns of behavior in others or in the organization.

Using a Surrogate: Using an intermediary to secure compliance in others.

Using Symbols: Reinforcing control through symbolic objects, ideas, or actions.

Training and Orienting Others: Transmitting skills, values, or specific behavior to others to instill in them our goals, values, philosophy, or desired behaviors.

The study coupled statistical data with observational data and interviews with organizational members at all levels and in a wide variety of working relationships. The responses received from survey documents, selected follow-up interviews, and comparison with other research studies confirm the tactics defined above. These power-use tactics reflect real-world behaviors. They describe a wide variety of behaviors that have as their main purpose getting others to behave in ways we desire—in ways that the target of these tactics probably would not have behaved if left alone. They define the essence of organizational politics.

Table A.2
Summary of Tactic Characteristics Used Toward Superiors

Tactic by Frequency of Use	p-value*	Tactic Effectiveness		Ethical Pattern		When Used	
		Rank among All Tactics	Rank toward Supervisor	Positive	Negative	Initial	Resistance
1 Productivity	.0001	5	2	P		I	
2 Use of Outside Experts	.0001	9	3		N		R
3 Charisma	.0001	4	1	P		I	
4 Rationalization	.0001	13	6		N		R
5 Using Ambiguity	.0001	12	5	P		I	
6 Image Building	.0001	10	4	P		I	

P = Seen as ethically positive.
N = Seen as ethically negative.
I = Used as an initial contact approach.
R = Used on encountering resistance.
* = Probability that the use of this tactic toward supervisors is effective.

Tactics Used Mostly Toward Our Superiors

In general respondents reported broad use of the tactics in all of their power relationships. However, survey findings confirm that some tactics are most often reserved for power relationships with those superior to us in the organizational structure. Others are used in peer contacts, and another group of power tactics is employed in our relations with subordinates. Tables A.2, A.3, and A.4 show these tactics and describe other descriptive factors relating to usage.

Table A.2 describes the most often-used tactics by people to impact their superiors in the organization. While all of the other tactics are used on occasion in power activity with superiors, these six are the most significantly used.

Tactics Used Mostly Toward Our Peers

Table A.3 shows statistical detail for the nine power tactics we use most often toward our peers. Table A.3 rankings are significant in that they represent largely trade-off tactics. All respondents used the trade-off behaviors most often. However, various classes of group members used the others in unique ways. Men, for example, lean more toward the use of group-oriented behaviors such as building coalitions, co-opting others to their position, and similar behaviors. Women rely a little more on personal tactics like placing others under obligation to them, controlling the action agenda, and allocating resources.

Table A.3
Summary of Tactic Characteristics Used Toward Peers

Tactic by Frequency of Use	p-value*	Tactic Effectiveness		Ethical Pattern		When Used	
		Rank among All Tactics	Rank among Supervisors	Positive	Negative	Initial	Resistance
Quid Pro Quo	.0001	15	6	P		I	
Resources	.0001	1	1	P		I	
Coalitions	.0001	7	2	P			R
Co-opting Others	1.0	8	3	P			R
Obligation	.0001	20	8		N		R
Use of Surrogate	.0001	11	5	P			R
Control Agenda	.0001	18	7		N		R
Brinkmanship	.0238	22+	9+		N		R
Building Image	.0001	10	4	P		I	

+ = Not effective.
P = Seen as ethically positive.
N = Seen as ethically negative.
I = Used as an initial contact approach.
R = Used on encountering resistance.
* = Probability that the use of this tactic toward peers is effective.

Tactics Used Mostly Toward Our Subordinates

Table A.4 summarizes cogent elements of data developed from research about uses of these nine clusters of power behavior directed toward those subordinate to us hierarchically.

Power Tactics Use by Class of Organization

Power use is not fundamentally limited by the kind of organization in which we work. People working in, say, business do not use power more than those employed by not-for-profit organizations or any other classification of employment. However, this study did identify some interesting variations on power use. Four different classifications of employment were specified in this study: business, higher education, government, and nonprofit organizations. Data were collected from workers in each class.

While members of each kind of organization make full use of all of the twenty-two power tactics identified in this study, each makes somewhat different use of them. Table A.5 displays some of the variety in this use. Generally speaking, developing others and proactivity are the most commonly used tactics in orga-

Table A.4
Summary of Tactic Characteristics Used Toward Subordinates

Tactic by Frequency of Use	p-value[*]	Tactic Effectiveness		Ethical Pattern		When Used	
		Rank among All Tactics	Rank among Supervisors	Positive	Negative	Initial	Resistance
Training/Orienting	.0001	3	2	P		I	
Developing Others	.0001	2	1	P		I	
Dispensing Rewards	.7414	21[+]	9[+]		N		R
Control Decisions	.0001	16	5	P		I	
Legitimizing	.0001	14	4	P			R
Organizational Placement	.0001	19	7		N	I	
Using Symbols	.0001	17	6		N	I	
Ritualism	.0001	6	3	P			R
Obligation	1.0	20	8		N		R

+ = Not effective.
P = Seen as ethically positive.
N = Seen as ethically negative.
I = Used as an initial contact approach.
R = Used on encountering resistance.
[*] = Probability that the use of this tactic toward subordinates is effective.

nizations. Brinkmanship and using outside experts are the least used. While these tactics are treated in about the same manner in each of the four types of organization, others are not. Some of these findings are instructive. For example, charisma is a frequently used tactic in business, higher education, and not-for-profit organizations. It is less frequently used by workers in government organizations. Rather, these workers rely more on system-based tactics.

Business makes more use of the tactics of symbols, obligation, and legitimizing control than do the others. This runs counter to the conventional wisdom that government workers are more involved in these kinds of activities. The fact that those in higher education make little use of obligation or symbols is also a new insight on academic behavior. That they do employ the using ambiguity tactics more than workers in other kinds of organizations is also unusual, given their avowed purpose to communicate understanding.

Higher education workers also make use of the use of resources tactic (probably information) more than their business or governmental colleagues, whom one would expect to use this tactic frequently. Higher education workers also use the rationalization tactic more frequently than their counterparts in other types of organizations. Table A.5 lists tactics by overall frequency of use and for each individual classification of organization.

Table A.5
Comparison of Frequency of Power Use by Organizational Class

Rank	Overall Tactic	Business (n = 30) Most Frequently	Education (N = 13) Used Tactic	Government (n = 55)	Not-for-Profit (n = 10)
1	Developing Others	1	1	2	2
2	Proactivity	3*	2	1	1
3	Ritualism	2	4	4	1
4	Training/Orienting Others	3*	3	3	2
5	Displaying Charisma	3*	3	5	2
6	Allocating Resources	4	2	4	3
7	Legitimizing Control	3*	5	4	2
8	Building Image	6	4	6	2
9	Using Ambiguity	8	2	8	3
10	Forming Coalitions	4	6	7	4
11	Co-opting Others	6	4	8	3
12	Rationalization	7	3	7	4
13	Quid Pro Quo	8	4	8	3
14	Decision Criteria	7	5	10	4
15	Use of Surrogates	9	4	9	4
16	Using Symbols	6	7	10	5
	Least Frequently Used Tactics				
17	Organizational Placement	10	6	11	5
18	Controlling the Agenda	12	8	12	4
19	Dispensing Rewards	11	8	12	4
20	Incurring Obligation	9	8	13	6
21	Using Outside Experts	14	5	14	5
22	Brinkmanship	15	8	15	7

*These numbers indicate rank order of frequency of use by each class of organization with "1" equalling the most frequently used tactic, "2" the next most frequently used, et cetera. Duplicate ranking numbers in a column indicate that respondents used these tactics with equal frequency.

Data amassed about the perceptions of the effectiveness of these tactics by workers in the four classes of organization are interesting. This data is summarized in Table A.6 and interpreted in Chapter 8. Table A.7 shows these and other comparisons on this measure. This table highlights the classification of organization studied that ranks each tactic most (or least) ethical or for which ethicality rankings were similar.

All four classes of organization workers find using ambiguity, charisma, developing others, building a favorable image, proactivity, allocating resources, ritualism, and training and orienting others to be initial-use power behaviors. Some difference is seen (see Tables A.8 and A.9) in other tactics, but the

Table A.6
Comparison of Effectiveness of Power Use by Organization Class

Business	Higher Education	Government	Not-for-Profit
Allocation of Resources	*Developing Others	Allocating Resources	*Developing Others
Forming Coalitions	*Building a Favorable Image	Developing Others	*Training & Orienting Others
Ritualism	*Training & Orienting Others	Training & Orienting Others	Displaying Charisma
*Displaying Charisma	*Using Surrogates	Proactivity	Allocating resources
*Developing Others	Allocating Resources	Displaying Charisma	Forming Coalitions
Proactivity	Displaying Charisma	Ritualism	Using Symbols
Using Symbols	Co-opting Opposition Members	Using Outside Experts	Legitimization
*Training & Orienting	*Legitimizing Control	Using Surrogates	Ritualism
*Legitimizing Control	*Using Outside Experts	Forming Coalitions	*Building a Favorable Image
Co-opting Opposition Members	Organizational Placement	Building a Favorable Image	*Quid Pro Quo
Using Ambiguity	Using Symbols	*Co-opting Opposition Members	Co-opting Opposition Members
Controlling the Agenda	*Using Ambiguity	*Quid Pro Quo	Rationalization
Controlling Decision Criteria	*Proactivity	Controlling Decision Criteria	*Using Outside Placement
Building a Favorable Image	*Rationalization	Using Ambiguity	Proactivity
*Using Outside Experts	Quid Pro Quo	Organizational Placement	Use of Surrogates
*Rationalization	Controlling Decision Criteria	Controlling the Agenda	*Controlling the Agenda
Use of Surrogates	Ritualism	Legitimizing Control	*Controlling Decision Criteria
Quid Pro Quo	*Forming Coalitions	*Rationalization	*Legitimizing Control
Incurring Obligation	*Controlling the Agenda	*Using Symbols	Using Ambiguity
Organizational Placement	Incurring Obligation	Dispensing Rewards	Dispensing Rewards
¹Dispensing Rewards	Brinkmanship	¹Incurring Obligation	¹Brinkmanship
¹Brinkmanship	Dispensing Rewards	¹Brinkmanship	

¹ Not Effective
* Same Ranking

preponderance of use is initially also for controlling decision criteria, organizational placement, and quid pro quo.

Power tactics used to counter resistance for all four classes of workers based on organization include: controlling the agenda, brinkmanship, co-opting opposition members, rationalization, dispensing rewards, and using a surrogate (see Table A.9). Most people in most classes also see forming coalitions, using outside experts, and legitimizing control as resistance-coping behaviors.

Power Tactic Use by Supervisors and Nonsupervisors

The conventional wisdom has it that supervisors use power—mostly authority power—and nonsupervisors are (relatively) powerless. This research explodes that myth. Both supervisors and nonsupervisors report frequent use of power tactics in getting their way. They both use all twenty-two of the tactics identified, albeit in somewhat different ways.

Table A.10 summarizes data collected about supervisor–nonsupervisor uses of power. This table points out key use ranking factors associated with their respective use of the twenty-two power tactics in their organizational activities. The six most frequently used power tactics for nonsupervisors are proactivity, allocating resources, displaying charisma, training and orienting others, ritualism, and legitimizing control. For supervisors the six most frequently used tactics

Table A.7
Most Ethical Tactics Used by Organizational Class

Tactics	Business	Education	Government	Not-for Profit	All
Agenda Preparation	Most	Most			
Using Ambiguity		Most	Least		
Brinkmanship*		Most			
Displaying Charisma					Same
Forming Coalitions		Most			
Co-opting Opposition Members		Most			
Controlling Decision Criteria					Same
Developing Others					Same
Using Outside Experts					Same
Building a Favorable Image					Same
Legitimizing Control					Same
Incurring Obligation*		Most			
Organizational Placement		Most			
Proactivity	Most				
Quid Pro Quo					Same
Rationalization					Same
Allocating Resources					Same
Dispensing Rewards*		Most			
Ritualism			Most		
Using Surrogates			Most		
Using Symbols					Same
Training & Orienting Others					Same

* Not Ethical

are developing others, proactivity, training and orienting others, ritualism, legitimizing control, and allocating resources.

In terms of frequency of use, it is evident that nonsupervisors make as much use of the tactics as their supervisors do. (See Table A.11.) Nonsupervisory workers in our organizations are fully engaged in power activity. It is a part of their organizational life, one in which they gain considerable practice. This finding casts the nonsupervisory worker in a new, more proactive role in our organizations.

Frequency of use is only one measure of tactic utility. The effectiveness of the individual tactics is also key. Comparison of supervisor and nonsupervisor effectiveness perceptions is displayed in Table A.12. Overall, Table A.12 data confirm a general uniformity in effectiveness rankings. These data compare supervisors' and nonsupervisors' feelings about the effectiveness of individual

Table A.8
Initial Style of Power Use by Organizational Class

Tactics	Business	Education	Government	Not-for Profit
Co-opting Others	*	*	*	2
Brinkmanship	*	*	*	3
Training/Orienting Others	3	1	2	5
Developing Others	2	7	3	*
Decision Criteria	6	4	3	*
Using Symbols	1	6	6	8
Ritualism	10	11	7	1
Building Favorable Image	7	3	5	9
Using Ambiguity	5	2	11	11
Proactivity	9	13	4	2
Displaying Charisma	4	9	9	13
Legitimizing Control*	*	*	12	4
Forming Coalitions	*	*	10	6
Allocating Resources	8	8	8	7
Controlling the Agenda	*	*	*	9
Organizational Placement	12	5	10	*
Using Outside Experts	11	*	*	*
Incurring Obligation	13	12	*	*
Quid Pro Quo	*	10	12	6
Rationalization**				
Dispensing Rewards**				
Using Surrogates**				

* Tactic not used in this style.
** Tactic not used at all by this group.

tactics. Most differences in effectiveness rankings come on the using ambiguity tactic.

Table A.13 displays the ethical rankings of power tactics used by supervisors and nonsupervisors in terms of which group sees a particular power tactic most ethical. Nonsupervisors find a few tactics significantly more ethical than supervisors.

Supervisors and nonsupervisors are unanimous in their choice of the timing of specific tactic use. Both groups selected the same lists as initial approach behaviors and as resistance-countering tactics.

Power Tactic Use: Perceptions of Men and Women

While data collected in this study showed responses for only a few women, some interesting and potentially useful information results from data analysis.

Table A.9
Resistance Style of Power Use by Organizational Class

Tactics	Business	Higher Education	Government	Not-for-Profit
Brinkmanship	1	1	2	*
Forming Coalitions	4	3	*	*
Co-opting Others	3	2	5	*
Dispensing Rewards	1	2	4	3
Use of Surrogates	5	5	5	1
Controlling Decision Criteria	*	*	*	6
Building a Favorable Image	7	3	5	9
Legitimizing Control	6	7	*	*
Incurring Obligation	9	4	*	*
Rationalization	4	7	8	6
Use of Outside Experts	7	10	7	*
Organizational Placement	*	*	*	8
Quid Pro Quo	8	*	*	*
Controlling the Agenda	*	9	8	9
Training and Orienting Others	8	*	*	*
Using Ambiguity**				
Displaying Charisma**				
Developing Others**				
Proactivity**				
Allocating Resources**				
Ritualism**				
Using Symbols**				

**Tactic not used in this style.
**Tactic not used at all by this group.

Table A.14 summarizes pertinent information developed from survey data about actual uses of the twenty-two power tactics by men and women.

Review of Table A.14 shows that both men and women workers make routine use of all tactics, mostly in similar ways. Both use more than half of the tactics about equally. Both sexes are similar in finding most of the same tactics to be effective or ineffective. They agree also on their ethical evaluations. And, both use the tactics in about the same way as either initial contact tactics or as methods to counter target resistance along with incurring obligation, dispensing rewards, and controlling the agenda.

Table A.15 compares frequency of use decisions of both men and women. This table and Table A.14 highlight the tactics most frequently used by men and those most often employed by women along with those used about equally frequently. Men and women differ significantly in how often they use the de-

Table A.10
Power Use by Supervisors and Nonsupervisors

Tactics	Rank Order of Use									
	Frequency		Effectiveness		Ethics		When Used			
							Initial		Resistance	
	S	N	S	N	S	N	S	N	S	N
Controlling the Agenda	18	10	19	15	20*	18*	+	+	8	7
Using Ambiguity	7	4	16	5	11*	8	5	8	+	+
Brinkmanship	20	11	22#	21#	22*	21*	+	+	1	4
Displaying Charisma	6	2	4	4	9	7	8	7	+	+
Forming Coalitions	9	5	6	9	8	10	+	+	6	9
Co-opting Opposition Members	9	8	9	8	7	5	+	+	3	3
Controlling Decision Criteria	3	9	15	14	10	12*	4	5	+	+
Developing Others	1	4	1	3	1	1	1	1	+	+
Using Outside Experts	19	11	8	12	16*	11*	+	+	7	10
Building a Favorable Image	8	5	13	7	5	2	7	3	+	+
Legitimizing Control	4	3	14	13	13	16*	+	+	5	5
Incurring Obligation	17	12	20	20#	21*	19*	+	+	9	6
Organizational Placement	15	10	18	18#	17*	17*	10	12	+	+
Proactivity	2	1	5	6	2	3	6	10	+	+
Quid Pro Quo	11	6	12	6	14*	13*	12	11	+	+
Rationalization	10	7	11	17#	18*	14*	+	+	10	2
Allocating Resources	5	2	2	1	6	6	9	9	+	+
Dispensing Rewards	16	11	21	19#	19*	20*	+	+	2	1
Ritualism	3	3	7	2	4	8	11	6	+	+
Use of Surrogates	12	7	10	11	12	15	+	+	+	8
Using Symbols	16	6	17	10	15*	9*	3	4	+	+
Training & Orienting Others	3	3	3	2	3	4	2	2	+	+

S = Supervisor   # = Not Effective * = Not Ethical
N = Nonsupervisor   + = Not Used in this Style

veloping others tactic. Men use this cluster of power behaviors most frequently. Women use three other tactics more frequently. Women favor using outside experts, by three rankings. Men use building a favorable image more frequently. They rank their frequency of use of this tactic eighth to the women's ranking of fourteenth, a difference of six rankings. Women use quid pro quo more frequently than do men (by four rankings). Women also opt for allocating resources by four rankings. Men favor training and orienting others much more than women—a difference of five rankings.

Men appear to favor power tactics associated with enhancing followers along with traditional tactics associated with authority and system. Women, contrary to some popular wisdom, find reason for more frequent use of proactivity,

Table A.11
Most Frequently Used Power Tactics by Supervisors and Nonsupervisors

Tactics	Supervisor	Nonsupervisor	Both
Controlling Agenda Preparation		Most	
Using Ambiguity		Most	
Brinkmanship		Most	
Displaying Charisma		Most	
Forming Coalitions		Most	
Co-opting Opposition Members			Same
Controlling Decision Criteria		Most	
Developing Others	Most		
Using Outside Experts		Most	
Building a Favorable Image	Most		
Legitimizing Control			Same
Incurring Obligation		Most	
Organizational Placement		Most	
Proactivity			Same
Quid Pro Quo		Most	
Rationalization		Most	
Allocating Resources		Most	
Dispensing Rewards		Most	
Ritualism			Same
Using Surrogates		Most	
Using Symbols		Most	
Training and Orienting Others			Same

ritualism, and allocation of organizational resources, which are more system-based than some "male" tactics. They also employ power in personal (personality) terms more frequently than do their male counterparts.

Women rate all tactics except brinkmanship and dispensing rewards as effective. Men follow suit; they rate only two tactics as ineffective: brinkmanship and incurring obligation.

The above comparison shows that, while both men and women use charisma, women use it more often and find it somewhat more effective. We also find significant difference in effectiveness rankings between men and women in their use of charisma. According to Table A.14, women find this the most effective tactic they use, favoring this by four rankings over men. Men, on the other hand, use developing others more often than do women and find it more effective than their female counterparts. They also value ritualism (ten ranks' difference), rationalization (seven ranks' difference), and building a favorable image (three ranks' difference) as significantly more effective than do women. In addition to charisma, women ranked using symbols (sixteen ranks), quid pro quo (seven ranks), using outside experts (three ranks), and incurring obligation (also three

Table A.12
Most Effectively Used Power Tactics by Supervisors and Nonsupervisors

Tactics	Supervisor	Nonsupervisor	Both
Controlling Agenda Preparation		Most	
Using Ambiguity		Most	
Brinkmanship			Same
Displaying Charisma			Same
Forming Coalitions	Most		
Co-opting Opposition Members			Same
Controlling Decision Criteria			Same
Developing Others	Most		
Using Outside Experts	Most		
Building a Favorable Image		Most	
Legitimizing Control			Same
Incurring Obligation			Same
Organizational Placement			Same
Proactivity			Same
Quid Pro Quo	Most		
Rationalization	Most		
Allocating Resources			Same
Dispensing Rewards		Most	
Ritualism		Most	
Using Surrogates			Same
Using Symbols		Most	
Training and Orienting Others			Same

ranks' difference) significantly more effective than men. Table A.15 reveals more of the interesting shades of difference between men and women in their use of these power tactics. Both sexes rank the effectiveness of these tactics similarly: using ambiguity, forming coalitions, proactivity, and dispensing rewards. Table A.16 compares tactics by perceived effectiveness and summarizes similarities and differences in effectiveness perceptions.

Table A.17 provides a similar breakdown based on perceived distinctions of the ethics of individual power tactic use. As noted, men find three tactics most ethical: building a favorable image, legitimizing control, and allocating resources. Women perceive use of using ambiguity, displaying charisma, and co-opting opposition members as the most ethical. They agree on the ethicality of using all of the other tactics.

Men and women are also generally agreed as to when to use the power tactics—as initial or resistance-countering strategies. Table A.18 summarizes research findings in this area of interest. It shows the tactics both men and women use on initial contact and those used when either encounters resistance.

Table A.13
Most Ethical Tactics Used by Supervisors and Nonsupervisors

Tactics	Supervisors	Nonsupervisors	Both
Controlling Agenda Preparation			Same*
Using Ambiguity		Most#	
Brinkmanship			Same*
Displaying Charisma		Most	
Forming Coalitions	Most		
Co-opting Opposition Members		Most	
Controlling Decision Criteria	Most+		
Developing Others			Same
Using Outside Experts		Most*	
Building a Favorable Image		Most	
Legitimizing Control	Most+		
Incurring Obligation		Most*	
Organizational Placement			Same*
Proactivity			Same
Quid Pro Quo			Same*
Rationalization		Most*	
Allocating Resources			Same
Dispensing Rewards			Same*
Ritualism	Most		
Using Surrogates	Most		
Using Symbols		Most*	
Training and Orienting Others			Same

*-Not seen as ethical by both groups.
#-Not seen as ethical by supervisors.
+-Not seen as ethical by nonsupervisors.

SUMMARY

These research findings provide specific information about operational uses of power by all kinds of people in all kinds of organizations in American society. While this data have to be described as preliminary, they do point to a fuller use of power in society by participants at all levels of the hierarchy than the conventional wisdom suggested to be the case. These data need to be confirmed and enlarged by further research. Nevertheless, even at this beginning stage of our understanding, they focus our attention on some important and interesting power phenomena: the tactics of a power-use technology.

Table A.14
Power Use by Males and Females

Tactics	Frequency M	Frequency W	Effectiveness M	Effectiveness W	Ethics M	Ethics W	Initial M	Initial W	Resistance M	Resistance W
Controlling the Agenda	18	20	17	15	20*	20*	+	+	6	8
Using Ambiguity	9	8	12	11	13*	5	7	6	+	+
Brinkmanship	22	22	22#	19#	22*	22*	+	+	1	3
Displaying Charisma	6	5	5	1	8	6	10	5	+	+
Forming Coalitions	10	11	7	7	9	7	+	+	4	7
Co-opting Opposition Members	11	10	8	10	7	8	+	+	2	5
Controlling Decision Criteria	15	16	14	10	10	11	3	7	+	+
Developing Others	1	4	1	5	1	1	1	4	+	+
Using Outside Experts	21	18	11	8	17*	14*	+	14	8	+
Building a Favorable Image	8	14	9	12	3	10	6	2	+	+
Legitimizing Control	5	6	15	13	11	16*	+	+	5	4
Incurring Obligation	20	21	21#	18	21*	19*	+	13	7	+
Organizational Placement	17	18	18	16	18*	17*	1	10	+	+
Proactivity	3	1	6	6	2	2	4	8	+	+
Quid Pro Quo	13	9	16	9	15*	13*	12	12	+	+
Rationalization	12	13	10	17	16*	21*	+	+	10	6
Allocating Resources	7	3	2	4	6	9	8	9	+	+
Dispensing Rewards	19	19	20	20#	19*	18*	+	+	3	1
Ritualism	4	2	4	14	5	4	9	11	+	+
Using Surrogates	14	14	13	8	12	12	+	+	9	2
Using Symbols	16	15	19	3	14*	15*	5	1	+	+
Training and Orienting Others	2	7	3	2	4	3	2	3	+	+

M = Men   # = Not Effective   * = Not Ethical
W = Women   + = Not Used in this Style

Table A.15
Most Frequently Used Tactics by Men and Women

Tactics	Men	Women	Both
Controlling Agenda Preparation			Same
Using Ambiguity			Same
Brinkmanship			Same
Displaying Charisma			Same
Forming Coalitions			Same
Co-opting Opposition Members			Same
Controlling Decision Criteria			Same
Developing Others	Most		
Using Outside Experts		Most	
Building a Favorable Image	Most		
Legitimizing Control			Same
Incurring Obligation			Same
Organizational Placement			Same
Proactivity		Most	
Quid Pro Quo		Most	
Rationalization			Same
Allocating Resources		Most	
Dispensing Rewards			Same
Ritualism		Most	
Using Surrogates			Same
Using Symbols			Same
Training and Orienting Others	Most		

Table A.16
Most Effectively Used Tactics by Men and Women

Tactics	Men	Women	Both
Controlling Agenda Preparation			Same
Using Ambiguity			Same
Brinkmanship		Most	
Displaying Charisma		Most	
Forming Coalitions			Same
Co-opting Opposition Members			Same
Controlling Decision Criteria		Most	
Developing Others	Most		
Using Outside Experts		Most	
Building a Favorable Image	Most		
Legitimizing Control			Same
Incurring Obligation		Most	
Organizational Placement			Same
Proactivity			Same
Quid Pro Quo		Most	
Rationalization	Most		
Allocating Resources			Same
Dispensing Rewards			Same
Ritualism	Most		
Using Surrogates		Most	
Using Symbols		Most	
Training and Orienting Others			Same

Table A.17
Most Ethical Tactics Used by Men and Women

Tactics	Men	Women	Both
Controlling Agenda Preparation			Same
Using Ambiguity		Most	
Brinkmanship			Same
Displaying Charisma		Most	
Forming Coalitions		Most	
Co-opting Opposition Members			Same
Controlling Decision Criteria			Same
Developing Others			Same
Using Outside Experts			Same
Building a Favorable Image	Most		
Legitimizing Control		Most	
Incurring Obligation			Same
Organizational Placement			Same
Proactivity			Same
Quid Pro Quo			Same
Rationalization			Same
Allocating Resources	Most		
Dispensing Rewards			Same
Ritualism			Same
Using Surrogates			Same
Using Symbols			Same
Training and Orienting Others			Same

Table A.18
Tactic Use: Comparison of When Used

Used Initially	Used on Resistance
Using Ambiguity	Controlling the Agenda
Displaying Charisma	Brinkmanship
Controlling Decision Criteria	Forming Coalitions
Developing Others	Co-opting Opposition Members
Building a Favorable Image	Legitimizing Control
Organizational Placement	Rationalization
Proactivity	Dispensing Rewards
Quid Pro Quo	Using Surrogates
Allocating Resources	
Ritualism	
Using Symbols	
Training and Orienting Others	

* There is no difference in this comparison between men and women.

Bibliography

Abrahams, Ray. "Maria's Macho: Demythologizing Power in Male–Female Relations: A Critique of Machismo-Marianismo Complex." *Vakgroep CANSA Culturele Antropologie* 8, no. 3, University of Amsterdam, Fall 1989, 42–52.

Adler, Alfred. *The Individual Psychology of Alfred Adler*. H. L. Ansbacher and R. R. Ansbacher, eds. New York: Basic Books, 1956.

Allen, Robert W.; Madison, Dan L.; Porter, Lyman W.; Renwick, Patricia; and Mayes, Bronston T. "Organizational Politics: Tactics and Characteristics of Its Actors." *California Management Review* 22, no. 1, 1979, 475–83.

Allen, Robert W., and Porter, Lyman W. *Organizational Influence Processes*. New York: Scott, Foresman, 1983.

Arendt, Hannah. *The Origins of Totalitarianism*. New York: Harcourt, Brace and World; 1951.

Azim, Ahmad N., and Boseman, F. Glenn. "An Empirical Topology of Power and Involvement within a University Setting." *Academy of Management Journal* 18, December 1975.

Bachrach, Peter, and Baratz, Morton S. *Power and Poverty: Theory and Practice*. New York: Oxford University Press, 1970.

———. "Two Faces of Power." *American Political Science Review* 56, 1972, 947–52.

Bacherach, Samuel B., and Lawler, Edward J. "Power Dependence and Power Paradoxes in Bargaining." *Negotiation Journal* 2, no. 2, 1986, 167–74.

Barnard, Chester I. *The Functions of the Executive*. Cambridge, Mass.: Harvard University Press, 1948.

Bass, Bernard M. *Leadership, Psychology and Organizational Behavior*. New York: Harper, 1960.

———. *Stogdill's Handbook of Leadership*, New York: The Free Press, 1981.

Bass, B.; Wurster, C. R.; and Alcock, W. A. "A Test of the Proposition: We Want to be Esteemed Most by Those We Esteem Most Highly." *Journal of Abnormal Psychology* 63, 1963, 650–53.

Bell, David V. J. *Power, Influence, and Authority: An Essay in Political Linguistics.* New York: Oxford University Press, 1975.

Benne, Kenneth, and Chin, Robert, eds *The Planning of Change: Readings in Applied Behavioral Science.* New York: Holt. 1961.

Bennis, Warren G. *Changing Organizations.* New York: McGraw-Hill, 1966.

Berle, Adolf. *Power.* New York: Harcourt, Brace and World, 1959.

Berlo, David K. *The Process of Communication.* New York: Holt, Rinehart, and Winston, 1960.

Bierstadt, Robert. "An Analysis of Social Power." *American Sociological Review* 15, 1950, 730–33.

———. *Power and Progress: Essays on Sociological Theory.* New York: McGraw-Hill, 1974.

Buckley, Walter. *Sociology and Modern Systems Theory.* Englewood Cliffs, N.J.: Prentice-Hall, 1967.

Cartright, D. "Influence, Leadership, Control." In J. G. March, ed., *Handbook of Organizations.* Chicago: Rand-McNally, 1965.

Cavanaugh, Gerald F.; Moberg, Dennis J.; and Velasquez. M., "The Ethics of Organizational Politics." *The Academy of Management Review* 6, no. 3, 1981, 423–39.

Cialdini, Robert. "The Triggers of Influence." *Psychology Today,* February 1984, 40–45.

Coenen, L., and Hofstra, N. A. "Informational Choice: The Development of Systems-Related Power in Organizations. *Sociological Abstracts,* Association Paper, 1988.

Cribbin, James J. *Effective Managerial Leadership.* New York: American Management Association, 1972.

Crozier, Michael. *The Bureaucratic Phenomenon.* Chicago: University of Chicago Press, 1964.

Culbert, S. A., and McDonough, J. J. *The Invisible War.* New York: John Wiley & Sons, 1980.

Daft, Richard L. *Organization Theory and Design.* 3rd ed. New York: West Publishing. 1989.

Dahl, Robert A. "The Concept of Power." *Behavioral Science* 2, 1957, 201–15.

———. *Who Governs.* New Haven, Conn.: Yale University Press, 1961.

Dansereau, Fred, Jr.; Graen, George; and Haga, William J. "A Vertical Dyad Linkage Approach to Leadership within Formal Organizations." *Organizational Behavior and Human Performance* 13, no. 1, 1975, 181.

Desmond, Morris. *The Human Zoo.* New York: McGraw Hill. 1969.

Drake, R. M. "A Study of Leadership." *Character and Personality* 12, 1944, 285–89.

Duke, James T. *Conflict and Power in Social Life.* Provo, Utah: Brigham Young University Press, 1976.

Duncan, W. S.; Smiltzer, L. R.; and Leap T. L. "Humor and Work: Applications of Joking Behavior to Management." *Journal of Management* 16, no.2, 1990, 255–78.

Easton, David. "The Perception of Authority and Political Change." In Carl J. Friedrich, ed., *Authority.* Cambridge, Mass.: Harvard University Press, 1958, 170–96.

Easton, Lloyd D., and Guddat, Kurt H., eds. *Writings of the Young Marx on Philosophy and Society.* New York: Doubleday, 1967, 278.

Emerson, Richard M. "Power Dependence Relations." *American Sociological Review*, 1962, 31–41.

Emerson, R. W. "Self Reliance." *The Selected Writings of Ralph Waldo Emerson*. Brooks Athinson, ed. New York: Modern Library, 1950.

Etzioni, Amitai. *A Comprehensive Analysis of Complex Organizations*. New York: The Free Press, 1961.

Fairholm, Gilbert W. "Sixteen Power Tactics Principals Can Use to Improve Management Effectiveness." *Bulletin*, National Association of Secondary Schools Principals, May 1984.

———. "Power Tactics on the Job." *Personnel*, May 1985.

———. *Values Leadership: Toward a Philosophy of Leadership*. New York: Praeger, 1991.

Falbo, T. "Multi-dimensional Scaling of Power Strategies." *Journal of Personnel Social Psychology* 35, 1977, 537–47.

Falbo, T.; New, B. L.; and Gaines, Margie. "Perceptions of Authority and the Power Strategies Used by Clergymen." *Journal for the Scientific Study of Religion* 26, no. 4, December 1987, 499–507.

Follett, Mary Parker. *Dynamic Administration: The Collected Papers of Mary Parker Follett*. Henry C. Metcalf and L. Urwick, eds. New York: Harper & Brothers, 1942.

French, John R. P., and Raven, Bertram. *Studies in Social Power*. Dorwin Cartwright, ed. Ann Arbor, Mich.: Institute for Social Research, University of Michigan, 1959, 150–65.

French, Wendell L.; Bell, Cecil H.; and Zawacki, Robert A. *Organization Development: Theory, Practice, and Research*. Plano, Texas: Business Publications, 1983.

Friedrich, Carl J., and Blitzer, Charles. *The Age of Power*. Ithaca, N.Y.: Cornell University Press, 1957.

Frost, Peter J., and Hayes, David C. "An Exploration in Two Cultures of a Model of Political Behavior in Organizations." In *Organizational Functioning in a Cross-Culture Perspective*. Kent, Ohio: Kent State University Press, 1979.

Frost, P. J.; Mitchell, V. E.; and Nord, W. R. *Organizational Reality: Reports from the Firing Line*. New York: Scott, Foresman, 1982.

Galbraith, John Kenneth. *The Anatomy of Power*. Boston: Houghton Mifflin, 1983.

Gandz, Jeffrey, and Murray, Victor V. "The Experience of Workplace Politics." *Academy of Management Journal* 23, no. 2, 1980, 237–51 and 440–54.

Gardner, John W. *Self-Renewal: The Individual and the Innovative Society*. New York: Harper Colophon Books, 1964.

Gellerman, Saul W. *Motivation and Productivity*. New York: American Management Association, 1963, 109.

Gerlach, Luther P., and Hine, Virginia H. *People, Power, Change: Movements of Social Transformation*. New York: Bobbs-Merrill, 1970.

Goldhammer, Herbert, and Shils, Edward A. "Types of Power and Status." *American Journal of Sociology* 45, 1972, 171–82.

Goodstadt, Barry E., and Hjelle, Larry A. "Power to the Powerless: Locus of Control and the Use of Power." *Journal of Personality and Social Psychology* 27, no. 2, 1973, 144–54.

Gouldner, A. W. "The Norm of Reciprocity: A Preliminary Statement." *American Sociological Review* 25, 1960, 161–78.

Grimes, A. J. "Authority, Power, Influence and Social Control: A Theoretical Synthesis." *Academy of Management Review*, October 1978, 724–35.

Handy, Charles B. *Understanding Organizations*. Middlesex, England: Penguin Books, 1976.

Harragan, Betty Lehan. "Games Mother Never Taught You." Reprinted excerpts in P. J. Frost, V. E. Mitchell, and W. R. Nord, *Organizational Reality: Reports from the Firing Line*. New York: Scott, Foresman, 1982.

Hartsock, Nancy C. M. *Money, Sex, and Power*. New York: Longman, 1983.

Harward, Donald W. *Power: Its Nature, Its Use, and Its Limits*. Cambridge, Mass.: Schenkaran, 1982.

Hickson, D. J.; Hinings, C. R.; Lee, C. R.; Schneck, R. E.; and Pennings, J. M. "A Strategic Contingencies' Theory of Intraorganizational Power." *Administrative Science Quarterly* 16, no. 2, June 1971, 33–52.

Hodgkinson, Christopher. *Toward a Philosophy of Administration*. New York: St. Martin's Press, 1978.

Hoffer, Eric. *Working and Thinking of the Waterfront*. New York: Perennial Library, 1969.

Hollander, E. P. *Leadership Dynamics: A Practical Guide to Effective Relationships*. New York: The Free Press, 1978.

Homans, G. C. *The Human Group*. New York: Harcourt, Brace, 1950.

———. "Social Behavior as Exchange." *American Journal of Sociology* 63, 1958, 597–606.

Hunter, Floyd. *Top Leadership, USA*. Chapel Hill, N.C.: University of North Carolina Press, 1959.

———. *Community Power Structure: A Study of Decision Makers* New York: Anchor Books, 1963.

Johns, Gary. *Organizational Behavior*. Glenview, Ill.: Scott, Foresman, 1983.

Kahn, Robert L. *Power and Conflict in Organizations*. New York: Basic Books, 1964.

Kanter, Rosabeth Moss. "Power Failure in Management Circuits." *Harvard Business Review*, July/August 1979.

Kaplan, Abraham. *Power and Conflict in Organizations*. New York: Basic Books, 1964.

King, Dennis C., and Glidewell, John C. "Power." *The 1976 Handbook for Group Facilitators*. New York: University Associates, 1976, 131–42.

Kipnis, David. *The Powerholders*. Chicago: University of Chicago Press, 1976.

Kipnis, David; Schmidt, Stuart M.; and Wilkinson, Ian. "Intraorganizational Influence Tactics: Explorations in Getting One's Way." *Journal of Applied Psychology* 65, no. 4, 1980, 440–52.

Korda, Michael. *Power! How to Get It, How to Use It*. New York: Ballantine Books, 1975.

Kotter, John P. "Power, Dependence, and Effective Management." *Harvard Business Review*, July/August 1977, 125–36.

Krech, D., and Crutchfield, R. S. *Theory and Problems of Social Psychology*. New York: McGraw-Hill, 1948.

Kreiger, L., and Stern, F., eds. *The Responsibilities of Power*. London: Macmillan, 1968.

Krupp, Sherman. *Pattern in Organization Analysis*. New York: Holt, Rinehart, and Winston, 1961.

Laeyendecker, L. "Resistance to Change in a Religious Institution." *The Netherlands Journal of Social* Sciences 25, no. 1, April 1989, pp. 4–17.

Lasswell, H. D., and Kaplan, A. *Power and Society*. New Haven, Conn.: Yale University Press, 1950.

Leavitt, Harold J. *Managerial Psychology*, 2d ed. Chicago: University of Chicago Press, 1958.

Lee, James A. "Perspectives in Leader Effectiveness." In Paul Hersey and John Stinton, eds., *Leader Power*. Athens, Ohio: The Center for Leadership Studies, Ohio University, 1980.

Lumsden, George J. *Impact Management: Personal Power Strategies for Success*. New York: AMACOM, 1979.

Maccoby, Michael. *The Leader*. New York: Simon and Schuster, 1981.

Madison, Dan L.; Allen, Robert W.; Porter, Lyman W.; Renwick, Patricia A.; and Mayes, Bronston T. "Organizational Politics: An Exploration of Managers' Perceptions." *Human Relations* 33, no. 2, 1980, 455–74.

Martin, N. H., and Sims, J. H. "Power Tactics." In D. A. Kolb, I. M. Rubin, and J. M. McIntire, eds., *Organizational Psychology: A Book of Readings*. Englewood Cliffs, N.J.: Prentice-Hall, 1974, 177–83.

Maslow, Abraham. *The Further Reaches of Human Nature*. Middlesex, England: Penguin Books, 1971.

May, Rollo. *Power and Innocence*. New York: W. W. Norton, 1972.

Mayes, Bronston T., and Allen, Robert W. "Toward a Definition of Organizational Politics." *The Academy of Management Review* 2, no. 4, 1977, 672–78.

McClelland, David C. *Power, The Inner Experience*. New York: Irvington, 1975.

McClelland, D. C., and Burnham, J. "Power Is the Great Motivator." *Harvard Business Review*, March/April 1976.

McKeachie, Wilbert J. *Teaching Tips: A Guidebook for the Beginning College Teacher*. Lexington, Mass.: D. C. Heath, 1969.

McKinney, J. B., and Howard, L. C. *Public Administration: Balancing Power and Accountability*. Oak Park, Ill.: More, 1979.

McMurray, Robert N. "Power and the Ambitious Executive." *Harvard Business Review*, 1973, 140–45.

———. *The Maverick Executive*. New York: AMACOM, 1974.

Mechanic, David. "Sources of Power of Lower Participants in Complex Organizations." *Administrative Science Quarterly* 7, no. 2, December 1962, 349–64.

Merrell, V. Dallas. *Huddling: The Informal Way to Management Success*. New York: AMACOM, 1979.

Michner, A., and Schwartfeger, M. "Liking as a Determinant of Power Tactic Preference." *Sociometry* 35, 1972, 190–202.

Milgram, S. *Obedience to Authority: An Experimental View*. New York: Harper and Row, 1974.

Mills, C. Wright. *The Power Elite*. New York: Oxford University Press, 1957.

Molm, Linda D. "Structure, Action, and Outcomes: The Dynamics of Power in Social Exchange." *American Sociological Review* 55, no. 3, June 1990, 427–47.

Morris, Desmond. *The Human Zoo*. New York: McGraw-Hill, 1969.

Mueller, Robert Kirk. *Risk, Survival and Power*. New York American Management Association, 1970, 161.

Muscovici, S. "Social Influence I: Conformity and Social Control." In C. Nemeth, ed., *Social Psychology: Classical and Contemporary Integrations*. Chicago: Rand McNally, 1974, 179–216.

Nettl, Peter. "Power and the Intellectuals." In Connor Cruise O'Brien and W. D. Vanech, eds., *Power and Consciousness*. New York: New York University Press, 1969, 17.

Neustadt, Richard E. *Presidential Power: The Politics of Leadership*. New York: John Wiley & Sons, 1960.

Nord, Walter R. "Dreams of Humanization and the Realities of Power." *The Academy of Management Review* no. 3, 3, 1978, 674–79.

Ng, Sik Hung. *The Social Psychology of Power*. New York: Academic Press, 1980.

Nyberg, David. *Power Over Power*. Ithaca, N.Y.: Cornell University Press, 1981.

O'Brian, Conner, and Banech, W. D. *Power and Consciousness*. New York: New York University Press, 1969.

O'Day, Rory, "Intimidation Rituals: Reaction to Reform." *The Journal of Applied Behavioral Science* 10, no. 3, 1974, 373–86.

Patchen, M. "The Locus and Basis of Influence on Organizational Decisions." *Organizational Behavior and Human Performance* 11, 1974, 195–221.

Pelz, Donald C. "Influence: A Key to Effective Leadership in the First-Line Supervisor." *Personnel*, November 1952, 209.

Pettigrew, A "Information Control as a Power Source." *Sociology* 6, 1972, 187–204

Pfeffer, Jeffery. "The Ambiguity of Leadership." *Academy of Management Review* 2, 1977, 104–12.

———. *Power in Organizations*. Marshfield, Mass.: Pittman, 1981.

———. *Managing With Power*. Cambridge, Mass.: Harvard University Press, 1992.

Pfiffer, John M., and Sherwood, Frank P. *Administrative Organization*. Englewood Cliffs, N.J.: Prentice-Hall, 1960.

Plott, Charles R., and Levine, Michael E. "A Model of Agenda Influence on Committee Decisions." *American Economic Review* 68, 1978, 146–60.

Porter, Lyman W.; Allen, Robert W.; and Angle, Harold L. "The Politics of Upward Influence in Organizations." *Research in Organizational Behavior* Vol 3. 1981, L. L. Cummings and Barry M. Staw, eds. 408–22.

Rose, Arnold M. *The Power Structure*. New York: Oxford University Press, 1967.

Rosen, S.; Levinger, G.; and Lippitt, R. "Perceived Sources of Social Power." *Journal of Abnormal Social Psychology* 62, 1961, 439–41.

Rost, Joseph C. *Leadership for the Twenty-First Century*. New York: Praeger, 1991.

Rubinoff, Lionel. *The Pornography of Power*. New York: Ballantine Books, 1968.

Russell, Bertrand. *Power: A New Social Analysis*. New York: W. W. Norton, 1938.

Salancik, Gerald R., and Pfeffer, Jeffrey. "Who Gets Power—And How They Hold on to It: A Strategic-Contingency Model of Power." *Organizational Dynamics*, 1977, 52–71.

Schattschneider, E. E. *The Semisovereign People: A Realist's View of Democracy in America*. New York: Holt, Rinehart, and Winston, 1960.

Schermerhorn, Richard A. *Society and Power*. New York: Random House, 1961.

Schuman, Patricia Glass. "Women, Power, and Libraries." *Library Journal*, January 1984, 42–47.

Simon, Herbert A. *The Models of Man*. New York: John Wiley & Sons, 1957.

Simon, Herbet A.; Smithburg, Donald W.; and Thompson, Victor A. *Public Administration*. New York: Alfred A. Knopf, 1950.

Siu, R. G. H. *The Craft of Power*. New York: John Wiley & Sons, 1979.

Smith, C. G., and Tannenbaum, A. S. "Organizational Control Structure and Member Consensus." *Human Relations* 16, 1963, 265–72.

Strauss, George. "Tactics of Lateral Relationship: The Purchasing Agent." *Administrative Science Quarterly* 7, no. 2, September 1962. pp 161–86.

Szilagyl, Andrew D., and Wallace, Marc J., Jr. *Organizational Behavior and Performance*. Glenview, Ill.: Scott, Foresman, 1983.

Thibaut, J. W., and Kelley, H. H. *The Social Psychology of Group*. New York: John Wiley & Sons., 1959.

Wagner, Karan Van, and Swanson, Cheryl. "From Machiavelli to Ms.: Differences in Male–Female Power Styles." *Public Administration Review*, January/February 1979, 66–72.

Weber, Max. *On Charisma and Institution Building*. Chicago: University of Chicago Press, 1968.

White, Judy. "Helping Themselves to Power: The Burgeoning of Women in Leisure Management." *Center for Urban and Regional Studies*, University of Birmingham, England, B–15, 1990.

Wildavsky, A. "Budgeting as a Political Process." In David E. Sills, ed., *The International Encyclopedia of the Social Sciences*. New York: Crowell, Collier and Macmillan, 1968, 192–99.

Winter, David G. *The Power Motive*. New York: The Free Press, 1973.

Wrong, Dennis H. *Power: Its Forms, Bases and Uses*. New York: Harper, 1979.

Yukl, Gary A. *Leadership in Organizations*. Englewood Cliffs, N.J.: Prentice-Hall, 1981.

Zald, Mayer N., ed. *Power in Organizations*. Nashville, Tenn.: Vanderbilt University Press, 1970.

Zaleznik, Abraham. "The Human Dilemma of Leadership." *Harvard Business Review*, July/August 1963, 49–55.

Index

About the Author

GILBERT W. FAIRHOLM is Associate Professor of Public Administration at Virginia Commonwealth University in Richmond. His career includes both academic and practical experience in leadership and management. He is a frequent facilitator in executive development and strategic vision-setting retreats. He is the author of *Values Leadership: Toward a New Philosophy of Leadership* (Praeger, 1991).